Zoroastrians

Zoroastrianism is of enormous importance in the history of religions. Elements in it can be traced back to a remote, possibly even Indo-European, past, and these, and others from Indo-Iranian times link it with the beliefs of ancient (Vedic) India, and survive as a subordinate part of what is the earliest known revealed religion. Zoroaster's own teachings have, moreover, a highly spiritual and ethical content, which makes them a deeply rewarding subject for study in themselves.

This book, now re-issued with a new introduction by Mary Boyce, is the first attempt to trace the continuous history of the faith from the time it was preached by Zoroaster down to the present day – a span of about 3,500 years. First taught on the Inner Asian steppes, Zoroastrianism became the state religion of the three great Iranian empires and, as such, had a remarkable influence on other world faiths: to the east on northern Buddhism; to the west on Judaism, Christianity and Islam. With the conquest of Iran by the Muslim Arabs, Zoroastrianism lost its secular power, but survives as a minority faith, and one of the oldest living religions.

Mary Boyce is Professor Emerita of Iranian Studies at the University of London and is the author of a number of works on Zoroastrianism and Manichaenism.

The Library of Religious Beliefs and Practices
Series editor:
John Hinnells

This series provides pioneering and scholarly introductions to different religions in a readable form. It is concerned with the beliefs and practices of religions in their social, cultural and historical setting. Authors come from a variety of backgrounds and approach the study of religious beliefs and practices from their different points of view. Some focus mainly on questions of history, teachings, customs and ritual practices. Others consider, within the context of a specific region, the interrelationships between religions; the interaction of religion and the arts; religion and social organisation; the involvement of religion in political affairs; and, for ancient cultures, the interpretation of archaeological evidence. In this way the series brings out the multi-disciplinary nature of the study of religion. It is intended for students of religion, philosophy, social sciences and history, and for the interested lay person.

Other titles in the series include:

Hindus
Their Religious Beliefs and Practices
Julius Lipner

Mahayana Buddhism
The Doctrinal Foundations
Paul Williams

Muslims
Their Religious Beliefs and Practices
Andrew Rippin

Religions of Oceania
Tony Swain and *Garry Trompf*

Theravada Buddhism
A Social History from Ancient
Benares to Modern Colombo
Richard Gombrich

Zoroastrians
Their Religious Beliefs and Practices
Mary Boyce

Zoroastrians

Their Religious Beliefs and Practices

Mary Boyce

Routledge
Taylor & Francis Group

LONDON AND NEW YORK

First published 1979 by Routledge & Kegan Paul Ltd

This edition first published 2001
by Routledge
11 New Fetter Lane, London EC4P 4EE

Simultaneously published in the USA and Canada
by Routledge
29 West 35th Street, New York, NY 10001

Reprinted 2002, 2003

Routledge is an imprint of the Taylor & Francis Group

© 1979, 2001 Mary Boyce

Printed and bound in Great Britain by
St Edmundsbury Press Ltd, Bury St Edmunds, Suffolk

British Library Cataloguing in Publication Data
A catalogue record for this book is available from the British Library

Library of Congress Cataloging in Publication Data
A catalog record for this book has been requested

ISBN 0–415–23902–8 (hbk)
ISBN 0–415–23903–6 (pbk)

Dedicated
in gratitude
to the memory of

HECTOR MUNRO CHADWICK

Elrington and Bosworth Professor of Anglo-Saxon
in the University of Cambridge

1912–41

Contents

Contents

Contents

Contents

Contents

Maps

Foreword to this edition

There have been notable advances in the study of Zoroastrianism since this book was published in 1979, and although a number of corrections were made in the text in the second reprint of 1983, it now seems desirable to indicate certain large developments which need to be borne in mind during a reading of the early chapters.

The approximate date first proposed for Zoroaster, of 1700 BC, has already been modified, partly because the earliest compilation of Rigvedic hymns is now assigned to about 1500 BC, and the 'Old Avestan' language spoken by the Prophet is very close to Vedic. It may be, however, that it evolved more slowly, because his people appear to have been more settled and conservative than their Indo-Aryan cousins; and calculations based on the language and content of the 'Old Avestan' and 'Young Avestan' texts suggest a date of about 1200 BC for the former, and not later than 800 BC for the latter. Archaeologists, however, have been led by their findings to assign the main movements by Iranians into the land that came to be called after them, 'Iran', to about 1000 BC, so that attributing the date of 1200 BC to Zoroaster still means that he lived before these movements took place, somewhere, therefore, on the Inner Asian steppes. Sites have been excavated in northern Kazakhstan which may, it is thought, have belonged to ancient Iranians of about this time. Their inhabitants were sedentary pastoralists with a mainly Stone Age culture, but making some use of bronze.

Foreword

A new edition of the Yasna Haptanhaiti ('Worship of the Seven Chapters') has led to a very important development in Zoroastrian studies, namely the attribution of this short liturgy (which, with the Gathas and the two most sacred manthras, makes up the whole corpus of Old Avestan texts) to Zoroaster himself. This discovery is of incalculable value, for not only does it add substantially to the store of the Prophet's own utterances, but, because the liturgy is almost entirely in prose and is intended for communal worship, it is rather more readily understood than the Gathas. The ancient text still has its own obscurities, but some important points are instantly clear, notably that the key theological expression 'Amesha Spenta' was used (and almost certainly coined) by Zoroaster himself. In general, the liturgy shows even more plainly than the Gathas to what an extent the Prophet drew on old religious beliefs of his people in evolving his own profoundly original and influential doctrines; and its testimony makes it all the more necessary to abandon the long-held academic theory (touched on in this book) that the Indo-Iranians venerated personified 'abstractions'. It is plain that this is anachronistic, and that what they in fact revered were the invisible forces (Avestan *mainyu-*, Sanskrit *manyu-*) which they apprehended in all things, animate or inanimate, some of which were felt to be very powerful.

Additional evidence from the Yasna Haptanhaiti confirms what is to be gleaned from the Gathas, that Old Avestan society had a simple structure, with only one distinct professional group, that of priests. Its other members were in general referred to simply as 'men' and 'women', with the men presumably fulfilling various roles as needed, of herdsmen, hunters or fighters; but their way of life seems to have been essentially peaceful and ruled by law. In Zoroaster's day, however, as his own words show, it was being violently threatened by the activity of roving marauders. When Zoroaster was thought to have lived in Iran itself, it was supposed (on the pattern of later history) that these were nomadic tribesmen, raiding across that country's borders; but now, not only has the Prophet to be regarded as living on the steppes, but archaeologists have established that nomadism (dependent as it is on ridden horses) did not begin to develop there until about 900 BC. Another explanation has therefore to be found for the emergence of these lawless robber bands, and the most likely one (reflected in later steppe-history) is that they were formed of men returning from mercenary service in kingdoms to the south, through which they had acquired superior weapons, new fighting skills, and a taste for adventure and quick gains by the sword rather than a quiet life of cattle-tending. These are recognized ingredients for a 'Heroic Age'; and it is yet another unique feature of the Old Avestan texts that they give glimpses of such an age from the point of view, not of the 'heroes' and their bards, but of the quiet, honest people who suffered from their exploits. Turbulent times such as this are recognized as conducive to the birth of salvation faiths, with hopes of peace and justice shifting from this world to the next; and Zoroastrianism is in fact the oldest of such faiths, and has been the prototype for many others.

Breakdown of social order on the steppes may well have been one of the major causes of the Iranians' mass migrations, which brought about radical changes for them. The Young Avestan texts mirror a new society, with three fixed groups: priests, warrior nobles (who included kings) and peasant farmers. These social groupings (which also evolved in parallel circumstances among the Indo-Aryans) used to be wrongly attributed (in the present book, as generally) to the Old Avestan people likewise; and so it was thought that among them the earthly representative of Ahura Mazda, 'Lord of Wisdom', was probably conceived of as the kingly ruler – an unknown figure, it seems, in traditional steppe society (where the exact status of 'Kavi' Vishtaspa remains undetermined). There, however, it is more likely to have been the leading priest who was felt to fulfil this role, since priests were the guardians of wisdom, and a wise priest may well have had an authoritative voice in the counsels of the elders of his community.

Another subject whose handling in this book needs revision is that of the Zoroastrian calendar. The author now thinks that the evidence points to the existence of a 'Young Avestan' calendar of 12 months of 30 days, each day being dedicated to a divine being, and a thirteenth month being added from time to time to keep this calendar in harmony with the seasons; and accepts that it was under the Achaemenians that a 365-day calendar was introduced, with 5 more days inserted at the year's end, that is, just before the spring No Ruz; and the 12 months, now firmly fixed without an irregular thirteenth, also receiving divine dedications; and considers that there was only the one Sasanian calendar reform, around 500 AC, by which No Ruz was moved from 1 Fravardin to 1 Adar.

Foreword

This was to bring it back into correspondence with the spring equinox, from which it had been slowly receding because of the deficiency in the 365-day calendar against the natural year.

There are two single points of some importance also to be revised. One concerns the story that Zoroaster died at the hand of an assassin, which has been shown to be a well-intentioned fabrication. The other is about the figure in a winged circle, which has gained significance through being adopted by Zoroastrians as one of their chief religious symbols. They now interpret it (as should have been said) as representing the fravashi. The idea that it could represent Ahura Mazda has been abandoned among academics, who now generally consider it to have represented khvarenah.

The above matters have been discussed in some detail in the writer's Zoroastrianism, its antiquity and constant vigour, Columbia Lectures on Iranian Studies 7, Costa Mesa and New York, 1992, with references and bibliography to that date.

Mary Boyce
May 2000

Preface

Zoroastrianism is the most difficult of living faiths to study, because of its antiquity, the vicissitudes which it has undergone, and the loss, through them, of many of its holy texts. Originating over 3500 years ago in a Bronze Age culture on the Asian steppes, it became the state religion of three mighty Iranian empires in succession, and so was endowed for many centuries with temporal power and wealth. Its lofty original doctrines came accordingly to exert their influence throughout the Middle East – an area where Judaism developed, and Christianity and Islam were born. To the east Iranian rule extended into Northern India, and there Zoroastrianism made a contribution to the development of Mahayana Buddhism. Some knowledge of the teachings of Zoroaster and of the history of his faith is therefore needed by every serious student of world religions; and the recent expansion of religious studies in universities has created a demand for an introductory book on this theme. The present work is an attempt to meet that demand. In it it has been sought to treat Zoroastrianism not merely as a mighty seminal influence, but also as a noble faith in its own right, which has held the loyalty of its followers over millennia and through harsh persecutions. Instead, therefore, of stopping, as is usual, with the worldly eclipse of Zoroastrianism by Islam, the book traces the continual history of the community through the subsequent years of oppression, down into the prosperity of modern times.

Preface

In the interests of clarity and conciseness only basic references are given, and this has occasionally entailed embodying the results of recent work by other scholars without due acknowledgment. A fuller treatment of the subject-matter of the earlier chapters already exists in the author's *A History of Zoroastrianism*, vol.I,II (Handbuch der Orientalistik, Leiden 1975,1982); and it is intended in the remaining volumes of that work to cover in detail the whole field of the present book, when detailed references and acknowledgments will be possible. A selection of primary sources is now available, edited and translated by the author, in *Textual Sources for the Study of Zoroastrianism*, Manchester University Press, 1984.

In compliance with the usage of the present series, words are supplied with diacritics only in the index. Zoroastrian technical terms are set between apostrophes at their first occurrence, and thereafter appear undifferentiated; but those which recur regularly are to be found in the glossary at the beginning of the book. Since Zoroastrian covers not only a great span of time, but also vast physical distances, the two maps are designed primarily to give a clear picture of its spheres of influence and of survival, and not every town or archaeological site referred to in the text is to be found on them; but it should always be possible to locate each place fairly closely by region.

The photograph on the jacket shows Dastur Firoze M. Kotwal, high priest of the Wadia Atash Bahram, Bombay, tending a ritual fire. I am indebted to him for his generous permission to use it

It remains for me to express my gratitude to my friend, Professor J.R. Hinnells, the general editor of the series, both for inviting me to undertake this work, and for helping, with patience, labour and wise counsel, to bring it to fruition. I am also indebted to the editorial staff of Messrs Routledge & Kegan Paul for their courtesy and helpful advice.

Glossary

Note: A word sometimes occurs in more than one form, according to different periods of history. In such cases the older form is given first.

agiary	Parsi term for a Zoroastrian place of worship, a fire temple
Ahuna Vairya, Ahunvar	the holiest Zoroastrian prayer, equivalent to the Lord's Prayer in Christianity
akabir	Arabic plural, 'great ones', used for elders or leading men
Amesha Spenta	'Holy Immortal', a term for one of the divine beings of Zoroastrianism, evoked by God; often used especially of the six greatest among them
anjoman	'assembly', a gathering or council of local Zoroastrians
asha	'order, truth, justice', a principle which governs the world
ashavan	'righteous, true, just'
atakhsh, atash	'fire'
Atakhsh i Aduran, Ataš Aduran	'fire of fires', a sacred fire of the second grade
Atakhsh i Varahram, Atash Bahram	'Victorious Fire', a sacred fire of the highest grade

Glossary

atash-zohr	'offering to fire'
Avesta	the sacred books of the Zoroastrians
Avestan	the Iranian language spoken by Zoroaster, in which the Avesta is composed
barashnom	ritual ablution, part of a prolonged rite of purification
baresman, barsom	bundle of twigs held by the officiating priest at acts of worship
behdin	'the good religion' i.e. Zoroastrianism; also 'of the good religion' i.e. a Zoroastrian
Dadgah	a sacred fire of the third grade
daeva, dev	an evil god, abjured by Zoroaster; later, a demon
dakhma	'grave'; later a place of exposure for the dead, a 'tower of silence'
dastur	one in authority, a high priest
dhimmi	'people of the covenant', a category of peoples subject to Islamic rule
drug	'disorder, falsehood', a principle opposed to asha
frasho-kereti, frashegird	end of the present state of the world, the Last Day
fravashi, fravahr, fravard	a spirit which has pre-existed this life and will survive after death; often a synonym for the soul
gabr, gaur, gor	a Muslim term, probably meaning 'infidel', applied in Iran especially to a Zoroastrian
gahambar	one of six holy days of obligation enjoined on his community by Zoroaster
Gathas	the hymns composed by Zoroaster
getig	'physical, tangible, corporeal' (opposed to menog)
haoma, hom	the sacred plant crushed for its juice at the main Zoroastrian act of worship
herbad, ervad	name for a Zoroastrian priest; in modern usage one less highly qualified than a mobad
Hudinan peshobay	'Leader of those of the good religion', title of the head of the Zoroastrian community under early Islam
jizya	poll-tax paid by non-Muslims
kavi, kay	title of Vishtaspa, Zoroaster's royal patron, and of others of his dynasty

Glossary

khrafstra	'noxious creature', held to belong to the world of evil
khvarenah	'divine grace'; also the divine being who personifies this
khvaetvadatha, khvedodah	'next-of-kin marriage'
kusti	'sacred cord', worn as girdle by Zoroastrians
magus (plural, magi)	Latin form of Old Persian magu, 'priest'
menog	'spiritual, intangible' (opposed to getig)
mobad	leading priest; in modern usage one more highly qualified than a herbad
No Ruz	'New Day', the holiest day of the Zoroastrian devotional year, and the seventh feast of obligation
Pahlavi	the language of the later Zoroastrian books
Saoshyant	the coming World Saviour
spenta	'holy, furthering, increasing', an adjective which characterizes the good creation
Staota Yesnya	the central and oldest part of the yasna
urvan	'soul'
Vahram fire	see Atakhsh i Varahram
Vendidad	'Code against demons', a book of the Avesta, read during a night office
Visperad	'(Service of) All the Masters', solemnized especially at the gahambars and No Ruz
yasht	a hymn to an individual divinity
yasna	'act of worship', the main Zoroastrian religious service
Yasna Haptanhaiti	'Yasna of Seven Chapters', part of the Staota Yesnya
yazata, yazad	'worthy of worship', one of the Zoroastrian terms for a divine being evoked by God
Yenhe hatąm	a short, ancient prayer
zand	translation of the Avesta, with commentary, in a vernacular

Signs and abbreviations

*	before a name indicates a restored form
AVN	Arda Viraz Namag
Dk	Dinkard
DkM	*Dinkard*, text edition, ed. D. M. Madan, 2 vols, Bombay 1911
Ep Man	Epistles of Manushchihr
GBd	Greater Bundahishn
MHD	Madigan i Hazar Dadestan
Pahl. Riv. Dd.	*The Pahlavi Rivayat accompanying the Dadestan i dinig*, ed. B. N. Dhabhar, Bombay 1911
RV	Rigveda
Saddar Bd	Saddar Bundahesh
SBE	Sacred Books of the East, ed. Max Müller
SM	Sar-Mashhad
Vd	Vendidad
Y	Yasna
Yt	Yasht
Zadspram	Wizidagiha i Zadspram
ZZZ	R. C. Zaehner, *Zurvan, a Zoroastrian Dilemma*

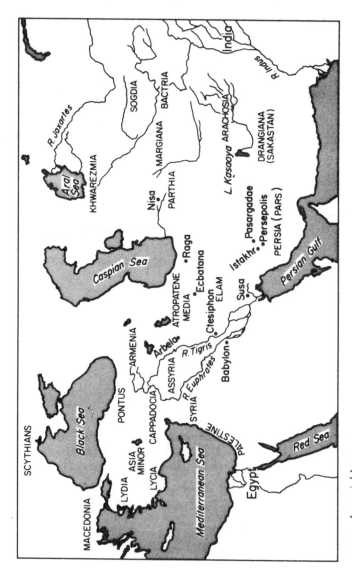

MAP I *Imperial Iran*

xxiv

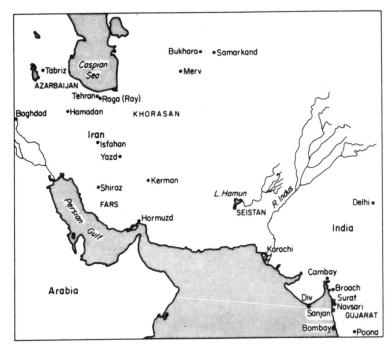

MAP II   *After the Arab conquest*

CHAPTER ONE

The background

Introduction

Zoroastrianism is the oldest of the revealed credal religions, and it has probably had more influence on mankind, directly and indirectly, than any other single faith. In its own right it was the state religion of three great Iranian empires, which flourished almost continually from the sixth century B.C. to the seventh century A.C., and dominated much of the Near and Middle East. Iran's power and wealth lent it immense prestige, and some of its leading doctrines were adopted by Judaism, Christianity and Islam, as well as by a host of Gnostic faiths, while in the East it had some influence on the development of northern Buddhism. Today external forces have reduced the Zoroastrians themselves to tiny scattered minorities, living mostly in Iran and India; but beliefs first taught by their prophet are still subscribed to by other peoples throughout the world.

Zoroastrianism was already old when it first enters recorded history; and it has its roots in a very distant past. Indeed, so tenacious are the Iranians of tradition that there are elements in living Zoroastrianism which go back, it seems, to Indo-European times. These elements, blended with later revealed doctrines, make it a richly complex faith, knowledge of which increases understanding of man's spiritual progress over millennia. It is also a noble one, with some unique and remarkable doctrines, which has been able to give its adherents purposeful and satisfying lives, awaking in them deep devotion. It is thus fully deserving of study for its own sake, as well as for its place in man's religious history.

Zoroastrianism has been so named in the West because its prophet, Zarathushtra, was known to the ancient Greeks as Zoroaster. He was an Iranian, and lived in what for his people were prehistoric times. It is impossible, therefore, to establish fixed dates for his life; but there is evidence to suggest that he flourished when the Stone Age was giving way for the Iranians to the Bronze Age, possibly, that is, between about 1400 and 1200 B.C.

The Indo-Iranians

In still remoter times the ancestors of both the Iranians and the Indians had formed one people, identified as the proto-Indo-Iranians. They were a branch of the Indo-European family of nations, and they lived, it is thought, as pastoralists on the south Russian steppes, to the east of the Volga. They were, it seems, semi-migratory, herding their cattle, sheep and goats over limited areas on foot with the help of dogs (for the horse had not yet been tamed). Their society was divided into two main groups: priests and the laity (whose men would have been herdsmen and hunters). The demands of life on the steppes allowed little room for development or change; and during centuries of this slow, stable way of existence – perhaps from the fourth to the third millennium B.C. – the proto-Indo-Iranians forged a religious tradition of immense strength, so that to this day elements from it are preserved by their descendants, the Brahmans of India and the Zoroastrians of Iran.

Eventually – it is thought early in the third millennium – the proto-Indo-Iranians drifted apart, to become identifiable by speech as two distinct peoples, the Indians and Iranians. They were still pastoralists; and they had contact, presumably through trade, with the settled peoples to the south of them. From Mesopotamia they learnt the use first of wooden carts pulled by oxen, and then of the war-chariot. To draw these chariots they lassoed and tamed the wild horses of the steppes; and at about the same time bronze came into use. The mountains flanking the Inner Asian steppes – notably the Altai – contained rich deposits of copper and tin; and so the steppe-dwellers were able to equip themselves formidably as fighting-men.

The old Iranian word for 'warrior' was 'nar', which also means simply 'man'; but as the use of the war-chariot spread, an especial term was coined, 'rathaeshtar', literally 'one who stands in a chariot'. With the horse-drawn chariot the old way of life seems to have given place to a more restless, dangerous one, a typical 'heroic age', in which chieftains and their followers set out in quest of gain and glory, and were as ready to raid a neighbouring tribe as to pillage alien settlements. In an ancient verse in the Zoroastrian scriptures supernatural spirits are said to contend 'even as a mighty chariot-warrior should fight, having girt on his sword-belt, for his well-gotten treasure' (Yt 13.67). Sometimes the warrior's booty consisted of herds of cattle, carried off by force; and the fame of a great champion had to be paid for with the blood of the slain, and the sufferings of the weak and unprotected. It was during this turbulent and restless age, it seems, when might ruled rather than law, that Zoroaster lived, and sought a revelation of the purpose of man's troubled days on earth.

Zoroaster himself was a priest; and to understand the nature of his revelation it is necessary to learn what one can of the old religion which nurtured him. Fortunately much can be discovered through a comparison of the most ancient elements in the Zoroastrian scriptures and cult with the oldest religious works of India (notably the Rigveda) and the Brahmanic rituals. The Zoroastrian scriptures are known collectively as the 'Avesta' (a title which probably means something like 'Authoritative Utterance'); and the language in which they are composed is called simply 'Avestan', since it is known only from this source. By comparing these diverse materials one can reconstruct the essentials of the proto-Indo-Iranian faith, and trace some of the subsequent developments among the Iranians before Zoroaster himself was born.

The old religion

THE CULT

Cult, it is generally admitted, is more enduring than theology, and the basic objects of the Zoroastrian cult are still those of the ancient Stone Age pastoralists, namely water and fire. Water made life on the steppes possible (they had been barren desert, it is held, down to the fifth millennium B.C., through lack of rain); and the proto-Indo-Iranians personified the waters as goddesses, the Apas, praying to them and offering them libations (called in Avestan 'zaothra', a word which came to mean 'offering' in general). In Zoroastrianism the libation to the waters consists essentially of three ingredients, namely milk and the sap or leaves of two plants. The number three was a sacred one for the proto-Indo-Iranians, and still regulates many Zoroastrian and Brahmanic observances. In the libation the three ingredients represent the vegetable and animal kingdoms, which are nourished by water; and so, consecrated by prayer, the zaothra was believed to return to that element the vital force which it had given out, and thus keep it itself pure and abundant. As in traditional Zoroastrianism, the libation was probably made regularly of old by each household to the nearest pool or spring, as well as forming part of the priestly rites.

The other chief cult object, fire, was also essential for the steppe-dwellers, the source of warmth in the bitter winters, and the means of cooking the meat which (whether from wild or domestic animals) was the staple of their diet. In ancient times, when it was a labour to light a fire, it was prudent to keep a hearth fire always burning (the live embers could be carried in a pot on migration); and a cult of ever-burning fire seems to have been widespread among the Indo-Europeans, who saw a divinity in its flames. The Brahmans knew him by the old name of Agni (cognate with Latin 'ignis'), but the Zoro-astrians called him Atar. They made a threefold offering also to fire, consisting of clean dry fuel, incense (such as the dried leaves of herbs), and a small portion of animal fat. (It was this third offering which in particular was called the zaothra to fire.) Thus fire, like water, was strengthened by two offerings from the plant world, and one from the animal one. Fuel and incense were probably given thrice daily, at the times ordained for prayer (sunrise, noon and sunset), while the zaothra of fat was presumably offered whenever the family had meat to cook, of which the fire thus received its share. By this it was visibly strengthened, as the melting fat made its flames blaze up.

The offerings to fire and water formed the basis also of the daily priestly act of worship, called by the Iranians the 'yasna', by Indians the 'yajña' (from the verbal root yaz- 'sacrifice', 'worship'). At this service the zaothra to fire was obtained from the blood sacrifice, which was evidently regularly made. The Indo-Iranians felt a sense of awe and danger at taking life, and never did so without consecrating the act by prayer, whereby, they believed, the creature's spirit was enabled to live on. There was a strong sense of kinship between man and beast, which is expressed in an ancient part of the yasna liturgy: 'We reverence our (own) souls, and (those) of the domestic animals which nourish us . . . and the souls of useful wild animals' (Y 39. 1– 2). Among the Iranians the belief grew up that the spirits of animals which died a consecrated death became absorbed in a divine being whom they venerated as Geush Urvan, the 'Soul of the Bull'; and they believed that the blood sacrifice strengthened this divinity, who cared for all useful animals on earth, and helped them to flourish.

At the solemnization of the yasna/yajña, grasses were scattered under the feet of the sacrificial beast, and over the ritual precinct. The reason given for this in a Sanskrit text is that it was done 'because the victim has grass as its body; verily thus he (the priest) makes the victim have its full body' (Aitareya Brahmana II.2.11). The officiating priest also held a bunch of this grass (called by the Iranians 'baresman') in his left hand while solemnizing the service, perhaps in further acknowledgment that 'all flesh is grass', and that man and beast are kin. Later in both Iran and India twigs were substituted for the bunch of grass.

The ritual offering to the waters made at the end of the yasna was prepared from milk, the leaves of one plant and the juice obtained from pounding the stems of another. The pounded plant was called in Sanskrit 'soma', in Avestan 'haoma', a name which means simply 'that which is pressed'. The identity of the original plant used by the proto-Indo-Iranians is uncertain, but it may well have been a species of ephedra (as is the 'hom' used by the Zoroastrians today). They ascribed great qualities to this plant, whose juice, they held, could exhilarate men and heighten their powers. Warriors drinking it would quickly be filled with battle-fury, poets be inspired, and priests become more open to divine promptings. The pounding of the plant in a stone mortar, and the preparation from it of the offering to the waters, forms a major part of the yasna ritual; and a concept developed from this ritual of the 'green-eyed' god Haoma, the divine priest, who was invoked also as a healer, and one who could protect cattle, give strength to fighting men, and ward off drought and famine. As the divine priest, Haoma received a ritual share of each sacrifice, namely the tongue and left jaw-bone, which were consecrated to him and set apart. Otherwise the Iranians believed that the gods were content with the odour of the sacrifice, and the intention of the gift to them. The consecrated meat was shared therefore after the service between the celebrating priests and the worshippers; and it is probable that, as in historic times, domestic animals were never killed except thus in offering to the gods. (The hunter was required to say a brief prayer of consecration at the moment when he took a creature's life.)

The sacred precinct in which the high rituals were performed (later called by the Zoroastrians the 'pavi' or 'pure place') was very simply made. (This was necessary for a semi-wandering people, who could not establish fixed places of worship.) It consisted merely of a small level piece of ground, rectangular in Iranian usage, and marked off by a furrow ritually drawn with prayers, to exclude all evil influences. The enclosed area was then sprinkled with pure water to cleanse it, and consecrated by more prayers. The priest sat cross-legged on the ground, with fire in a small container before him. All vessels used in the service were first cleansed, then consecrated; but they had no inherent sanctity, and after it was over they might be freely handled by anyone, and so could readily be packed up for a move to another place. This remains essentially the character of the Zoroastrian ritual precinct and vessels to this day, with parallels in Brahmanic usage.

The importance of purity in the service of the gods, and as a guard against evil, was very great for the Indo-Iranians – hence the need to purify the ground and to wash all vessels with the utmost care before they were blessed. As a disinfectant after what they felt to be actual contamination (such as touching a dead body), they used what was available, namely cattle-urine with its ammonia content. It is probable that the elaborate purification rites administered later by both Zoroastrians and Brahmans have their origin in simpler rituals already practised by their Stone Age ancestors.

THE GODS

As for the gods to whom the Indo-Iranians offered their worship (for the yasna/yajña is always dedicated by name to a particular divinity), these were many. As well as the cult-gods (Fire, the Waters, Haoma and Geush Urvan) there were 'nature' gods, who personified some physical phenomenon: Sky and Earth, whom the Iranians called Asman and Zam; Sun and Moon, for them Hvar and Mah; and two gods of the Wind, Vata and Vayu. Vata was simply god of the wind that blows, and he was venerated as the being who brought the rain-clouds. Vayu is a more mysterious being, called in the Rigveda the 'soul of the gods', and regarded by the Iranians, it seems, as god of the breath of life itself – beneficent while he sustains it, but terrible in the moment when he makes it depart.

With Vata the rain-bringer was associated *Harahvati Aredvi Sura, the Sanskrit Sarasvati, whose name means 'Possessing waters'. She personified a mythical river, held to pour down from a huge mountain at earth's centre into a great sea, called in Avestan Vourukasha, 'Of many bays'. From this sea other rivers flow out and carry water to every land. The clouds too should take up rain each year from the waters of Vourukasha, and to ensure that they do so is the task of Tishtrya, god of the Dog Star. Every year, the myth tells, Tishtrya goes to the shores of Vourukasha in the shape of a splendid white stallion; but there he is met by Apaosha, demon of Dearth, in the shape of another stallion, hairless, black and ugly, and they fight. If through the year men have failed in their prayers and offerings to Tishtrya, Apaosha will be stronger and will drive the god back; but if he has been truly venerated, Tishtrya is the mightier and conquers the demon. Then he rushes into the sea. In this myth its waves are conceived of as mares, which through their encounter with Tishtrya produce water in abundance; and Vata snatches it up into the clouds and scatters it over the 'seven karshvars'. Mixed with the water are the seeds of plants, which sprout as the rain falls. These seeds came, it was held, from the 'Tree of All Seeds', which grew in the sea Vourukasha, and which was also called the 'Tree of All-Healing'. Belief in it was probably linked with actual tree-cults, that is, veneration of great trees growing beside streams and springs, whose fruits or bark were thought to be curative.

As for the expression 'the seven karshvars', the Indo-Iranians believed that the world was divided into seven regions. These the Iranians thought of as solid circles, the biggest, Khvaniratha, being the one which man inhabits. It, they held, was in the middle, with the other six in a ring around it, separated by water or thick forests (not an unreasonable picture of the world for dwellers on the south Russian steppes). The peak of Hara (the high mountain from which *Harahvati descends) rose in the very centre of Khvaniratha, and the sun, they believed, revolved around it, so that half the world was always in darkness, the other half in light.

The Indo-Iranians held that there was a natural law which ensured that the sun would thus maintain its regular movement, the seasons change, and existence continue in an orderly way. This law was known to the Indians as 'rta', to the Avestan people by the corresponding word 'asha'. The offering of worship and sacrifice by men was felt to be a part of this natural process, and in itself it helped to maintain 'asha', by strengthening both the beneficent gods themselves and the natural world in which man lived.

The concept of 'asha' had ethical implications also, in that it was thought that it should likewise govern human conduct. Truth, honesty, loyalty, and courage were felt to be proper for mankind. Virtue, that is, belonged to the natural order, and vice was its betrayal. So asha is a difficult word to translate, and different English terms are needed to render it in different contexts: order where the concept refers to the physical world, truth or righteousness in connection with the moral one.

The principle of falsehood or distortion which was opposed to asha the Avestan people called 'drug' (Sanskrit 'druh'); and their moralists divided mankind accordingly into the 'ashavan', the righteous who upheld asha, and the wicked, the 'drugvant'. Much of their pondering, plainly, was concerned with social relations, as vital to Stone Age steppe-dwellers as to an urban society – for one tribe must agree with its neighbours as to the extent of their pasture-grounds, one man with his fellow about herding their cattle, and all were concerned with common human matters such as betrothal and marriage, the barter of goods and the rules of hospitality. One matter which evidently meant much to lawmakers and priests was the sacredness of a man's given word, and the importance of enforcing respect for this as a vital aspect of asha. Two sorts of pledges were evidently recognized: the solemn oath, called, it seems, '*varuna' (probably from the IE verbal root *ver, 'bind, tie'), by which a man bound himself to do or not to do some specified act; and the compact or covenant, called 'mithra' (probably from IE *mei, 'exchange'), whereby two parties agreed together over something. In both cases a power was felt to be latent in the spoken pledge, and this power came to be recognized as a divinity who would support and further the upright man who kept his word, but smite down with terrible vengeance the liar who betrayed it.

This vengeance was made visible through the ordeal. Cases inevitably arose when a man was accused of breaking his word and denied it; and then he might be obliged to submit to an ordeal by water (if it were an oath that was in question) or fire (if a covenant) to test his veracity. One type of ordeal by water is described in the Sanskrit Yajñavalkya, 2.108 f.: The accused man had to submerge himself, holding the thighs of a man standing upright. As he went under, he should utter the words 'Through truth protect me, Varuna.' At that instant an archer shot an arrow, and a swift runner darted away to retrieve it. If when he returned the accused were still alive beneath the water, then Varuna, lord of the oath, was held to have spared him as an ashavan. If he were dead this was because he was guilty, and the matter was ended. One of the ordeals by fire consisted of making the accused man run along a narrow gap between two blazing piles of wood. Again, if he lived, Mithra, lord of the covenant, was held to have declared his innocence. Molten copper was evidently also used in fiery ordeals, being poured on the bared breast of the accused.

As a result of such judicial procedures, Mithra and Varuna became closely linked with the elements by which they slew or spared. Varuna received the by-name 'Son of the Waters', Apąm Napat, by which alone he is known in the Avesta; and he was thought of as having his dwelling in the waters of Vourukasha. Mithra correspondingly became lord of fire, and was believed to accompany the sun, the greatest of all fires, in its daily course across the sky, gazing down as he did so to see who upheld the covenant, who broke it. Both he and Varuna were deeply venerated, and grew to be great gods, with many beliefs attached to them; and their concepts broadened out, so that they may be regarded as personifications of Loyalty and Truth respectively. Both received the title 'asura', in Avestan 'ahura', which means simply 'lord'.

The ordeals at which these two mighty beings were invoked were plainly highly dangerous, and in historic times the decision to require one lay with the king or leader of a local community. This figure of the wise ruler, in ultimate control of the law, seems to have been the origin of the concept of the third and greatest of the 'lords', in Avestan Ahura Mazda, the Lord Wisdom. He is a lofty being, exalted far above the fraternal pair, Mithra and Apąm Napat, whose actions he directs and rules. Nor is he connected with any physical phenomenon, but hypostatizes the power of wisdom, which should control all actions of gods and men alike. In the Rigveda he is known simply, it seems, as the Asura, 'the Lord'; and in one passage the two lesser 'lords' are addressed in these words; 'You two make the sky rain through the supernatural power of the Asura; . . . you two protect your ordinances through the supernatural power of the Asura. Through ṛta you rule the universe' (RV 5.63.7). The three 'lords' are all highly ethical beings, who uphold asha/ṛta, and themselves submit to it. These lofty concepts must have been evolved by the proto-Indo-Iranians early in the Stone Age, for they are deeply interwoven in the religions of both the descendant peoples.

The proto-Indo-Iranians venerated a number of other 'abstract' gods, for they evidently had the capacity to personify what would now be termed abstractions, and to apprehend them as strong, ever-present divinities. Instead, that is, of defining a divine personality by saying, for instance, 'God is Love', the Indo-Iranians would begin by believing that 'Love is a god', and would gradually create a divine personality from this concept. How far the process went of enriching the 'abstract' divinity with character and myths seems to have depended on how closely he was associated with human needs or religious observances, and how popular he therefore became. Mithra, for instance, hypostatizing loyalty to the covenant, became worshipped in time as a war-god, fighting on behalf of the ashavan and smiting the treaty-breaker with ruthless power; as a great judge, impartially assessing the deeds of men; and as a solar deity, as splendid as the sun whom he accompanies on high. After the leading Iranian tribesmen acquired the war-chariot, they came to think of their gods too as chariot-riders; and Mithra is said to be drawn across the sky by white horses, shod with silver and gold, which cast no shadow. In his chariot he carries weapons of both the Stone and Bronze Ages: he is armed, that is, with a mace 'cast in the yellow metal' (Yt 10.96), and has also spear, bow and arrows, knife and slingstones (Yt 10.102, 129–31).

Around Mithra were grouped other lesser 'abstract' divinities: Airyaman (Sanskrit Aryaman), personifying the power of friendship – which, ritually established, was a form of covenant; Arshtat, 'Justice'; Ham-vareti, 'Courage'; and Sraosha, 'Obedience', who is also the guardian of prayer. Another divine being associated with both Mithra and Apạm Napat is Khvarenah, who personifies 'divine grace' or 'glory' – a quality that dwells with kings and heroes and prophets, but departs if they are false to asha. Khvarenah in his turn is sometimes linked with Ashi, goddess of Fortune, who should bestow her prizes only on the righteous, the ashavan. The same is true of Verethraghna, god of Victory, who has the standing epithet of 'created by the Ahuras'. Most of the Indo-Iranian gods were conceived anthropomorphically, but Verethraghna's characteristic manifestation is the wild boar, proverbial among the Iranians for its fierce courage; and it is thus that he is pictured in the Avestan hymn to

Mithra (Yt 10), rushing along in front of the Ahura, sharp-tusked and powerful, ready to crush the faithless, the treaty-breakers.

Verethraghna was not worshipped by the Vedic Indians, for their ancestors, it seems, had allowed the ancient god of Victory to be displaced by Indra, a divinity who was the prototype of the Indo-Iranian warrior of the heroic age – bountiful to his followers, valiant in combat, reckless, drinking deep of soma. He is amoral, and demands of his worshippers only lavish offerings, for which he will reward them amply with material gains. The contrast between him and the ethical Ahuras is strikingly expressed in a Rigvedic hymn (RV 4.42), in which he and Varuna in turn state their different claims to greatness. Varuna declares: 'Lordship belongs indeed to me, the perpetual sovereign, as all the Immortals (acknowledge) to us . . . I let the dripping waters rise up, through ṛta I uphold the sky. Through ṛta I am the lord who rules through ṛta.' Indra responds by declaring: 'Men who drive swiftly, having good horses, call on me when surrounded in battle. I provoke strife, I the bountiful Indra. I whirl up the dust, my strength is overwhelming. All things have I done. No godlike power can check me, the unassailable. When draughts of soma, when songs have made me drunk, then both the unbounded regions grow afraid.' The two gods are thus conceived as utterly different beings, who have their prototypes on earth in the ethical ruler, concerned to maintain the law from which he derives his own authority, and the bold warrior-chief, caring for little beyond his personal prowess and fame.

In the lines just quoted Varuna speaks of 'the Immortals'. The title 'Immortal' (in Vedic 'Amṛta', in Avestan 'Amesha') was one of those used by the Indo-Iranians for their gods. Another was 'Shining One', in Vedic 'Deva', in Avestan 'Daeva'. Both words are Indo-European in origin. Yet another term used by the Iranians was Baga, 'He who distributes (good things)'. For some reason Zoroaster himself restricted the use of the ancient title Daeva to Indra and other martial gods whom he saw as destructive forces, opposed to the ethical Ahuras.

Although each act of worship performed by the Iranian priests was dedicated to one of the gods, the rites themselves (with the regular offerings to fire and water) seem to have been always the same. Some priests came to ponder, evidently, on the details of the rituals, and the nature of the physical world which they were designed to sustain; and they evolved thereby a lucid picture of the cosmogony. This can be reconstructed from Zoroastrian writings as follows: the gods created the world in seven stages. First they made the sky of stone, solid like a huge round shell. In the bottom half of this shell they put water. Next they created earth, resting on the water like a great flat dish; and then at the centre of the earth they fashioned the three animate creations in the form of a single plant, a single animal (the 'Uniquely-created Bull') and a single man (Gayo-maretan, 'Mortal Life'). Seventh, they created fire, both visibly as itself and also as an unseen, vital force pervading the animate creations. The sun, part of the creation of fire, stood still overhead as if it were always noon, for the world was brought into being motionless and unchanging. Then the gods offered a triple sacrifice: they crushed the plant, and slew the bull and man. From this beneficent sacrifice more plants, animals and men came into existence. The cycle of being was thus set in motion, with death followed by new life; and the sun began to move across the sky and to regulate the seasons in accordance with asha.

These natural processes, to judge from Indian sources, were regarded as unending. Having been started by the gods, they would go on forever, if men also did their part. So the priests saw themselves as re-enacting every day, with plants and animals, the original sacrifice, to ensure that the world continued in its proper course; and by this daily rite they consciously purified, blessed and strengthened every one of the seven creations, which were all represented there: earth in the ritual precinct itself, and water and fire in vessels before the priest; the stone of the sky in the flint knife and the stone pestle and mortar; plants in the baresman and haoma; and animals in the sacrificial beast (or in animal products, milk and butter). Finally, man was there in the person of the celebrating priest, who was thus a partner with the gods in the task of maintaining the world in a state of strength and purity.

DEATH AND THE HEREAFTER

No end being foreseen for the world as long as this partnership continued, no end was foreseen either for the generations of men, which were thought to follow one another ceaselessly. There was belief in life after death for the individual, and according to its earliest form the disembodied spirit, the 'urvan', lingered on earth for three days before departing downward to a subterranean kingdom of the dead, ruled over by Yima (Sanskrit Yama) who had been the first king to rule on earth and the first man to die. (Gayo-maretan is the prototype of humanity rather than an actual man.) In Yima's realm the spirits lived a shadowy existence, and were dependent on their descendants still living on earth to satisfy their hunger and to clothe them. Offerings for this purpose had to be ritually made, at specified times, so that they could pass through the barrier of matter; and they were given most frequently during the first year, when the newly departed spirit was thought of as lonely, and not yet fully accepted into the brotherhood of the dead. The responsibility for making the offerings fell upon the dead man's heir, usually his eldest son; and it was his duty to perform them for thirty years – three decades, or roughly the span of a generation.

The rituals of the first three days were held to be vitally important, both to protect the soul from evil powers while it waited to depart, and to give it strength to reach the underworld. There seems to have been an old concept of some dangerous place, perhaps a ford or ferry over a dark river, which the soul must cross in order to arrive there. This was called in Avestan the 'Chinvato Peretu', thought to mean the 'Crossing of the Separator'. To give the departed all possible help, the family would mourn during the three days, fast, and have their priest say many prayers. Then a blood sacrifice would be made, with the ritual offering to fire; and meat from it, and clothing, would be blessed during the third night, so that the soul could depart fed and clad on its lonely journey at dawn the next day. Thereafter (to judge from later Zoroastrian usage) food offerings would be consecrated daily on its behalf for thirty days, ending with a second blood sacrifice on the thirtieth day; and then once every thirtieth day, or month by month, till the end of the first year, when there would be the third and last blood sacrifice. After that the soul's need of material cherishing was felt to be less, and there would simply be annual offerings for thirty years on the anniversary of death. Then the soul was believed to be fully one of the great company of the dead, so that it could be sustained simply by sharing in the general offerings made by each family for their ancestors at the feast of All Souls, called by the Avestan people Hamaspathmaedaya. This feast was celebrated on the last night of the year, the souls returning to their old homes, it was believed, at sunset, and departing again as the sun rose on New Year's day.

The funeral rite connected with the belief in an underworld home of the dead was burial. The Zoroastrian word 'dakhma' (coming through '*dafma' from an IE verbal root dhṃbh 'bury') meant originally, it seems, a grave. The proto-Indo-Iranians are held to have been one group among the 'pit-grave' peoples of the steppes, who buried members of their leading families at the bottom of deep shafts covered by earthen barrows. The ordinary people were presumably laid in simple graves in the earth, of which no trace remains.

It seems probable that it was just before the Indians and Iranians separated that they conceived a new hope concerning the hereafter. This was that some at least among them – princes and warriors and the priests who served the gods – might escape the dreaded fate of an eternally joyless existence, and that their souls might mount upward at death to join the gods in sunlit Paradise, where they would know all imaginable delights. With this hope the 'Crossing of the Separator' became thought of as a bridge, with one end resting on the mountain peak of Hara, the other on the road up to heaven. Only those who were worthy – perhaps through having offered many sacrifices – could cross this bridge. Other souls, attempting it, would fall off, down to the subterranean kingdom of the dead. Among those held to be thus doomed were probably all lowly persons – including all women and children. The souls who attained Paradise would naturally have no need of offerings to be made for them by their descendants; but because of tradition, and also no doubt because of uncertainty about each individual fate, these offerings were still made piously for all the departed.

With the hope of attaining Paradise there developed a belief in the resurrection of the body. It was evidently impossible to conceive of experiencing the joys of heaven in spirit only; and (to judge from Indian evidence) it came to be held that within the first year after death the bones of the physical body would be raised up and, clothed in immortal flesh, be reunited with the soul in heaven. It was probably in connection with this belief that the Indians gradually changed their funerary rite to cremation, whereby the mortal flesh was swiftly destroyed. The bones were then carefully gathered up and buried to await resurrection. The Iranians, however, seem to have had too great a respect for fire to use it to consume polluting matter; and it may be that already in pagan times some among them adopted instead the rite of exposure known later from Zoroastrianism. This consisted of laying the corpse down in some barren place where vultures and scavenging beasts would quickly devour it. The sun's rays made a path to draw the spirit skyward, and the corrupting flesh was swiftly disposed of. Thereafter, the bones were collected and buried, as in the Indian rite.

What complicates the study of pagan Iranian beliefs about the hereafter is the use of another term besides urvan for the departed spirit, namely '*fravarti', Avestan 'fravashi'. The etymology of this word (like that of urvan) is doubtful; but it seems possible that it may derive from the same verbal root as Ham-vareti 'Courage', and that the fravashi was originally the departed soul of a hero, one particularly potent to help and protect his descendants. If this is so, there must once have existed a hero-cult among the ancient Iranians, as among the Greeks. The fravashis were conceived, something like the Valkyries, as female beings, winged and inhabiting the air, through which, if satisfied by offerings, they would fly swiftly to men's aid. They strove each year to bring rain to their own families, and to see that children were born to them, and in time of war they fought, invisibly, beside their descendants.

Probably there were similarities from the earliest period between the specialized fravashi-cult and the general cult of the urvan which must have helped beliefs about the two to blur and mingle. The growth of hope for some of an after-life in Paradise may well have added confusion. One might expect that it would be the powerful fravashi who would be first thought of as dwelling on high with the gods, but it is in fact the urvan who is chiefly spoken of in this connection. Possibly an age-old belief in the fravashis as ever-present helpers and guardians prevented their being readily conceived of as dwelling afar; and it may also have been difficult to associate these winged spirits with the doctrine of the resurrection of the body. Nevertheless, it seems that already in pagan times the concepts of mighty fravashi and helpless urvan had to a large extent become fused. In the Avestan hymn to the fravashis (Yt 13), which contains ancient elements, it is they who are represented as returning to their homes at Hamaspathmaedaya, seeking offerings of meat and clothing; but in other verses of the same hymn they are invoked as godlike in their powers. In the liturgy of the Zoroastrian yasna the identification of fravashi and urvan is at times complete, and is expressed by the recurrent words: 'We worship the souls (urvan-) of the dead, which are the fravashis of the just.' Yet a broad distinction between the two persists to this day (without, it seems, the support of clearly formulated doctrine) which is that in general one prays to the fravashi, but for the urvan.

Conclusion

In sum, it seems that the religion of the pagan Iranians centred on rituals and observance, but that the beliefs concerning the gods contained noble elements, which were linked with the concepts of asha and the Ahuras. These elements were part of a traditional faith, which restricted hope of happiness hereafter to the leaders among men. They were mixed, moreover, with amoral concepts, so that those who chiefly worshipped Indra and the warlike divinities associated with him could nurture the hope of buying prosperity in this life and salvation in the next with abundant offerings. Both moral and amoral elements go back, evidently, to the proto-Indo-Iranian period, that is, to a pastoral Stone Age; but the latter were almost certainly strengthened with the coming of the Bronze Age, and all the opportunities which developed then for the ruthless acquisition of wealth and power.

CHAPTER TWO

Zoroaster and his teachings

Introduction

The prophet Zarathushtra, son of Pourushaspa, of the Spitaman family, is known to us primarily from the Gathas, seventeen great hymns which he composed and which have been faithfully preserved by his community. These are not works of instruction, but inspired, passionate utterances, many of them addressed directly to God; and their poetic form is a very ancient one, which has been traced back (through Norse parallels) to Indo-European times. It seems to have been linked with a mantic tradition, that is, to have been cultivated by priestly seers who sought to express in lofty words their personal apprehension of the divine; and it is marked by subtleties of allusion, and great richness and complexity of style. Such poetry can only have been fully understood by the learned; and since Zoroaster believed that he had been entrusted by God with a message for all mankind, he must also have preached again and again in plain words to ordinary people. His teachings were handed down orally in his community from generation to generation, and were at last committed to writing under the Sasanians, rulers of the third Iranian empire. The language then spoken was Middle Persian, also called Pahlavi; and the Pahlavi books provide invaluable keys for interpreting the magnificent obscurities of the Gathas themselves.

Much valuable matter is preserved also in the 'Younger Avesta'.

Zoroaster and his teaching

The dialect which Zoroaster himself spoke is known only from the Gathas and a few other ancient texts. (This linguistic isolation increases the difficulties of interpreting his hymns, since these are full of otherwise unknown words.) The rest of the surviving Avesta consists of liturgical texts preserved in various later stages of the same language (but not in exactly the same dialect). To his followers all these works embodied different aspects of Zoroaster's revelation, and were to be reverenced accordingly. Although Western scholars distinguish the post-Gathic texts collectively as the 'Younger Avesta', some of them contain matter which is very old. This is particularly true of certain of the yashts, hymns addressed to individual divinities.

Zoroaster and his mission

Zoroaster's date cannot be established with any precision, since he lived in what for his people were prehistoric times. The language of the Gathas is archaic, and close to that of the Rigveda (whose composition has been assigned to about 1700 B.C. onwards); and the picture of the world to be gained from them is correspondingly ancient, that of a Stone Age society. Some allowance may have to be made for literary conservatism; and it is also possible that the 'Avestan' people (as Zoroaster's own tribe is called for want of a better name) were poor or isolated, and so not rapidly influenced by the developments of the Bronze Age. It is only possible therefore to hazard a reasoned conjecture that Zoroaster lived some time between 1700 and 1500 B.C.

In the Gathas he refers to himself as a 'zaotar', that is, a fully qualified priest; and he is the only founder of a credal religion who was both priest and prophet. (In the Younger Avesta he is spoken of by the general word for priest, 'athaurvan'.) He also calls himself a 'manthran', that is, one able to compose 'manthra' (Sanskrit 'mantra'), inspired utterances of power. Training for the priesthood began early among the Indo-Iranians, probably at about the age of seven, and was carried out orally, for they had no knowledge of writing. It must have consisted, basically, of learning both rituals and doctrines, as well as acquiring skill in extemporizing verses in invocation and praise of the gods, and learning by heart great manthras composed by earlier sages. The Iranians held that maturity was reached at fifteen, and it was presumably at that age that Zoroaster was made priest. His own Gathas suggest that he must thereafter have sought all the higher knowledge which he could gain from various teachers; and he further describes himself there as a 'vaedemna' or 'one who knows', an initiate possessed of divinely inspired wisdom. According to Zoroastrian tradition (preserved in the Pahlavi books), he spent years in a wandering quest for truth; and his hymns suggest that he must then have witnessed acts of violence, with war-bands, worshippers of the Daevas, descending on peaceful communities to pillage, slaughter and carry off cattle. Conscious himself of being powerless physically, he became filled with a deep longing for justice, for the moral law of the Ahuras to be established for strong and weak alike, so that order and tranquillity could prevail, and all be able to pursue the good life in peace.

According to tradition Zoroaster was thirty, the time of ripe wisdom, when revelation finally came to him. This great happening is alluded to in one of the Gathas (Y 43), and is tersely described in a Pahlavi work (Zadspram XX–XXI). Here it is said that Zoroaster, being at a gathering met to celebrate a spring festival, went at dawn to a river to fetch water for the haoma-ceremony. He waded in to draw it from midstream; and when he returned to the bank – himself in a state of ritual purity, emerging from the pure element, water, in the freshness of a spring dawn – he had a vision. He saw on the bank a shining Being, who revealed himself as Vohu Manah 'Good Purpose'; and this Being led Zoroaster into the presence of Ahura Mazda and five other radiant figures, before whom 'he did not see his own shadow upon the earth, owing to their great light'. And it was then, from this great heptad, that he received his revelation.

Ahura Mazda and his Adversary

This was the first of a number of times that Zoroaster saw Ahura Mazda in vision, or felt conscious of his presence, or heard his words calling him to his service, a summons which he whole-heartedly obeyed. 'For this' (he declares) 'I was set apart as yours from the beginning' (Y 44.11). 'While I have power and strength, I shall teach men to seek the right (asha)' (Y 28.4). It was as the master of asha (order, righteousness and justice) that he venerated Ahura Mazda. This was in accordance with tradition, since Mazda had been worshipped of old as the greatest of the three Ahuras, the guardians of asha; but Zoroaster went much further, and in a startling departure from accepted beliefs proclaimed Ahura Mazda to be the one uncreated God, existing eternally, and Creator of all else that is good, including all other beneficent divinities.

One cannot hope to retrace with any certainty the processes of thought which led Zoroaster to this exalted belief; but it seems probable that he came to it through meditating on the daily act of worship which he as priest performed, and on the cosmogonic theories connected with this. Scholar-priests, as we have seen, had evolved a doctrine of the genesis of the world in seven stages, with the seven creations all being represented at the yasna; and they had postulated primal unity in the physical sphere, with all life stemming from one original plant, animal and man. From this, it would seem, Zoroaster was inspired to apprehend a similar original uniqueness in the divine sphere also, with, in the beginning, only one beneficent Being existing in the universe, Ahura Mazda, the all-wise, and also the wholly just and good, from whom all other beneficent divine beings emanated.

Harsh experience had evidently convinced the prophet that wisdom, justice and goodness were utterly separate by nature from wickedness and cruelty; and in vision he beheld, co-existing with Ahura Mazda, an Adversary, the 'Hostile Spirit', Angra Mainyu, equally uncreated, but ignorant and wholly malign. These two great Beings Zoroaster beheld with prophetic eye at their original, far-off encountering: 'Truly there are two primal Spirits, twins, renowned to be in conflict. In thought and word and act they are two, the good and the bad. . . . And when these two Spirits first encountered, they created life and not-life, and that at the end the worst existence shall be for the followers of falsehood (drug), but the best dwelling for those who possess righteousness (asha). Of the two Spirits, the one who follows falsehood chose doing the worst things, the Holiest Spirit, who is clad in the hardest stone [i.e. the sky] chose righteousness, and (so shall they all) who will satisfy Ahura Mazda continually with just actions' (Y 30.3–5).

An essential element in this revelation is that the two primal Beings each made a deliberate choice (although each, it seems, according to his own proper nature) between good and evil, an act which prefigures the identical choice which every man must make for himself in this life. The exercise of choice changed the inherent antagonism between the two Spirits into an active one, which expressed itself, at a decision taken by Ahura Mazda, in creation and counter-creation, or, as the prophet put it, in the making of 'life' and 'not-life' (that is, death); for Ahura Mazda knew in his wisdom that if he became Creator and fashioned this world, then the Hostile Spirit would attack it, because it was good, and it would become a battleground for their two forces, and in the end he, God, would win the great struggle there and be able to destroy evil, and so achieve a universe which would be wholly good forever.

The heptad and the seven creations

These teachings were fundamentally new; but it was the old cosmogony which provided the basis for Zoroaster's thought. So the first act which he conceived Ahura Mazda as performing was the evocation, through his Holy Spirit, Spenta Mainyu, of six lesser divinities, the radiant Beings of Zoroaster's earliest vision. These divinities formed a heptad with Ahura Mazda himself, and they proceeded with him to fashion the seven creations which make up the world. The evocation of the six is variously described in Zoroastrian works, but always in ways which suggest the essential unity of beneficent divinity. Thus Ahura Mazda is said either to be their 'father', or to have 'mingled' himself with them, and in one Pahlavi text his creation of them is compared with the lighting of torches from a torch.

The six great Beings then in their turn, Zoroaster taught, evoked other beneficent divinities, who are in fact the beneficent gods of the pagan Iranian pantheon. (He himself invokes a number of them in the Gathas, notably the 'other Ahuras', that is, Mithra and Apąm Napat; Sraosha, Ashi and Geush Urvan.) All these divine beings, who are, according to his doctrines, either directly or indirectly the emanations of Ahura Mazda, strive under him, according to their various appointed tasks, to further good and to defeat evil. Collectively they are known in Zoroastrianism as Yazatas, 'Beings worthy of worship', or Amesha Spentas, 'Holy Immortals'. Although the latter term does not occur in the Gathas, it was most probably coined by Zoroaster himself to distinguish those beings revealed to him as beneficent from the generality of pagan gods, who are invoked as 'All the Immortals' in the Vedas; for Zoroaster rejected with the utmost courage and firmness the worship of the warlike, amoral Daevas – that is, Indra and his companions – whom he regarded as being 'of the race of evil purpose' (Y 32.3). 'The Daevas chose not rightly, because the Deceiver came upon them as they consulted, so that they chose the worst purpose. Then together they betook themselves to Wrath, through whom they afflicted the life of man' (Y 30.6). To Zoroaster the Daevas were thus both wicked by nature and wicked by choice, like Angra Mainyu himself – false gods who were not to be worshipped because they stood for conflict among men, luring them through their greed for offerings to bloodshed and destructive strife.

The crucial word 'spenta', used by Zoroaster of Ahura Mazda and all his creation, is one of the most important terms in his revelation. Basically, it seems, it meant 'possessing power', and when used of beneficent divinities, 'possessing power to aid', hence 'furthering, supporting, benefiting'. Through constant religious use spenta acquired overtones of meaning, like the word 'holy', which similarly meant originally 'mighty, strong'. 'Holy' is therefore a close rendering for it; but to avoid suggesting concepts alien to Zoroastrianism, some scholars have preferred 'bounteous' as a standard translation. This, however, has the weakness that it has no religious associations in English, and so does not convey the sense of reverence implicit in Zoroastrian spenta. The rendering 'holy' has therefore been generally preferred in this book.

Although the title Amesha Spenta may be used of any of the divinities of Ahura Mazda's creation, it is applied especially to the great six of the prophet's own vision, the other lesser divinities being referred to as the Yazatas. The doctrine of the six Holy Immortals is fundamental to Zoroaster's teachings, and has far-reaching spiritual and ethical consequences, since these Beings hypostatize qualities or attributes of Ahura Mazda himself, and can in their turn (if rightly sought and venerated) bestow these upon men. For every individual, as for the prophet himself, the Immortal who leads the way to all the rest is Vohu Manah, 'Good Purpose'; and his closest confederate is Asha Vahishta, 'Best Righteousness' – the divinity personifying the mighty principle of asha, whom Zoroaster names in the Gathas more often than any other of the six. Then there is Spenta Armaiti, 'Holy Devotion', embodying the dedication to what is good and just; and Khshathra Vairya, 'Desirable Dominion', who represents both the power which each person should properly exert for righteousness in this life, and also the power and the kingdom of God. The final pair are Haurvatat and Ameretat, 'Health' and 'Long Life', who not only enhance this mortal existence but confer that eternal well-being and life, which may be obtained by the righteous in the presence of Ahura Mazda.

That divine attributes should be isolated, and then invoked and worshipped as independent beings, was a characteristic of the pagan Iranian religion, as we have seen in the case of Mithra, surrounded as he is by Friendship, Obedience, Justice, Courage and Divine Grace. So the mould was already old in which Zoroaster cast his new doctrines. He saw the great six as remaining similarly close to the supreme Lord; and it is said of them in the Younger Avesta (Yt 19.16–18) that they are 'of one mind, one voice, one act. . . . Of them one beholds the soul of the other, thinking upon good thoughts, good words, good deeds . . . they who are the creators and fashioners and makers and observers and guardians of the creations of Ahura Mazda.' The tendency also existed in the old Iranian religion to link 'abstract' divinities with physical phenomena, so closely that (as in the case of Mithra and Apam Napat) the phenomena could be regarded as representing the divinities themselves; and already in the Gathas the association of the seven Amesha Spentas with the seven creations was of this kind. The nature of the link in each case appears to have been understood by the prophet through his meditations upon the yasna, the daily act of worship by which the seven creations were sustained and blessed. In pondering on its rituals he came, it seems, to apprehend that within each of the things which he as priest saw or handled was an immaterial presence, a hidden divinity, so that through these rites, performed primarily for the sake of the physical world, priest and worshippers could at the same time seek a moral and spiritual good, honouring and striving to unite themselves with the great invisible Amesha Spentas. A new dimension was thus added to the age-old observance.

The link of each divinity with his creation is a reasonable one, for Zoroastrianism, once its intuitively held – or divinely revealed – premises are granted, is essentially a rational faith. So Khshathra Vairya, Desirable Dominion, is lord of the hard sky of stone, which arches protectively over the earth. Lowly earth itself belongs to Spenta Armaiti, Holy Devotion. Water is the creation of Haurvatat, Health, and plants belong to Ameretat, Long Life or Immortality. Vohu Manah, Good Purpose, is lord of the mild beneficent cow, who for the nomad Iranians was a powerful symbol of creative goodness, of that which sustains and nourishes. Fire, which pervades the other creations, and, through the sun, controls the seasons, is under the protection of Asha Vahishta, the Order which should pervade and regulate the world. Finally man himself, with his intelligence and power of choice, belongs especially to Ahura Mazda, the Lord Wisdom, who made the first choice of all. These associations, subtly alluded to in the Gathas, are plainly set out in the later literature. The order of the great heptad of divinities often does not correspond with the chronological sequence of the seven creations. This was because it was natural to name them usually according to spiritual dignity and worth, with Ahura Mazda in his rightful place at their head. Any of the great seven may be entreated by any individual worshipper – indeed he should invoke them all, if he is to become a perfect man; but two among them had particular links with two groups of society. Armaiti, as guardian of the enduring, fertile earth, mother of all things, was the natural protectress of women. In the words of an ancient text: 'This earth then we worship, her who bears us, together with women' (y.38.1). Her great partner, Khshathra, lord of the lofty, protective sky, and so of stone everywhere, was as fittingly the guardian of just men, who had the duty to use their weapons – their flint-tipped arrows and spears, their slingstones and heavy maces – to protect the poor and weak, and not to despoil or harm them. The priests, who were the learned class, trained in religious lore, evidently felt themselves especially under the protection of Ahura Mazda, the Lord Wisdom, whose creation, mankind, they represented at the yasna; but the supreme Lord's power is so all-encompassing that this link is not made so much of in the tradition.

Being the creation of Ahura Mazda, every man has the duty not only to cherish the six lesser creations, but also to watch over his own physical and moral well-being, and to care for his fellow-men, since each of them is likewise the special creature of God. The particular ethical code which Zoroaster gave his followers to live by demanded of them good thoughts, good words and good deeds – an admirable moral law which seems a generalization of the threefold demand made of the Iranian priest, who to perform an act of worship effectively needed good intention, right words and correct rituals.

The doctrine of the seven Amesha Spentas and the seven creations thus inspired a comprehensive morality, and inculcated in man a deep sense of responsibility for the world around him. He is the chief of the creations, but he is bound to the other six by the link of a shared purpose, for all spenta creation is striving for a common goal, man consciously, the rest by instinct or nature, for all were brought into existence for this one end, namely the utter defeat of evil.

Creation and the Three Times

Another aspect of the relationship between tangible and intangible was embodied in Zoroaster's teaching (best known to us from the Pahlavi books) that Ahura Mazda accomplished the act of creation in two stages. First he brought all things into being in a disembodied state, called in Pahlavi 'menog', that is, 'spiritual, immaterial'. Then he gave it 'material' or 'getig', existence. The getig existence is better than the previous menog one, for in it Ahura Mazda's perfect creation received the added good of solid and sentient form. Together, the fashioning of these two states constituted the act of Creation, called in Pahlavi 'Bundahishn'. The achievement of the getig state set the field for the battle with evil, for unlike the menog one it was vulnerable to assault; and Angra Mainyu straightway attacked. According to the myth as set out in the Pahlavi books, he broke in violently through the lower bowl of the stone sky, thus marring its perfection. Then he plunged upwards through the water, turning much of it salt, and attacked the earth, creating deserts. Next he withered the plant, and slew the Uniquely-created Bull and the First Man. Finally he fell upon the seventh creation, fire, and sullied it with smoke, so that he had physically blighted all the good creation.

The divine beings then rallied their forces. Ameretat took the plant, pounded it up (as haoma is pounded in the yasna-ritual), and scattered its essence over the world by cloud and rain, to grow up as more plants everywhere. The seed of the Bull and Man were purified in the moon and sun, and more cattle and men sprang from them. So in the Zoroastrian version of the ancient myth the beneficent sacrifice attributed originally to the pagan gods was assigned as an evil act to Angra Mainyu, for it was he who brought decay and death into the perfect, static world of Ahura Mazda. The Amesha Spentas were able, however, through their holy power to turn his malicious acts to benefit; and such must be the constant endeavour of all the good creation.

'Creation' was the first of the three times into which the drama of cosmic history is divided. Angra Mainyu's attack inaugurated the second time, that of 'Mixture' (Pahlavi 'Gumezisn'), during which this world is no longer wholly good, but is a blend of good and evil; for the cycle of being having been set in motion, Angra Mainyu continues to attack with the Daevas and all the other legions of darkness which he had brought into existence to oppose the Yazatas, and together they inflict not only physical ills but every moral and spiritual evil from which man suffers. To withstand their assaults man needs to venerate Ahura Mazda and the six Amesha Spentas, and to bring them so fully into his own heart and being that there is no room there for vice or weakness. He should also worship all the beneficent Yazatas, some of whom, like the two lesser Ahuras (twice invoked by Zoroaster himself in the Gathas) will also help him in his moral struggles, while others, such as Sun and Moon, will play their part in keeping the physical world strong and in accordance with asha.

According to Zoroaster's new revelation, mankind thus shared with the spenta divinities the great common purpose of gradually overcoming evil and restoring the world to its original perfect state. The glorious moment when this will be achieved is called 'Frasho-kereti' (Pahlavi 'Frashegird'), a term which probably means 'Healing' or 'Renovation'. Therewith history will cease, for the third time, that of 'Separation' (Pahlavi 'Wizarishn') will be ushered in. This is the time when good will be separated again from evil; and since evil will then be utterly destroyed, the period of Separation is eternal, and in it Ahura Mazda and all the Yazatas and men and women will live together for ever in perfect, untroubled goodness and peace.

In thus postulating not only a beginning but also an end to human history, Zoroaster made a profound break with earlier ideas, according to which the process of life, once started, was expected to continue forever, if men and gods both bore their part. The old concept of co-operation between divinity and worshipper, as necessary in order to maintain the world according to asha, persists in his teachings; but he gave this co-operation new significance by seeing it, not as directed simply to preserving the world as it is, but to reaching an ultimate goal of restored perfection. Moreover, his revelation lent man new dignity, for according to it he was created to be God's ally, working with him to achieve the victory over evil which is longed for by both.

The doctrine of the Three Times – Creation, Mixture, Separation – makes history in a sense cyclical, with the getig world restored in the third time to the perfection it possessed in the first one. Meanwhile all the sorrows and strivings of the present time of Mixture are part of the battle against Angra Mainyu. Zoroaster thus not only saw a noble purpose for humanity, but also offered men a reasoned explanation for what they have to endure in this life, seeing this as affliction brought on them by the Hostile Spirit, and not imputing to the will of an all-powerful Creator the sufferings of his creatures here below.

Death and the hereafter

The most general human affliction is death; and death forces individual souls, throughout the time of Mixture, to leave the getig world and return for a while to the deficient menog state. As each spirit departs, according to Zoroaster, it is judged on what it has done in this life to aid the cause of goodness. He taught that women as well as men, servants as well as masters, may hope to attain Paradise, for the physical barrier of pagan days, the 'Bridge of the Separator', becomes in his revelation a place of moral judgment, where each soul must depend, not on power or wealth of offerings in the life it has left behind, but on its own ethical achievements. Here Mithra presides over the tribunal, flanked by Sraosha and by Rashnu, who holds the scales of justice. In these are weighed the soul's thoughts, words and deeds, the good on one side, the bad on the other. If the good are heavier, the soul is judged worthy of Paradise; and it is led by a beautiful maiden, the personification of its own conscience ('daena') across the broad bridge and up on high. If the scales sink on the bad side, the bridge contracts to the width of a blade-edge, and a horrid hag, meeting the soul as it tries to cross, seizes it in her arms and plunges with it down to hell, 'the dwelling-place of Worst Purpose' (Y 32.13), where the wicked endure a 'long age of misery, of darkness, ill food and the crying of woe' (Y 31.20). The concept of hell, a place of torment presided over by Angra Mainyu, seems to be Zoroaster's own, shaped by his deep sense of the need for justice. Those few souls 'whose false (things) and what are just balance' (Y 33.1) go to the 'Place of the Mixed Ones', Misvan Gatu, where, as in the old underworld kingdom of the dead, they lead a grey existence, lacking both joy and sorrow.

Even for souls in Paradise bliss is not perfect during this time of Mixture, for complete happiness can come again only at Frashegird. The pagan Iranians had presumably held, like the Vedic Indians, that soon after each blessed soul reached Paradise it was reunited with its resurrected body, to live again a happy life of full sensation; but Zoroaster taught that the blessed must wait for this culmination till Frashegird and the 'future body' (Pahlavi 'tan i pasen'), when the earth will give up the bones of the dead (Y 30.7). This general resurrection will be followed by the Last Judgment, which will divide all the righteous from the wicked, both those who have lived until that time and those who have been judged already. Airyaman, the Yazata of friendship and healing, together with Atar, Fire, will melt all the metal in the mountains, and this will flow in a glowing river over the earth. All mankind must pass through this river, and, as it is said in a Pahlavi text, 'for him who is righteous it will seem like warm milk, and for him who is wicked, it will seem as if he is walking in the flesh through molten metal' (GBd XXXIV.18–19). In this great apocalyptic vision Zoroaster perhaps fused, unconsciously, tales of volcanic eruptions and streams of burning lava with his own experience of Iranian ordeals by molten metal; and according to his stern original teaching, strict justice will prevail then, as at each individual judgment on earth by a fiery ordeal. So at this last ordeal of all the wicked will suffer a second death, and will perish off the face of the earth. The Daevas and legions of darkness will already have been annihilated in a last great battle with the Yazatas; and the river of metal will flow down into hell, slaying Angra Mainyu and burning up the last vestige of wickedness in the universe.

Ahura Mazda and the six Amesha Spentas will then solemnize a last, spiritual yasna, offering up the last sacrifice (after which death will be no more), and making a preparation of the mystical 'white haoma', which will confer immortality on the resurrected bodies of all the blessed, who will partake of it. Thereafter men will become like the Immortals themselves, of one thought, word and deed, unaging, free from sickness, without corruption, forever joyful in the kingdom of God upon earth. For it is in this familiar and beloved world, restored to its original perfection, that, according to Zoroaster, eternity will be passed in bliss, and not in a remote insubstantial Paradise. So the time of Separation is a renewal of the time of Creation, except that no return is prophesied to the original uniqueness of living things. Mountain and valley will give place once more to level plain; but whereas in the beginning there was one plant, one animal, one man, the rich variety and number that have since issued from these will remain forever. Similarly the many divinities who were brought into being by Ahura Mazda will continue to have their separate existences. There is no prophecy of their re-absorption into the Godhead. As a Pahlavi text puts it, after Frashegird 'Ohrmazd and the Amahraspands and all Yazads and men will be together. . . ; every place will resemble a garden in spring, in which there are all kinds of trees and flowers . . . and it will be entirely the creation of Ohrmazd' (Pahl.Riv.Dd. XLVIII, 99, 100, 107).

Zoroaster was thus the first to teach the doctrines of an individual judgment, Heaven and Hell, the future resurrection of the body, the general Last Judgment, and life everlasting for the reunited soul and body. These doctrines were to become familiar articles of faith to much of mankind, through borrowings by Judaism, Christianity and Islam; yet it is in Zoroastrianism itself that they have their fullest logical coherence, since Zoroaster insisted both on the goodness of the material creation, and hence of the physical body, and on the unwavering impartiality of divine justice. According to him, salvation for the individual depended on the sum of his thoughts, words and deeds, and there could be no intervention, whether compassionate or capricious, by any divine Being to alter this. With such a doctrine, belief in the Day of Judgment had its full awful significance, with each man having to bear the responsibility for the fate of his own soul, as well as sharing in responsibility for the fate of the world. Zoroaster's gospel was thus a noble and strenuous one, which called for both courage and resolution on the part of those willing to receive it.

CHAPTER THREE

The establishing of Mazda worship

Introduction

Noble though they were, and a development of the old Ahuric religion, Zoroaster's teachings contained much to anger and trouble his people. In offering the hope of heaven to everyone who would follow him and seek righteousness, he was breaking, it seems, with an aristocratic and priestly tradition which consigned all lesser mortals to a subterranean life after death. Moreover, he not only extended the hope of salvation on high to the humble, but threatened the mighty with hell and ultimate extinction if they acted unjustly. His doctrines concerning the hereafter were thus doubly calculated to outrage the privileged; and to rich and poor alike his rejection of the Daevas must have seemed rash and dangerous, being calculated to draw down the wrath of those divine beings on the whole community. Further, the grand concepts of the one Creator, dualism and the great cosmic struggle, with the demand for continual moral endeavours, may well have been difficult to grasp, and, once grasped, too challenging for the ordinary easy-going polytheist.

In addition to all this, Zoroaster's own people evidently felt the usual scepticism towards a familiar person who claims a divine and unique revelation; and so the years he spent preaching among them were almost fruitless, bringing him only one convert, his cousin Maidhyoimanha. So he departed and went to another tribe, where, coming as a stranger, he gained a hearing from the queen, Hutaosa, and her husband, Vishtaspa, who 'came forward as the arm and help of this religion, the Ahuric, Zoroastrian' (Yt 13.100). Vishtaspa's conversion angered the neighbouring princes, who demanded his return to the old faith. On his refusal there was fighting, in which Vishtaspa was victorious; and so Zoroaster's teachings became established in his territory.

According to the tradition Zoroaster lived for many years after Vishtaspa's conversion, but little is known of his life either before or after this crucial event. Marriage was demanded of an Iranian priest, to fit him fully for his vocation, and the prophet was married three times. His first two wives, whose names are not recorded, bore him three sons and three daughters. The marriage of the youngest daughter, Pouruchista, is celebrated in one of the Gathas (Y 53). Her husband was Jamaspa, Vishtaspa's chief counsellor, who is proverbial among Zoroastrians for wisdom. He figures in the Gathas with his kinsman Frashaostra; and Zoroaster himself took Frashaostra's daughter Hvovi as his third wife. This marriage was childless.

The Zoroastrian badge

In the Gathas Zoroaster appears as prophet rather than lawgiver; but during the years which he spent at Vishtaspa's court he must have organized his community, and established its devotional forms and practices. It had been, it seems, an Indo-Iranian custom for men on initiation to put on a woven cord as a sign of their membership of the religious community. The Brahmans of India wear the cord over one shoulder. It is knotted for them by a priest, and they never untie it, but simply slip it aside when ritually necessary. This may well have been the general old usage, which Zoroaster adapted to give his followers a distinctive badge. All Zoroastrians, men and women alike, wear the cord as a girdle, passed three times round the waist and knotted at back and front. Initiation took place at the age of fifteen; and thereafter, every day for the rest of his life, the believer must himself untie and retie the cord repeatedly when praying. The symbolism of the girdle (called in Persian the 'kusti') was elaborated down the centuries; but it is likely that from the beginning the three coils were intended to symbolize the threefold ethic of Zoroastrianism, and so to concentrate the wearer's thoughts on the practice of his faith. Further, the kusti is tied over an inner shirt of pure white, the 'sudra', which has a little purse sewn into the throat; and this is to remind the believer that he should be continually filling its emptiness with the merit of good thoughts, words and deeds, and so be laying up treasure for himself in heaven.

The times and manner of praying

For the pagan Iranians three times of day – sunrise, noon and sunset – had been significant for prayer and worship, and these divided the daylight hours into two periods, with the morning one, Havani, under the protection of Mithra, and the afternoon one, Uzayara, under that of his brother Ahura, Apąm Napat. The night, it seems, constituted a third period, called Aiwisruthra, and this was assigned to the fravashis, the spirits of the dead. Zoroaster, it seems, made two new divisions of the twenty-four hours, and required of his followers accordingly five times of daily prayer. One of the new divisions, named Rapithwa, began at noon (the ideal moment at which time stood still at Creation, as it will again at Frasho-kereti), and extended into the first part of the afternoon, being thus taken from Uzayara. During summer, when the spenta powers are in the ascendant, this new period was dedicated to the spirit of noon, Rapithwina, and was set under the protection of Asha Vahishta, lord of fire and so of noontime heat; but during the Daeva-dominated winter Rapithwina was held to retreat beneath the earth, to cherish with his warmth the roots of plants and springs of water; and his division of the day was then assigned, like the morning one, to Mithra, and became the Second Havani. So all through summer the prayers said at noon helped the devout to think of asha and of the present and future triumph of goodness, while Rapithwina's withdrawal during winter was an annual reminder of the menacing power of evil, and the need to resist it. So Zoroaster used both the times of day and seasons of the year to imprint essential doctrines firmly in the minds of his followers.

The other new division of the twenty-four hours began at the opposite moment, midnight. Zoroaster thus divided the night into two, leaving the first half to the fravashis, but devoting the second half, called Ushah (from midnight till sunrise) to Sraosha, lord of prayer; and during that time, when the powers of darkness are at their strongest and prowl about, his followers were to rise, put fuel and incense on the hearth fire, and strengthen the world of goodness by their prayers.

The five daily prayers were a binding duty on every Zoroastrian, part of his necessary service to God, and a weapon in the fight against evil. The ritual of prayer, as known from living practice, is as follows: first the believer prepares himself by washing the dust from face, hands and feet; then, untying the sacred cord, he stands with it held in both hands before him, upright in the presence of his Maker, his eyes on the symbol of righteousness, fire. Then he prays to Ahura Mazda, execrates Angra Mainyu (flicking the ends of the cord contemptuously as he does so), and reties the cord while still praying. The whole observance takes only a few minutes, but its regular repetition is a religious exercise of the highest value, constituting both a steady discipline and a regular avowal of the fundamental tenets of the faith.

The seven festivals

The other strict obligation which Zoroaster laid on his followers was to celebrate annually seven high feasts, dedicated to Ahura Mazda and the Amesha Spentas, and to their seven creations. Six of these feasts, known later as the 'gahambars', made a uniform chain, and the tradition duly ascribes their foundation to the prophet himself; but in origin they appear to have been pastoral and farming festivals which he rededicated to his own faith, and as such they are scattered irregularly through the year. Their names (preserved in Younger Avestan forms) are as follows: Maidhyoi-zaremaya, 'Mid-spring'; Maidhyoi-shema, 'Mid-summer'; Paitishahya, '(Feast of) bringing in the corn'; Ayathrima, '(Feast of) the home-coming', that is, of the herds from pasture; Maidhyairya, 'Mid-winter'; and Hamaspath-maedaya, a name of uncertain meaning, given to the feast of the fravashis, which was celebrated on the last night of the year, before the spring equinox.

Each Zoroastrian congregation celebrated these festivals by attending religious services early in the day, devoted always to Ahura Mazda, and then by gathering in joyful assemblies, with feasts at which food was eaten communally which had been blessed at the services. Rich and poor met together on these occasions, which were times of general goodwill, when quarrels were made up and friendships renewed and strengthened. The first festival, Maidhyoi-zaremaya, was held in honour of Khshathra Vairya and the creation of sky, and the last, Hamaspathmaedaya, was devoted to Ahura Mazda himself and his creation, man, with an especial honouring of the fravashis of the just, who had 'conquered for righteousness'.

The seventh creation, fire, remains always apart from the others, being their pervasive life-force; and the seventh feast likewise is separated a little from the rest. It is called in Persian No Ruz, 'New Day' (the Avestan form of the name does not survive); and it appears that Zoroaster established it at the spring equinox, re-dedicating what was probably an ancient celebration of spring to Asha Vahishta and fire. As the last of the seven feasts it looks forward to the Last Day, with the ultimate triumph of righteousness, which will also be the New Day of eternal life. Since the festival ushers in the Ahuric season of summer, it marks a yearly defeat for the Hostile Spirit, and in Zoroastrian usage (attested from early medieval times) Rapithwina is welcomed back above ground at noon on the 'New Day', to bring in the season of warmth and light. Thereafter he is honoured daily in the prayers of his own noontime watch, which is now called Rapithwa again, instead of Second Havani, and Asha Vahishta is then invoked throughout the summer months.

In imposing on his followers these two obligations – the individual one of praying five times daily, and the communal one of celebrating the seven feasts – Zoroaster created a devotional system which gave his religion enormous strength and ensured its survival over millennia; for these religious exercises reminded Zoroastrians constantly of the essential doctrines of their faith, fixing them in the minds of simple as well as learned; and they made the community moreover disciplined and self-reliant, while developing in it a strong corporate sense.

The oldest prayers

Zoroaster also composed for his followers a short prayer, which is for the Zoroastrian what the Lord's Prayer is for the Christian. This is the 'Ahuna Vairya' (later called the 'Ahunvar'). It is the first prayer taught to every Zoroastrian child, and it may be uttered, at need, in place of all other forms of worship or supplication. It is, naturally, in the ancient Gathic dialect spoken by the prophet, and there has been much discussion among scholars about the exact meaning of its venerable lines. The following version represents a conflation of recent renderings: 'He (Ahura Mazda) is as much the desired Master as the Judge according to asha. (He is) the doer of the acts of good purpose, of life. To Mazda Ahura (is) the kingdom, whom they have established as pastor for the poor.' The word translated as 'poor', 'drigu', a forerunner of Persian 'darvish', had a special sense, that of a devout and humble person, a true adherent of the faith.

There is one other short Gathic prayer, which was perhaps composed by one of the prophet's earliest disciples, since (unlike the Ahunvar) it is not attributed traditionally to him himself. This is called the 'Airyema ishyo', and it invokes Airyaman, who, with Fire, will cleanse the world at Frasho-kereti. It runs: 'May longed-for Airyaman come to the help of the men and women of Zoroaster, to the help of their good intention. The conscience which deserves the desirable recompense, for it I ask the longed-for reward for righteousness, which Ahura Mazda will measure out.' This prayer is still uttered daily in Zoroastrian acts of worship, and at every marriage ceremony.

The creed

Zoroaster created a community which was united by clearly defined doctrines, shared moral endeavour, and common observances. This unity, and the conviction of his followers that all who would not accept his revelation were likely to be damned, must have been a provocation to the unconverted; and according to the tradition Zoroaster himself met a violent end in old age from the dagger of a pagan priest. Some disaster also overwhelmed Vishtaspa's kingdom, and it seems that for a time the young faith had to struggle to survive. It evidently found the strength not only to do so, but gradually to spread among the Iranian peoples. The Zoroastrian creed, the 'Fravarane', uttered daily, appears to have taken form during those early, difficult times, and represents, it has been suggested, the declaration of faith required then of each new convert. The ancient text begins (Y 12.1): 'I profess myself a worshipper of Mazda, a follower of Zoroaster, rejecting the Daevas, accepting the Ahuric doctrine; one who praises the Amesha Spentas, who worships the Amesha Spentas. To Ahura Mazda, the good, rich in treasures, I ascribe all things good.' It is noteworthy that the word chosen before all others to define a believer is 'Mazdayasna', a worshipper of Mazda. This occurs eight times in the longer version of the creed (preserved as Y 12), and only four times is it further qualified by 'Zarathushtri', that is, a follower of Zoroaster. Plainly it was by exalting Ahura Mazda as God, and devoting to him, ultimately, all worship, that the Zoroastrian distinguished himself essentially from adherents of the pagan faith.

Dualism is also avowed in the opening lines of the Fravarane, with rejection of the Daevas. (Angra Mainyu himself appears to belong solely to Zoroaster's own revelation, and so no denial of him was needed explicitly from a convert.) Only what is good is ascribed to Ahura Mazda. The text continues (after Gathic citations): 'Holy Armaiti, the good, I choose for myself. Let her be mine! I renounce the theft and carrying off of cattle, and harm and destruction for Mazda-worshipping homes' – words which suggest the sufferings and harassment of the early community. Thereafter comes a more detailed, emphatic rejection of the evil powers: 'I forswear . . . the company of Daevas and of the followers of Daevas, of demons, and the followers of demons, of those who do harm to any being by thoughts, words, deeds or outward signs. Truly I forswear the company of all this as belonging to the Drug, as defiant (of the good). . . . Even as Zoroaster forswore the company of Daevas. . . at all encounterings at which Mazda and Zoroaster spoke together, so I forswear, as Mazda-worshipper and Zoroastrian, the company of Daevas. . . . As was the choice of the Waters, the choice of the Plants, the choice of the beneficent Cow, the choice of Ahura Mazda, who created the cow, who (created) the just Man, as (was) the choice of Zoroaster, the choice of Kavi Vishtaspa, the choice of Frashaostra and Jamaspa . . . by that choice and by that doctrine am I a Mazda-worshipper . . .'. These last lines emphasize the characteristic Zoroastrian doctrine that by choosing the good each individual is allying himself as a humble fellow-worker with God and the whole spenta cosmos. Ahura Mazda is honoured here as the Creator. There is no reason to suppose that he was thus regarded by the pagan Iranians, for in so far as they assigned creative activity to any one divinity it seems rather to have been to the lesser Ahura, Varuna (perhaps as carrying out the behests of the remote Lord Wisdom). So this was probably another distinctively Zoroastrian doctrine.

The Fravarane ends with the believer engaging himself to uphold the threefold Zoroastrian ethic, and the faith in general: 'I pledge myself to the well-thought thought, I pledge myself to the well-spoken word, I pledge myself to the well-performed act. I pledge myself to the Mazda-worshipping religion, which . . . is righteous, which of all (faiths) which are and shall be is the greatest, the best, the most beautiful, which is Ahuric, Zoroastrian.'

The establishing of Mazda worship

The liturgy and Yenhe hatạm

Apart from verses from his Gathas, which are the supreme Zoroastrian manthras, and the Ahuna Vairya for daily use, Zoroaster does not seem to have established any fixed devotional utterances for his disciples, being content, presumably, that otherwise they should worship and pray with words of their own choice. But at some stage his followers must have decided to create a fixed liturgy to accompany the daily act of worship, the yasna. This seems to have been done at a time when the Gathic dialect was fading away – a development which may, indeed, have prompted their action, with the desire that for this service, which embodied so much that was central to the prophet's thought, his community should continue to use words as close as possible to those with which he himself had prayed. The result was the putting together of the 'worship of the seven chapters', Yasna Haptanhaiti (Y 35–41). This is a liturgy in seven short sections (one in verse), which perhaps represents a collection of what old priests still remembered then of ancient manthras in the Gathic dialect, such as were used at the daily offerings to fire and water. These manthras even contain what appear to be pre-Zoroastrian elements; but in its existing form the liturgy is devoted naturally to Ahura Mazda, and it is here (Y 39.3) that the term Amesha Spenta first appears. Another little text in Younger Avestan was appended to the seven chapters, as Y 42; and then this and the Yasna Haptanhaiti were enclosed by the Gathas themselves, arranged according to metre in five groups. Zoroaster's own words, mighty in spiritual power, were thus set like protective walls on either side of the rituals and the liturgy which accompanied them, so that they could shield the whole act of worship from malign influences.

One group of the Gathas, known as 'Gatha Ahunavaiti', is by far the longest, and it was placed before the seven chapters, as Y 28–34; and the four other groups follow them, as Y 43–51, 53. The Gatha Ahunavaiti was accompanied by the Ahuna Vairya (from which it takes its name), together with two other short and very sacred prayers. One of these, the Yenhe hatạm, consists of a remodelling of the Gathic verse Y 51.22, which runs as follows: 'At whose sacrifice Ahura Mazda knows the best for me according to righteousness. Those who were and are, those I shall worship by their names and shall approach with praise.' Zoroaster's first words here presumably referred to a particular divinity to whom an act of worship had just been offered; but the whole verse was altered rather awkwardly to create a prayer of general application, which may be rendered thus: 'Those of the Beings, male and female, whom Ahura Mazda knows to be best for worship according to righteousness, those we shall worship.' The intention was evidently to offer veneration with these words to all divinities of the spenta creation, omitting none through inadvertence, and so this prayer forms a regular part of the litanies of the faith.

The Ashem vohu

The other very sacred prayer is the Ashem vohu, with which most Zoroastrian devotions end. This seems to be a brief manthra designed to concentrate the mind upon asha, and to invoke the aid of Asha Vahishta, the word or name occurring thrice within the twelve words of the prayer. The following translation is perhaps the least forced: 'Asha (is) good, it is best. According to wish it is, according to wish it shall be for us. Asha belongs to Asha Vahishta.' This prayer, together with the Ahuna Vairya and Yenhe hatąm, precedes the Gatha Ahunavaiti, while the second great Gathic prayer, the Airyema ishyo, is set protectively after the last Gatha, as Y 54. The whole liturgy, from the Ahuna Vairya to the Airyema ishyo, was called the Staota Yesnya, '(Words) of praise and worship', and once it had been accepted as the standard form of words to accompany the yasna, it must have become obligatory for every practising priest to know it by heart. The safe-keeping of the Gathas themselves was thus assured, the prophet's great hymns being reverently transmitted in this way, by word of mouth, from generation to generation.

The hymns

The other religious texts, notably the yashts, the hymns to individual yazatas, continued much longer in fluid oral transmission, partly learnt by heart, partly extemporized. Some of the oldest portions, coming down from pagan times, were recast in the light of Zoroaster's teachings, with Ahura Mazda exalted, and all revelation put in the mouth of his prophet; but many of the verses, being concerned with beneficent divinities, needed no particular revision; and others of a strikingly pagan cast survived unaltered, and are as incongruous to Zoroaster's message as are parts of the Old Testament to Christianity.

CHAPTER FOUR

The unrecorded centuries

The early days

It is thought to have been around 1500 B.C. – in the Bronze Age, that is, and the time óf chariot-warfare – that the Indian peoples moved south off the steppes and across Central Asia, shattering (as archaeologists have shown) a fairly advanced civilization there. Then, turning south-east, they pressed on through mountain-passes to conquer the land now called after them. The Iranians, following in their wake, branched instead south-westerly on to the plateau of Iran. The Avestan people appear to have been in the rear of this second great migration, for they seem to have settled in Central Asia itself – possibly in the region later known as Khwarezm. There is no means of tracing their movements precisely, however, for this whole area remained prehistoric – lacking, that is, any dateable records – for many more centuries.

There is, however, some material to be found in the Avesta itself about the early days of the faith, though this cannot be dated or given a precise location. Most of it is in the hymn to the fravashis, Yasht 13, which contains a great list of names of men and women of old whose fravashis are worthy of veneration. This list begins with 'The first teachers and first hearers of the doctrine' (Yt 13.17, 149), among whom are Maidhyoimanha, Kavi Vishtaspa and his queen Hutaosa, Jamaspa and a few others familiar from the Gathas or the tradition;

but these are followed by many unfamiliar names, all Iranian, but belonging to far-off, forgotten times. There are the names too of tribes who accepted the Zoroastrian religion – the Airyas (who included the 'Avestan' people), Tuiryas, Sairimas, Sainus and Dahis; and also of some lands, whose names are unknown to history.

The first piece of evidence to associate Zoroastrianism with familiar places comes from another of the old yashts, Yasht 19, in honour of Khvarenah (Divine Grace). Here it is said (v. 66) that the royal Khvarenah accompanies him 'who rules there where is the Lake Kạsaoya, which receives the Haetumant. . .'. The Haetumant is the modern Helmand, and Lake Kạsaoya must be the Hamun Lake in Drangiana (modern Seistan) in the south-east of Iran. It follows therefore that the Iranians of that area had adopted Zoroastrianism before the canon of Avestan scripture was closed – that is, at least by the sixth century B.C. There is further evidence for this in a prose Avestan text which forms the first chapter of a late compilation, the Videvdad (later corrupted into Vendidad), the 'Code against demons'. In this chapter are enumerated seventeen lands, headed by Airyanem Vaejah, the by then mythical homeland of the Iranians. Each land (it is said) was created excellent by Ahura Mazda, but suffers its own affliction from the Hostile Spirit. Some of these lands again are otherwise unknown, but some bear familiar names, notably Sughda (Sogdia), Mouru (Margiana), Bakhdhi (Bactria), Harakhvaiti (Arachosia) and Haetumant (Drangiana). All these belong to the north-east and east of Iran. Various suggestions have been made as to why the list was drawn up, but the most reasonable (in the light of its preservation as a religious work) seems to be that these were all lands which accepted Zoroastrianism relatively early. It is a puzzling fact, however, that Khwarezm is not included in the list, while Airyanem Vaejah appears to be a late addition.

Doctrinal developments

There is no information about the ecclesiastical organization of Zoroastrianism in the prehistoric period – whether, for instance, there was a single recognized head of the whole community, or whether there were autonomous local churches in each tribal area or kingdom. A scrap of evidence is, however, vouchsafed in the Avesta about the pursuit of religious learning, for in Yasht 13 (v. 97) Saena,

son of Ahum-stut, is honoured as the first among the faithful to have had a hundred pupils; and clearly, through all the migrations and conquests and new settlements, the Zoroastrian priests upheld the faith, and steadily developed its theology and liturgical practices.

One doctrinal problem which must early have confronted them, because of material progress, concerned Khshathra and his guardianship both of the sky of stone and of the men as warriors; for the general spread of the use of bronze, followed (from about the ninth century B.C.) by that of iron, meant that weapons could no longer be thought of as being of stone. Anything concerning one of the six Amesha Spentas was of the greatest doctrinal and ethical importance, and scholar-priests must have wrestled hard with this problem before they found an ingenious solution: they identified the stone of the sky as rock-crystal, and this substance they felt able to classify as a metal, presumably because it is found in veins in rock, like metallic ores. So Khshathra, lord of the crystal sky, could now be venerated as lord of metals, and hence as the protector still of fighting men. A metal knife must already have replaced the flint one in the yasna ritual, and gradually pestles and mortars of metal came to be used as well as stone ones (both are mentioned in the Avesta); so as lord of metals Khshathra continued to be represented at the daily act of worship.

A further development with regard to the six Amesha Spentas was that the pantheon of yazatas became organized around them. Thus Khshathra, as lord of the sky, had for his associates and helpers Hvar, the sun-yazata, Asman, spirit of the sky, and Mithra, while Spenta Armaiti, as guardian of the earth, received aid from the Waters and the divinities of water, Aredvi Sura and Apąm Napat. The earth-yazata herself, Zam, gave her support to Ameretat, lord of plants. Since, as these instances show, some of the yazatas personify what one or other of the Amesha Spentas protects, the Zoroastrian pantheon is a complex one, full of criss-crossing webs of alliance and interdependence; but this would have been no stumbling-block for Iranian converts, who were familiar with such relationships in the pagan faith. (Thus, to take one example, Mithra had long been venerated as lord of fire and the sun, although both fire and sun were themselves personified as gods.) Since all the spenta divinities of Zoroastrianism strive together for a common end, which they were evoked by Ahura Mazda to help achieve, there is no rivalry among them, no sense that one is too exalted to aid or be aided by another. So the divine pantheon itself creates a pattern for human society, in

which every man should help his fellows, according to his own abilities.

Belief in a world Saviour

An important theological development during the dark ages of the faith concerned the growth of beliefs about the Saoshyant or coming Saviour. Passages in the Gathas suggest that Zoroaster was filled with a sense that the end of the world was imminent, and that Ahura Mazda had entrusted him with revealed truth in order to rouse mankind for their vital part in the final struggle. Yet he must have realized that he would not himself live to see Frasho-kereti; and he seems to have taught that after him there would come 'the man who is better than a good man' (Y 43.3), the Saoshyant. The literal meaning of Saoshyant is 'one who will bring benefit'; and it is he who will lead humanity in the last battle against evil. Zoroaster's followers, holding ardently to this expectation, came to believe that the Saoshyant will be born of the prophet's own seed, miraculously preserved in the depths of a lake (identified as Lake Kạsaoya). When the end of time approaches, it is said, a virgin will bathe in this lake and become with child by the prophet; and she will in due course bear a son, named Astvat-ereta, 'He who embodies righteousness' (after Zoroaster's own words: 'May righteousness be embodied' Y 43.16). Despite his miraculous conception, the coming World Saviour will thus be a man, born of human parents, and so there is no betrayal, in this development of belief in the Saoshyant, of Zoroaster's own teachings about the part which mankind has to play in the great cosmic struggle. The Saoshyant is thought of as being accompanied, like kings and heroes, by Khvarenah, and it is in Yasht 19 that the extant Avesta has most to tell of him. Khvarenah, it is said there (vv. 89, 92, 93), 'will accompany the victorious Saoshyant . . . so that he may restore existence. . . . When Astvat-ereta comes out from the Lake Kạsaoya, messenger of Mazda Ahura . . . then he will drive the Drug out from the world of Asha.' This glorious moment was longed for by the faithful, and the hope of it was to be their strength and comfort in times of adversity.

Just as belief in the coming Saviour developed its element of the miraculous, so, naturally, the person of the prophet himself came to be magnified as the centuries passed. Thus in the Younger Avesta, although never divinized, Zoroaster is exalted as 'the first priest, the

first warrior, the first herdsman . . . master and judge of the world'
(Yt 13. 89, 91), one at whose birth 'the waters and plants . . .
and all the creatures of the Good Creation rejoiced' (Yt 13.99). Angra
Mainyu, it is said, fled at that moment from the earth (Yt 17.19); but
he returned to tempt the prophet in vain, with a promise of earthly
power, to abjure the faith of Ahura Mazda (Vd 19.6).

The extension of purity laws

There must have been developments in the early period in practice as
well as belief; and one area where there was probably steady extension
of the usages of the primitive community was the code of purity laws.
These, which are characteristic of Zoroastrianism, are rooted in the
prophet's dualistic teachings, and also in his linking of spiritual and
material, which means that, even as service of Ahura Mazda and the
six Amesha Spentas furthers spiritual salvation, so caring for their
seven creations helps to achieve Frasho-kereti physically. The seven
had been made perfect, and all that blemishes them – dirt and disease,
rust, tarnish, mould, stench, blight, decay – is the work of Angra
Mainyu and his legions. So to prevent or reduce any of these things
contributes to the defence of the good creation, and the weakening of
its attackers. This doctrine is one of the strengths of Zoroastrianism,
because it involves every member of the community in fighting
cosmic evil through the ordinary tasks of daily life, so that no one
need feel useless, or merely self-regarding in his endeavours.

Some of the individual purity laws go back evidently to Indo-
Iranian times, being observed more or less similarly by Zoroastrians
and Brahmans. So also does the use of cattle urine as a cleansing agent.
These ancient laws gained fresh force from association with
Zoroaster's new doctrines. So it is as the chief of the seven creations
that man should keep himself scrupulously clean, in person and
clothing. Having powers of reason and action, he should moreover be
vigilant in his care for the other six creations. Some of the basic
injunctions of Zoroastrianism – to keep earth fertile and unsullied, to
encourage plants and trees to healthy growth, to have regard for the
welfare of animals – are now being generally commended to
humanity. Food should be carefully prepared, with strict cleanliness,
and eaten almost reverently, since everything consumed belongs to
one or other of the creations; and there were special rules concerning
water and fire which are particular to the faith. Most people use water

heedlessly for washing; but for a Zoroastrian the cleanliness of water itself was to be protected, since it is the 'spenta' creation of Haurvatat. So nothing impure should be allowed in direct contact with a natural source of water, such as lake, stream or well. If anything ritually unclean was to be washed, water should be drawn off for this purpose, and even then, this was not to be used directly, but the impure object should first be cleaned with cattle-urine, and then dried with sand or in sunlight before water was allowed to touch it for the final washing.

Similarly with regard to fire, the general practice of using it to burn rubbish was unthinkable for the Zoroastrian, who laid only clean, dry wood and pure offerings on it, and set cooking pots over it with special care. Rubbish had therefore to be disposed of in other ways. Dry and clean waste-matter, such as broken pots, or sun-bleached bones, might be buried, since this would not harm the good earth; and as for the rest, orthodox custom came to be to cast it into a small building with only a chimney-like roof-opening, and to destroy it periodically with acid. Night-soil might be put on fields, and otherwise ancient communities produced little of the waste characteristic of modern times.

As for what constituted impurity, broadly speaking this included everything daevic, or under daevic influence. All creatures which were harmful or repulsive to man, from beasts of prey down to scorpion, wasp or ugly toad, were regarded as part of Angra Mainyu's counter-creation, and therefore unclean. They were grouped under the general term 'khrafstra'; and to kill them was meritorious, for it diminished the world of evil. Yet though there was no sin in bringing death on the creatures of him who created it, still death itself was daevic and a great uncleanness. So a dead khrafstra was even more polluting than a live one, and no orthodox Zoroastrian would willingly touch one with bare hands. The greatest pollution in death, however, the priests maintained, was from the bodies of righteous people, for a concentration of evil forces was necessary to overwhelm the good, and these continued to hover round the corpse. So from the moment of death the body was treated as if highly infectious, and only professional undertakers and corpse-bearers approached it, who were trained to take ritual precautions. If possible the funerary service was performed the same day, and the body was carried at once to a place of exposure. From medieval times this has been a funerary tower; but in ancient days (it would seem from the Avesta), it was

simply a bare mountain side or stretch of stony desert – it being essential that the polluting body, laid down naked for birds and beasts to devour, should not come into contact with the good earth, or with water or plants. After the bones had lain for a while to bleach in sun and wind, they were gathered together and buried, to await Judgment Day. The primary purpose of this funerary rite seems to have been, as we have seen, to secure the swift destruction of the polluting flesh, and to set the spirit free to mount up to heaven. (The old belief survived that the soul lingered on earth for three days after death, and it was held to be at daybreak on the fourth day that it went up, drawn by the rays of the rising sun, to face Mithra at the Chinvat Bridge. Probably Zoroaster, with his insistence on the responsibility of each man for his own fate hereafter, reduced the number of traditional rites and observances performed on behalf of the newly departed spirit; but if so, long usage and family piety led to their revival, and intercession for the dead, with many prayers and offerings, became the general practice among his followers.)

Another great source of uncleanness was any flow of blood, this being a breach in the ideal physical state. This purity law pressed hard on women, for it meant that during her monthly courses every woman was ritually unclean, and was segregated and forbidden to engage in normal activities. This was undoubtedly ancient practice, widespread among the peoples of the world; but it seems that the Zoroastrian priests gradually elaborated the restrictions, which became in the end severe. Yet though the rules were harsh, women in general seem to have accepted them stoically, as their inescapable part in the cosmic struggle against evil.

It was thus impossible for a woman, and difficult for a man, to avoid all ritual uncleanness; and purity being part of morality for Zoroastrians, various rites existed for restoring it. All involved actual washing from head to foot, and the simplest could be performed by lay people in their own homes. More elaborate ones, for heavier contaminations, were administered by priests, with recitation of holy words. The greatest of these consisted of successive triple cleansings with cattle-urine, sand and finally water, undergone by the polluted person as he moved through nine pits. Later the Zoroastrians substituted stones for the pits, probably to reduce the danger of contaminating the earth; and for them there followed nine days and nights spent in retreat, with further ablutions and prayers, in order that the cleansing should penetrate body and soul. They called this

form of purification accordingly the 'ablution of the nine nights', the 'barashnom-i no shaba'. The method by which it should be administered is set out in detail in the Vendidad (Vd 9).

Priests and worship

This elaborate purification was not only administered by priests, but often undergone by them; for in order to be fitted to invoke and worship the divine beings they had to be the purest of the pure. They were also equipped for this task by strict professional training, as their pagan forbears had been. The laity depended on priests to perform services for them at initiation, marriage and death, and on special family and public occasions, as well as relying on them to solemnize the daily yasna. The priests in their turn depended directly on the laity for subsistence, since they lived from what they received for each particular ceremony performed . There was thus a close and usually hereditary bond between individual lay and priestly families, among both rich and poor. That these families sometimes intermarried is shown by the fact that Zoroaster himself took Hvovi, Frashaostra's daughter, to be his wife; but it is probable that the priestly vocation descended only through the male line, as is still the case today.

Presumably, as in the pagan period, ceremonies were usually performed either at the priest's house or that of the man who asked for them. Early Zoroastrianism thus had no need of sacred buildings or fixed altars, and has left no traces for the archaeologist. The seven great feasts were probably celebrated either in the open, or at the house of a leading member of the local community, according to the season. Another form of corporate worship, inherited almost certainly from the pagan period, was performed by the people gathering together at certain times of the year and going up into the mountains to offer sacrifice there to the divine beings. This practice accorded perfectly with the spirit of Zoroastrianism, with worship being offered thus to the Amesha Spentas in the natural temple of their own creation; and it has been maintained by the Irani Zoroastrians down to the present day.

Conclusion

It is not possible to trace the spread of Zoroastrianism through eastern Iran, but Avestan was evidently regarded everywhere as the sacred

language of the faith, and to this day both private prayers and public services are said in this ancient tongue. How, or exactly when, the religion then reached western Iran, where it first enters recorded history, remains unknown. It seems, however, that by the time it did so, Zoroaster's great vision of a world faith had been largely lost, and his religion had come to be regarded as specifically that of the Iranian peoples. There must have been a number of reasons for this. Nothing is recorded of the fate of the earlier inhabitants of eastern Iran at the time of the great migrations, but those who were not overwhelmed were evidently absorbed by their conquerors. In any case, Zoroastrian missionaries would plainly have found it easiest to work among fellow-Iranians, both because of the absence of a serious language barrier, and because the common religious heritage provided a basis for acceptance of the new faith. These considerations must have been reinforced by inherent pride of race, which was naturally strengthened in the case of a conquering people. To Iranians in general the non-Iranian, the 'anarya' (Pahlavi 'aner') was as much a creature to be despised and disregarded as was the 'barbarian' to the Greeks; and so he might be left to follow what religion he pleased, provided only that it was peaceable. As the numerous Iranian peoples were brought gradually to accept Zoroaster's teachings, they came accordingly to regard these as part of their own racial heritage, to be treasured accordingly, rather than as a universal message of salvation for all mankind.

CHAPTER FIVE

Under the Achaemenians

The Medes, the Persians and Zoroaster

In ancient times mountain, desert and forest made formidable barriers between eastern and western Iran; and it seems probable that the Iranian peoples who settled in the West, the Medes and the Persians, invaded the land in a separate movement through the mountain passes to the west of the Caspian Sea. They are the first Iranians to enter recorded history, for from the ninth century B.C their names occur repeatedly in Assyrian records of military expeditions on to the Iranian plateau. According to Herodotus (I.101), the Medes, who settled in the north-west, were divided into six tribes, one of which comprised the 'magoi' (better known by the Latin plural 'magi', singular 'magus', from Iranian 'magu'). This tribe was, it seems, a learned, sacerdotal one, which provided priests not only for the other Medes but also for the Persians. The magi appear to have been a close-knit fraternity, and they may well have formed a stiff obstacle to the western spread of Zoroastrianism. Moreover, in their new homelands the Medes and Persians, having established themselves along the eastern side of the Zagros mountains, had sustained contact over several hundred years, partly as neighbours, partly as subjects, with ancient urban civilizations – Assyria and Urartu to the north, Elam and Babylon to the south – from which they learnt much. They may therefore have looked down on their fellow-

Iranians in the east, when communications were established between them, and have been slow to accept a religious revelation from that source.

The pride of the Medes had cause to swell when, in alliance with Babylon, they overthrew the Assyrian Empire in the years 614–612. Thereafter they annexed the northern Assyrian possessions, including part of Asia Minor, and went on to subject the Persians, who at about this time had finally made themselves masters of the kingdom of Anshan, in the south-west of Iran. (This region came thereafter to be known as Pars, or Persis to the Greeks.) The Medes also extended their sway over some of the Iranian peoples to the east, among whom Zoroastrianism was by then evidently generally established. The Median Empire flourished for about sixty years; and it is very probable that it was during this epoch that Zoroastrianism spread rapidly among the western Iranians. The efforts of missionary priests may well have been reinforced by the words and example of eastern princes, living as hostages at the Median court, and of eastern princesses, taken in political marriages; and in due course Raga, the most easterly of the Median cities, came to be regarded as a holy place by Zoroastrians.

In 549 the Persians, led by Cyrus the Great, of the Achaemenian family, a son-in-law of the reigning Median king, rebelled, defeated the Medes, and founded the first Persian Empire (in which the Medes still had a worthy part). Cyrus pressed on to conquer Asia Minor, and Babylonia (whose subject territories, up to the Mediterranean coast, then submitted to him), and brought all the Eastern Iranians under his rule. Notices by classical writers suggest that at this time of their first encounter with the Greeks, in Asia Minor, the Persians were already Zoroastrians; and learning about Zoroaster from them, the Greeks naturally considered him to be a Persian prophet, and 'master of the magi'. They learnt of him, moreover, as a figure of immense antiquity. Thus Hermodorus and Hermippus of Smyrna assigned him to 5000 years before the Trojan War, Xanthos of Lydia to 6000 years before Xerxes' invasion of Greece, and Eudoxus and Aristotle to 6000 years before the death of Plato. From this it is plain that the Persians told the Greeks that their prophet had lived in the remote past – information which Greek scholars then wove into their own schematic calculations.

This tradition of the venerable age of Zoroastrianism accords with the fact that the Medes and the Persians evidently received it as a

long-established faith, with its doctrines and observances already defined, and a canon of works in the Avestan tongue into which virtually no Western Iranian material was ever allowed to intrude. This last fact is the more remarkable because the Avesta continued in oral transmission throughout the Achaemenian period, and indeed long afterwards, and interpolation is naturally easier in unwritten texts. Such interpolation can indeed be shown, exceptionally, to have taken place; but its rarity is a sign of the respect in which the Medes and the Persians held what they believed to be the revealed word of God.

The reasons why the Avesta was not written down at this time are complex; but one was that, though the Medes and the Persians met several systems of writing in Western Iran, they plainly regarded the alien art with suspicion (in the Persian epic its discovery is attributed to the devil). So though in due course they adopted it for practical purposes, the priests, who were the scholars of ancient Iran, rejected it as unfit for recording holy words. Under the Achaemenians the chief means of written communication was Aramaic, a Semitic language with its own alphabet, which (because the Aramaeans were great traders) was already a lingua franca in the Middle East. The early Achaemenians ordered their own Persian language to be used, however, for royal inscriptions. For this, the earliest known setting down of any Iranian language, a special form of cuneiform script was evolved.

The early kings

CYRUS

Cyrus himself left only brief inscriptions, carved on the stones of his splendid new capital of Pasargadae, in the north of Pars. These inscriptions contain no declaration of his religious beliefs; but beside the palace ruins there is a sacred precinct with two massive stone plinths, it seems for public worship in the open, in traditional Iranian fashion. The fragments of three 'fire-holders' have also been recovered. These cannot be called altars in the strict sense – that is, 'raised structures, with a plane surface, on which to place or sacrifice offerings to a deity' for in Zoroastrian usage such an object is designed simply to hold the fire in whose presence believers pray. The offerings which they make to the fire while doing so are for its own sustenance,

and are practical in origin. Throughout Zoroastrian history personal and family prayers have been said in the presence of the hearth fire; but in the sixth century B.C., it seems, acquaintance with the stately religious rituals of the Middle East, and new imperial splendour, inspired the Persian priests to elevate the fire before which the king prayed. The object on which it was placed seems to be a modification of the type of a genuine altar excavated at the Median site of Nush-i Jan Tepe, near Ecbatana (Hamadan). This, attributed to the eighth century B.C., and serving an unknown cult, consists of a massive mud-brick pedestal, finely plastered, supporting a four-stepped top. In the top there is a shallow depression with marks of charring, perhaps from a sacrificial fire. The stone 'altars' of Pasargadae were more elegant, though still massive. They had a three-stepped base to balance a three-stepped top (the number three is prominent throughout Zoroastrian observance); and this top, instead of being almost flat, like that at Nush-i Jan, was deeply hollowed, so that the stand was capable of holding the thick bed of hot ashes needed to sustain an ever-burning fire. There is no evidence as to where these fire-holders originally stood; but since there is no structure at Pasargadae which can be identified as a temple, it is probable that they were set within the successive palaces, and bore what was as it were the 'hearth fire' or personal fire of the Great King, elevated in this way as a sign of his own majesty, and for the dignified performance of the Zoroastrian daily prayers.

In addition to this tangible testimony to Cyrus' religious beliefs, Greek writers record that he called one of his daughters 'Atossa', which appears to be their rendering of Iranian 'Hutaosa', the name of the queen of Vishtaspa, Zoroaster's royal patron. Cyrus' actions were, moreover, those of a loyal Mazda-worshipper, in that he sought to govern his vast new empire justly and well, in accordance with asha. He made no attempt, however, to impose the Iranian religion on his alien subjects – indeed it would have been wholly impractical to attempt it, in view of their numbers, and the antiquity of their own faiths – but rather encouraged them to live orderly and devout lives according to their own tenets. Among the many anarya who experienced his statesmanlike kindness were the Jews, whom he permitted to return from exile in Babylon and to rebuild the temple in Jerusalem. This was only one of many liberal acts recorded of Cyrus, but it was of particular moment for the religious history of mankind; for the Jews entertained warm feelings thereafter for the Persians, and

this made them the more receptive to Zoroastrian influences. Cyrus himself is hailed by 'Second Isaiah' (a nameless prophet of the Exilic period) as a messiah, that is, one who acted in Yahweh's name and with his authority. 'Behold my servant whom I uphold' (Yahweh himself is represented as saying). '(Cyrus) will bring forth justice to the nations. . . . He will not fail . . . till he has established justice in the earth' (Isaiah 42.1, 4). The same prophet celebrates Yahweh for the first time in Jewish literature as Creator, as Ahura Mazda had been celebrated by Zoroaster: 'I, Yahweh, who created all things . . . I made the earth, and created man on it. . . . Let the skies rain down justice . . . I, Yahweh, have created it' (Isaiah 44.24, 45. 8, 12). The parallels with Zoroastrian doctrine and scripture are so striking that these verses have been taken to represent the first imprint of that influence which Zoroastrianism was to exert so powerfully on post-Exilic Judaism.

Cyrus died fighting against fellow-Iranians – the Massagetes – who, still semi-nomads, threatened the frontier of his empire in the north-east; and his body was embalmed, brought back to Pasargadae, and laid in a tomb which still stands there on the plain. The fact that his corpse was not exposed according to the orthodox rite might seem at first sight to disprove his Zoroastrianism, but not only the Achaemenians, but also their successors, the Arsacids and the Sasanians, maintained a distinctive rite of embalming the bodies of kings and placing them in sepulchres of living rock or stone. There is no sanction for such a practice in the Avesta or in Pahlavi literature, indeed tombs for the dead are always referred to there with unqualified condemnation; so one can only suppose that a refusal by the Achaemenians to adopt the rite of exposure set a precedent for kings, who continued thereafter to regard themselves as above this particular religious law. The preservation of royal bodies was probably linked with the concept of the king's royal khvarenah, thought of as abiding at his tomb to the benefit of his successors and the people at large. There is scattered evidence for a special cult of the royal dead; and the practice of embalming their bodies, learnt presumably by the western Iranians from the peoples among whom they had settled, spread to their pagan kinsmen on the steppes, where it is well attested in the barrow burials of Scythian chiefs.

The tomb of Cyrus shows, however, with what care Zoroastrian kings prepared their sepulchres so that there should be no contact between the embalmed body – unclean in death, even though there

was no decay – and the living creations. The tomb-chamber is set high on a six-stepped stone plinth, which raises it far above the good earth, and it is itself all of stone. It consists of a single small chamber, thick-walled, windowless, with formerly a double stone roof and a narrow, low doorway. Over this doorway was set a carving of the sun, symbol of immortality in luminous Paradise; and Cyrus' successor, Cambyses, endowed, as well as a daily sacrifice of sheep, a monthly sacrifice of a horse, the especial creature of the sun, to be made at the tomb for his father's soul (Arrian, VI. 29. 7). These rites were maintained there for two hundred years, until Alexander conquered Persia, and the tomb was broken into and despoiled. One of those who entered it reported that it contained 'a golden couch, a table with cups, a golden coffin, and numerous garments and ornaments set with precious stones' (Strabo, XV. 3. 7).

CAMBYSES

Cambyses continued his father's expansion of the Persian Empire, adding Lower Egypt to its already vast possessions. Little good is recorded of him by the Greeks (our chief source for Achaemenian history), and as far as Zoroastrianism is concerned his main claim to notice is that he is the first person known to have practised 'khvaetvadatha', that is, next-of-kin marriage. According to the Pahlavi books, this form of marriage was highly meritorious, and never more so than when it took place within the close family circle – father with daughter, brother with sister, even mother with son. The term itself occurs in the Zoroastrian creed, the Fravarane; but it is oddly placed there, appearing towards the end in a section otherwise concerned with noble generalities, and so may well be interpolated. The passage in question (Y 12.9) runs: 'I pledge myself to the Mazda-worshipping religion, which throws off attacks, which causes weapons to be laid down, which upholds khvaetvadatha, which is righteous.' As for the earliest attestation of the custom, it has been suggested that since both Vishtaspa and his wife Hutaosa belonged to the Naotara clan, theirs may have been a khvaetvadatha-union; but there is no indication in the Avesta that they were closely related by blood. The same is true of the marriage of Cyrus to 'Cassandane, daughter of Pharnaspes, an Achaemenian' (Herodotus II .1, III .2). So the first certain marriages of this kind were those of Cambyses, their son, who wedded two of his full sisters. According to

Herodotus (III. 31) he fell in love with one sister, and, wishing to marry her, 'summoned the royal judges, since the thing he was planning was contrary to all custom, and enquired of them whether there was any law which gave the right to cohabit with his sister to any man who desired it. The judges gave a reply that was at once safe and in accordance with justice, saying that while they could not discover any law that gave to a brother the right to cohabit with a sister, they had nevertheless discovered another law which gave to the King of the Persians the right to do whatsoever he willed.' Accordingly Cambyses married first this and then a second sister (Atossa). If Herodotus' report could be trusted in all its details, it would show that khvaetvadatha was unknown to the western Iranians before Cambyses' day. Yet it would be strange if a practice originating in the caprice of a single monarch should have come to be regarded as a religious duty, generally incumbent on the faithful. Moreover, Xanthos of Lydia, a contemporary of Herodotus, is cited as saying: 'The Magian men co-habit with their mothers. They may also have like association with daughters and sisters.' The practice of consanguineous marriages is widely attested among ancient peoples; and perhaps in its earliest days the Zoroastrian community, promoting marriages among the faithful, found itself, because of their small numbers, solemnizing unions within the immediate family; and in time the priests came to believe that such close unions served actually to strengthen the religion. Thereafter khvaetvadatha is not only lauded in the Pahlavi books, but is actually attested, in literature, documents and historical records, as having taken place among princes, priests and commoners from the sixth century B.C. down to the tenth century A.C. (after which it survived only as the marriage of first cousins, still the favoured form of union in Iran).

DARIUS THE GREAT

Cambyses died in 522, and after a brief period was succeeded by Darius the Great, from a collateral branch of the family. Darius, who took as his queen Atossa/Hutaosa, the sister-widow of Cambyses, was himself the son of a Hystaspes (a Greek rendering of Vishtaspa), which suggests that his grandparents were, like Cyrus, pious Zoroastrians. Darius had to fight hard to establish his rule over the empire, and he left many cuneiform inscriptions to record his achievements, then and thereafter. In these he shows himself a devout believer, convinced, it seems, that he had a divine mandate to rule the world, with an authority parallel in the temporal sphere to Zoroaster's in the religious one, since it too had been conferred directly by Ahuramazda. (In Persia by the sixth century the name and title of the Lord Wisdom had been fused thus into a single word.) So he declares: 'A great God is Ahuramazda, who created this earth, who created yonder sky, who created man, who created happiness for man, who made Darius king, one king over many, one lord over many. . . . Ahuramazda when he saw this earth in commotion, thereafter he bestowed it upon me, he made me king. I am king. By the grace of Ahuramazda I set it in its place. . . . This which has been done, all that by the will of Ahuramazda I did. Ahuramazda bore me aid, until I did the work' (Naqsh-i Rustam A, 1–8, 31–36, 48–51). He was naturally a convinced dualist, and saw behind each individual rebellion against his rule the workings of Drauga 'Deceit'. (Drauga is Old Persian for the Drug, enemy of Asha, so repeatedly denounced in the Gathas and Fravarane). 'Thou who shalt be king hereafter', he exhorts his successor, 'protect thyself vigorously from Drauga' (Behistun IV. 37–8). All the troubles in his own time had begun, he is certain, when 'Drauga flourished in the land' (ibid. I. 34); and he prays: 'May Ahuramazda protect this country from a (hostile) army, from famine, from Drauga!' (Persepolis D, 15–18). He does not speak of Anra Mainyu (the Younger Avestan form of Angra Mainyu) preferring in this and other respects, it seems, familiar Persian terms to Avestan ones.

Having defeated these manifestations of Drauga Darius strove, so he declares, to live according to asha (Old Persian 'arta') and to dispense justice on earth: 'For this reason', he says, 'Ahuramazda bore me aid, and the other gods who are, because I was not hostile, I was not deceitful, I did not act falsely, neither I nor my family. I conducted myself according to justice. Neither to the weak nor to the powerful did I do wrong' (Behistun IV. 62–5). 'The man who was excellent, him I rewarded well; (him) who was evil, him I punished well' (ibid. I. 21–2). 'By the grace of Ahuramazda I am of such a sort that I am a friend to right, I am not a friend to wrong. It is not my desire that the weak man should have wrong done to him by the mighty; nor is that my desire, that the mighty man should have wrong done to him by the weak. What is right, that is my desire. . . . It is not my desire that a man should do harm; nor indeed is that my desire, if he should do harm, he should not be punished' (Naqsh-i Rustam B, 6–12, 19–21). Here is sought the strict equity which is at the heart of Zoroastrianism.

Although Darius invoked only Ahuramazda by name, he called generally upon 'the other gods who are' and upon 'all the gods', using in these doubtless ancient formulas the old word 'baga' rather than the 'yazata' preferred in the Avesta. (This usage persisted in Persia, prevailing also in Sasanian times.) These 'other gods' he plainly regarded, orthodoxly, as lesser divinities, subordinate to the Creator, Ahuramazda. His utterances further show that for him within Iran 'Mazda-worship' was the only true faith, all others leading to trouble and disorder. Thus he declares of the Elamites: 'Those Elamites were faithless and by them Ahuramazda was not worshipped. I worshipped Ahuramazda; by the favour of Ahuramazda, as was my desire, thus I did unto them. . . . Whoso shall worship Ahuramazda as long as (his) strength shall be, for him both living and dead (there is) happiness' (Behistun V. 15–20). Yet tablets inscribed in the Elamite language have been found at Persepolis which show that Darius in fact permitted these non-Iranian subjects of his, once subdued, to continue worshipping their own ancestral gods as well as Ahuramazda, even making them grants from his treasury for this purpose. He thereby displayed the same broad tolerance towards the beliefs and practices of the anarya as his predecessor, Cyrus, had done.

XERXES

It was certainly, therefore, action against fellow-Iranians which is recorded by Darius' son Xerxes (486–465), who relates in one of his inscriptions: 'When I became king . . . there was (a place) where previously the Daivas were worshipped. Afterwards, by the grace of Ahuramazda I destroyed that sanctuary of the Daivas, and I proclaimed: "The Daivas shall not be worshipped!" Where previously the Daivas were worshipped, there I worshipped Ahuramazda with proper rites, in accordance with asha' (Xerxes, Persepolis H, 35–41). Old Persian 'daiva' corresponds to Avestan 'daeva', and these lines show the religious struggle initiated by the prophet in eastern Iran being carried on centuries later by his followers in the west. Zoraster's name does not appear in the Achaemenians' inscriptions perhaps because of the lack of precedent for referring to a prophet in the ancient Near Eastern texts which served their scribes as models. (The same omission is found in the royal inscriptions of the later Sasanians, and even in those of their great high priest, Kirder.)

Achaemenian palaces and tombs

The Achaemenians, lords of a great empire, had several royal residences. They maintained one at the old Median city of Ecbatana (Hamadan), and Darius built an imposing new palace at Susa, an ancient Elamite capital. He also created another new palace of great magnificence at Persepolis in Pars, to the south of Pasargadae, which became, it seems, the symbolic home of his branch of the dynasty. This palace, raised on a stone platform overlooking a broad plain, was extended and enriched through successive reigns; and among its many splendours are superb carvings, up its wide stairways, showing processions of soldiers, courtiers, and the peoples of the empire, from the Persians and Medes themselves, and other Iranians, to far-dwelling Indians and Egyptians, Babylonians and Greeks. The representatives of these peoples come bearing offerings, and it is widely held that the processions represent the annual bringing of gifts to the King of kings at the New Day (No Ruz) feast. Some scholars have even sought a religious significance in the orientation of the palace in relation to sunrise at the spring equinox; and there are other fine carvings on its walls (notably those representing a lion and its prey) whose symbolism has been much discussed.

The royal tombs were near Persepolis. Darius had his own sepulchre cut high in the side of the mountain known as Naqsh-i Rustam, a few miles away, and three of his successors made theirs beside it, while three later kings of the dynasty were laid in similar graves in the mountain behind Persepolis itself. An impressive sculpture was carved above the entrance to Darius' tomb, and this was faithfully reproduced over all the others. In it the king is depicted standing upon a three-stepped dais, his right hand raised, apparently in prayer. He faces a fire burning brightly upon a raised stand, and this too has a three-stepped base and an inverted three-stepped top (like the fire-holders of Pasargadae), while its shaft is decorated with three recessed panels. King and fire are shown upon a broad platform supported by thirty bearers who, their inscribed names tell us, represent the thirty peoples who made up the Persian Empire. The scene is framed by narrow panels, in which six figures are set one above the other, three to each side. These represent the six noble Persians who helped Darius to gain the throne, who thus stand on either side of the Great King as the six Amesha Spentas stand, according to the Pahlavi books, on either side of Ahuramazda. Darius thus declared visually, it is suggested, his conviction that he ruled as Ahuramazda's representative on earth, being likewise the chief personage of a great heptad. The three nobles who face the king in the right-hand panel are all shown raising their left hands, covered by the sleeve, towards their mouths in a ritual gesture of mourning (a gesture which Zoroastrian priests still make today when reciting confessional texts for the dead).

Above the king's head, in the right-hand corner of the main panel, a moon symbol is carved, which shows the round disc of the full moon with a crescent moon within it, along the lower rim. This symbol is Egyptian in origin, and had earlier been adopted by the Assyrians for their moon-god. By night Zoroastrians may pray before the 'fire' of the moon. A little below it, hovering between king and fire, is carved what has come to be regarded (through its revival in modern times) as the characteristic Zoroastrian symbol. This again is of Egyptian origin, symbol of the sun god Horus. It is a circle with a wing on either side. Often there is a bird-tail beneath it, and two undulating appendages, deriving from the sacred snakes of the prototype. The Assyrians had adopted this symbol also, and they set within the circle the upper part of a male figure; and the Persians followed them in this, although they still made use also of the simple winged circle. Usually in Achaemenian art the symbol is placed above a person; and when that person is royal, then a male figure is regularly set within the circle, himself robed and crowned like a king, his right hand raised in benediction, the left holding a ring. The earliest known occurrence of the symbol in this form is on Darius' inscription at Behistun, made early in his reign; and thereafter it recurs repeatedly on the stone walls of the great Achaemenian palaces. There is no specific link, therefore, between it and death; and one interpretation of it is that it represents Khvarenah or Divine Grace, either as a general concept (conveyed by the simple winged circle) or, specifically, the Royal Khvarenah, symbolized by the addition of the kingly figures within the circle. The Khvarenah is linked with the sun, the heavenly fire before which Zoroastrians may pray by day.

The main themes of Darius' tomb sculpture are thus strikingly Zoroastrian: the king, Ahuramazda's royal representative, is shown flanked by his six noble helpers, the mortal counterparts of the Amesha Spentas, and praying, as the prophet had taught his followers to do, in the presence of fire. The sacred number three occurs in the three steps of dais and fire-holder, and in the triple panelling of the stand's shaft. The iconography is thus orthodox, although the kings kept to the unZoroastrian practice of preserving their bodies – even while regarding a corpse as unclean, and therefore to be scrupulously isolated. (Herodotus, I. 187, relates that it vexed Darius that he could not use one of the gates of Babylon, because the embalmed body of a former queen lay in a tomb-chamber above it.)

Even Persians of lesser rank seem to have adopted the rite of exposure only slowly, for Herodotus states that, although it was common knowledge in his day that the magi let a corpse be 'torn by bird or dog' before it was buried, the Persians were more reticent about this matter, their regular custom (he says) being 'to cover the corpse with wax and bury it in the earth'. The oldest archaeological evidence for the distinctive Zoroastrian rite comes from about 400 B.C., with a rock-cut sepulchre in a mountain cemetery in Lycia, in western Asia Minor. The other tombs there appear to be those of Lycian aristocrats, but this one is distinguished by inscriptions both in Greek and Aramaic. The latter declares that 'Artim son of Arzifiy made this ossuary (astodana)'. 'Artim' has been identified as being probably the Artimas who was appointed Persian governor of Lydia in 401 B.C.; and the ossuary, which (as the Greek inscription shows) he had made to receive the bones of himself and his descendants, consists of two small chambers, each with a rectangular cavity cut in the rock floor, that was once covered by a stone lid, for further security. Each cavity evidently held the bones of several persons, gathered up after the rite of exposure. Artimas was probably of royal blood; and the ossuary shows that the rite of exposure had found acceptance among even high-ranking nobles by the end of the fifth century.

There exist at Pasargadae and Naqsh-i Rustam two impressive free-standing structures, which some have thought to be connected in some way with funerary observances. They were evidently very much alike; but the one at Pasargadae, called in later times the Zindan-i Suleyman, 'Solomon's Prison', is in ruins, whereas the one at Naqsh-i Rustam, now termed the Ka'ba-yi Zardusht or 'Zoroaster's Box', is well preserved. This is a tower-like building set on a three-stepped stone base, and consists of massive blocks of masonry which enclose a solitary windowless chamber, raised high above the ground. Its one aperture, a narrow doorway, is reached by a steep flight of thirty stone steps. Details of the stonework show that the Zindan belongs to the time of Cyrus, and that the Ka'ba, evidently modelled on it, was not built until the reign of Darius I. The two structures are unique, and their purpose remains, for a variety of reasons, a matter of much debate. The strong probability is, however, that the two narrow chambers, thus raised and isolated, served as ossuaries for lesser members of the royal family, queens, princes and princesses.

Fires and fire-holders

Achaemenian tombs and funerary sculptures show a mixture of Zoroastrian orthopraxy (with scrupulous care for the purity of the creations) with alien usages and newly adopted symbols; and this mixture demonstrates the fact that, though the Persians received Zoroastrianism as an authoritative revelation come to them from the east, yet, as a great imperial people, they set their own imprint on it in a number of lasting ways. Their earliest known innovation in cult was that of setting fire upon a raised stand. Yet still at Persepolis it must be presumed that under the early Achaemenians such fire-holders existed only within their palaces, for there is still no evidence for separate sacred buildings at that period. Indeed, the Greeks stated positively that the Persians despised temples, considering it wrong, in Cicero's later words, 'to keep shut up within walls the gods whose dwelling place was this whole world'. The two great plinths which survive at Pasargadae testify to the persistence of the tradition of worship under the open sky; and Strabo records (XI. 8.4) that a temple founded by Cyrus at Zela, in Asia Minor, consisted originally simply of a great artificial mound encircled by a wall – a man-made hill rather than a building, which people could ascend to pray. It may have been sacred precincts such as these to which Darius referred when he spoke in the Behistun inscription (I. 63) of 'ayadana', that is, 'places of worship' (though the word is rendered, perhaps conventionally, in the Elamite and Babylonian versions as 'temples'). Still in the fifth century B.C. Herodotus could write of the Persians that they erected no statues or temples or altars. Nevertheless, fire exalted upon an altar-like stand was, it is clear, very important for the early Achaemenians, perhaps as a double declaration both of their Zoroastrian faith and of their sovereign rule (the king's hearth fire, exalted thus, becoming a symbol of his own majesty). The priests must also, in those settled times, have had their established precincts for performing the yasna and other high rituals, and these (to judge from an Aramaic inscription of 458 B.C.) were called 'brazmadana' or 'place of rites'.

The divine beings

Other developments in Zoroastrianism which can be identified as Persian innovations affected the pantheon. One was the assimilation of an alien goddess, presumably Assyro-Babylonian Ishtar, the Lady of the planet Venus, and of love and war, whose cult had absorbed that of various mother-goddesses. According to Herodotus (I. 131) the Persians had learnt to sacrifice to this 'Heavenly Goddess', whom later Greek writers named 'Aphrodite Anaitis' or simply 'Anaitis'. Plainly the royal family, however sincere in their conversion to Zoroastrianism, clung to the worship of this alien divinity, but equally plainly the Zoroastrian priests could not countenance her direct acceptance among the spenta beings declared worthy of worship by their prophet. The influence of the imperial house being very great, a compromise seems to have been reached, the first evidence for which comes from the reign of Artaxerxes II (404–359). This king broke with the tradition of his predecessors by invoking, not Ahuramazda alone, but 'Ahuramazda, Anahita and Mithra'. The explanation for this innovation has to be sought from the combined testimony of the Avesta and the Pahlavi books, Zoroastrian observance and Greek sources; and together these suggest that Ishtar came to be venerated by the western Iranians as 'the Immaculate One', *Anahitish, this being their own name for the planet Venus; and that *Anahitish was then assimilated by use of the Avestan adjective anahita, 'immaculate', to the yazata *Harahvati Aredvi Sura, who was always invoked thereafter in the Avestan liturgies by the triple epithets 'Aredvi Sura Anahita', her own proper name falling into oblivion. Evidently *Harahvati was chosen for the identification because as a river-goddess she too was worshipped for fertility. The assimilation meant the uniting of two powerful cults, and Artaxerxes' invocations show how dominant the resulting veneration of Aredvi Sura Anahita became; for if one compares his words with Zoroaster's own invocations in the Gathas of 'Mazda and the (other) Ahuras', it appears likely that 'Anahita', by assimilation a river-goddess, came to be accorded, in Achaemenian worship, the place of the third Ahura, the 'Son of the Waters', *Varuna Apąm Napat. Thereafter *Varuna faded into the background in popular devotion, although he retains his place to this day in Zoroastrian priestly rituals and prayers. The pattern set by Artaxerxes was followed by his successors, and the kings of the later Iranian empires continued to invoke the divine triad of Ahuramazda, Anahita and Mithra. These three beings, together with Verethraghna, yazata of Victory, became the chief objects of popular devotion also.

Another assimilation was of a god, probably the Babylonian Nabu, lord of scribes and of the planet Mercury, who, called in Persian Tiri (perhaps meaning 'the Swift One'), was identified with the Avestan Tishtrya. His cult is attested by the number of proper names, from the Achaemenian period onwards, which were formed with the element 'Tiri'. Apart from the slight similarity between the names of these two stellar divinities, Tishtrya and Tiri were both associated with the coming of rain. Thereafter Tiri's feast, the annual celebration call Tirikana, was kept as a great Zoroastrian festival, but the divinity invoked at all its services and prayers was Tishtrya, and it was celebrated as a rain festival, as befits a feast for this yazata.

Icons and temples

Tiri's assimilation to Tishtrya appears to have enhanced the popularity of the Avestan yazata, but it did not have any such far-reaching effects as the absorption of 'Anahita's' worship was to have on Zoroastrianism. The custom all over the Near East was to venerate the mother-goddess with statues; and Berossus, a Babylonian priest of the early third century B.C., recorded that Artaxerxes was the first Persian to introduce an image cult, in that he set up statues of 'Aphrodite Anaitis' in the chief cities of the empire, and enjoined their worship upon the people. Zoroastrians were evidently asked to venerate these statues as representing Aredvi Sura Anahita; and there are verses in the Avestan hymn to this yazata which seem directly inspired by such images, for whereas she is first pictured there as the personification of a rushing river, hastening in a chariot drawn by the steeds of wind, cloud, rain and sleet, in these later verses (Yt 5, vv. 126–8) she is invoked as a magnificently static figure, richly arrayed in a jewel-encrusted mantle, with golden shoes and earrings, necklace and radiate crown. Statues so adorned could only be set within the shelter of buildings, and there is no doubt that temples arose with the introduction of this image cult. Recent excavations have shown that a large complex of buildings to the north of the terrace of Persepolis, known as the 'Fratadara' Temple, belong to the time of Artaxerxes II, and in all probability this was one of that king's foundations in honour of 'Anahita'. (In its main columned hall a stone block was found which may well have been the pedestal for her statue.)

Such striking innovations must have demanded co-operation from the priesthood, and the composition of verses inspired by the 'Anahita' statues suggests willing promotion of the cult by some of their order. So much could be ensured by imperial power and influence. But other priests as well as laymen must have been shocked by the setting up of man-made icons as objects of veneration, and it seems probable that it was as a counter-measure to this image cult that the temple worship of fire was introduced. The orthodox, that is, yielded to the new fashion of erecting consecrated buildings as centres for worship, but in place of a statue with an altar before it, they set a fire in the sanctuary, so that those coming there to pray could still do so in the presence of the only icon of which their prophet had approved. The new temple fires were elevated upon altar-like stands, like the fires shown in the sculptures of the Achaemenian kings. The development must have needed royal assent, so presumably its sponsors gained the ear of the reigning monarch, perhaps Artaxerxes II himself, perhaps his successor, Artaxerxes III (359–338), for it seems that it was one or other of these kings who was the 'Artaxerxes' or 'Ardashir' so much honoured in Zoroastrian tradition. Whatever the exact date of its establishment, there is no doubt that by the end of the Achaemenian period the fire temple, like the image sanctuary, had a recognized place in Zoroastrian worship.

A ritual had presumably been already evolved for establishing the dynastic fire of each new king, and this may well have been adapted for the 'enthronement' (as it is called in Zoroastrian usage) of each new temple fire. Essentially, however, the temple fire, like the dynastic one, was still the traditional hearth fire, elevated and set apart. It remained always a wood fire, kept continually burning. It was venerated with the Atash Niyayesh, the traditional prayer to fire, some of whose verses refer to the cooking of the morning and evening meals; and it received the same offerings as the hearth fire, namely dry wood and incense at the five daily times of prayer, and regular oblations of fat from the animal sacrifice. Moreover, the terms used in connection with its cult (as recorded from Parthian and Sasanian times) were plain and ordinary ones. The building was called simply the 'place of fire', or 'house of fire', and the pedestal upon which the fire burnt the 'fire-stand', or 'fire-holder', or 'fire-place'. These prosaic usages may well represent deliberate efforts by those who instituted the temple cult (presumably highly conservative and orthodox men) to avoid any tincture of idolatry, and to keep the new 'houses of fire' simply as places of congregational worship, where prayers could be said in the presence of the enthroned fire as naturally as they were said before the hearth fire in the home.

Yet it was inevitable that the temple fires should become imbued with a special holiness, and awaken a new and deep devotion among worshippers. Their purity, set apart as they were in their sanctuaries, could be guarded with a strictness not possible with a hearth fire; and they were not only specially consecrated at their installation, but were kept continually sanctified by the many prayers said before them. Fire, moreover, so bright and living an icon, attracts veneration even more readily than idols of wood and stone; and later usage shows that each temple fire came to be endued by the congregation with its own personality and protective power (as happens with statues and images in other faiths). Fire came, therefore, to have an enhanced part in the devotional lives of Zoroastrians after the establishment of the temple cult. Herodotus (III. 16) speaks of the veneration of fire by the Persians, but he does not single this out as the distinctive feature of their religion, and it is only after the founding of temple fires that those of other faiths came to label Zoroastrians as 'fire-worshippers'. Nor does fire figure in Herodotus' accounts of Persian military rites, whereas Curtius Rufus states that Darius III, the last of the Achaemenians, had embers from 'the fire which the Persians called sacred and eternal' carried before his army when he marched out to battle.

Nothing is known directly of categories of Achaemenian temple fires; but it seems likely that by the end of the period two kinds of sacred fires were already in existence which are familiar from later times. The great fires, the 'cathedral fires', as it were, of Zoroastrianism, were all called, it seems, Atar- Verethraghan- , 'Victorious Fire' (the name is known only in its later forms, as Atakhsh i Varahram, Atash Bahram). These were created from the embers of many kinds of ordinary fires, purified and consecrated through

Second Story
Books

REG   10-31-2013 19:56

000115

DEPT01   T1 $8.00
TAX-AMT 1 $8.00
TAX 1 $0.46
TOTAL $8.46
CASH $20.00
CHANGE $11.54

prolonged rites. The lesser fires were known simply as 'Fire of Fires' (in later parlance Atakhsh i Aduran, Atash Aduran). These were formed from embers from the hearth fires of representatives of each social class, and their temples were roughly equivalent to the parish churches of Christendom. Just why the great fires were dedicated to Verethraghna remains a matter for speculation; but later Pahlavi texts show that all fires were regarded as warriors fighting for the spenta creation – not only on the physical plane, against darkness and cold, but also on the spiritual one, against the forces of vice and ignorance. It would seem natural, therefore, to devote the greatest of them to Victory, in a spirit of courage and hope; and hence the custom can readily be understood of carrying embers from such a 'Victory' fire before a Zoroastrian army when it advanced to combat the infidel.

The establishing of temple cults had many consequences. Early Zoroastrianism was rich in doctrine and observance, but made, it seems, few material demands on its followers. Offerings to the hearth fire served a practical purpose also, in that they helped to support something which was necessary in every home; and congregational worship, whether in high places or at the seasonal feasts, required no special buildings or separate order of priests. By contrast the new sacred fires had no worldly use; and for them, as for the 'Anahita' images, buildings had to be constructed and maintained, and priests employed to serve them. This gave new scope for the wealth of imperial Persia to be lavished on the faith, and magnificent temples were built which were embellished with gold and silver, and endowed with great estates. (Records of such temples come only from after the downfall of the Achaemenians, for the latter part of their epoch is poorly documented.)

The priesthood

All the great temples must have had many priests. Sacred fires in particular need constant attendance, and the high priest of a fire temple (to judge from later evidence) was called '*magupati', 'lord of priests', having serving priests under his authority. These priests would have been supported both by income from endowments and by offerings from the faithful; and so a new branch of the ecclesiastical hierarchy came into being, less directly involved than the family priests with the laity in their daily lives, but partly dependent on them nevertheless, and so creating a new charge on the community.

Colleges of scholar-priests must also have existed, either independently or perhaps in conjunction with the great religious foundations. Another form of pious endowment (older, evidently, than the founding of temples) is also attested in the Achaemenian period. This was the establishing of religious services and offerings on behalf of the souls of the eminent departed, to be maintained as far as possible in perpetuity. The offerings instituted by Cambyses at his father's tomb exemplify this usage, and the rites which he established were maintained by the same family of priests, living by the tomb, for over two hundred years. Such chantry priests formed yet another group within the ecclesiastical body.

The growth of Zoroastrianism as a great imperial faith, possessed of temples, shrines and broad estates, and served by an ever increasing number of priests, can thus be traced through the Achaemenian period. Nothing is known from this time, however, about the organization of the religious community – whether the priests of east and west, the 'athaurvan' and 'magu', were joined in a single body with a united hierarchy, or whether the local priesthoods enjoyed a measure of autonomy under the general leadership of Persia. The latter state of affairs appears more probable, and would reflect secular conditions in the Achaemenian Empire, in which each province or satrapy retained its own customs and language, and a degree of independence. Even the Iranian satrapies (which in general corresponded to old tribal divisions) kept their own tongues (Parthian, Sogdian and the like) instead of adopting Persian. This was evidently largely because the language of written communication throughout the empire continued to be Aramaic, and so Persian, though the speech of the ruling Iranian people, gained little general currency.

At the beginning of the Achaemenian period the use of this foreign language, Aramaic, and the foreign art of writing which went with it, were practised by alien scribes; but long before the era ended both skills must have been acquired by members of the Iranian learned class, namely the priests, who (as in medieval Europe) came in due course to provide the judges, administrators and 'clerks' needed in an increasingly complex society. Such men presumably underwent the basic training for their own hereditary calling, up to the age of fifteen or so, and then studied the special art of scribesmanship, acquiring a practical knowledge of written Aramaic. The scribe was called by a half-foreign name, 'dipivara', Middle Persian 'dibir', from an old Akkadian word 'dipi', meaning 'writing, record'; and he received his training at an institution called in Middle Persian 'dibirestan' that is, 'place of scribes'. Each Iranian satrapy must have had its own institutions of this kind; and there was a natural tendency for the calling to become in its turn hereditary, so that by Sasanian times the scribes were recognized as a special group within society.

A few representations of priests survive from the Achaemenian period, which show them wearing a long-sleeved, belted tunic reaching to the knees, loose trousers and a sleeved mantle. For headgear there was a hood-like cap with side-pieces which could be brought forward to cover the mouth. Tradition suggests that cap and garments would all have been white, the priestly colour; but in these representations, where colour cannot be shown, the priest is distinguished by carrying a tall bundle of baresman-rods, for he would otherwise have resembled many of the Iranian laity. This style of dressing was, it seems, evolved by the Scythians of the steppes when they became horse-riders instead of charioteers, and was adopted from them by the Medes and other settled Iranian peoples in the north. Even the Persians wore similar garments in the field, but when at leisure dressed in flowing robes. That priests should have chosen the garb of horsemen may seem at first sight strange, but this clothing was practical for them also. Close-fitting garments were more suitable than loose robes for wear while solemnizing rituals, when there must be no danger of a fold of cloth touching consecrated objects; and although the original purpose of the hood-like cap with its mouth-pieces was evidently to give protection against cold, heat and dust, this headgear also served admirably to cover the hair of head and beard, for purity's sake, and to prevent the breath reaching what was consecrated. The Zoroastrian priests continued accordingly to wear this style of dress for many centuries, the fashion presumably spreading during the Achaemenian period throughout the community.

The Zurvanite heresy

As for unity in more important matters, the lucid and comprehensive doctrines taught by Zoroaster left little scope for heresy or schism. Yet they must have given the western magi much new matter to ponder upon. One of the most striking elements in the prophet's teachings was the wholly original concept of history having an end. This concept, embodied in the doctrine of the Three times – Creation, Mixture and Separation – accustomed his followers to the idea of events taking place within a fixed chronological framework. The magi had also evidently become familiar with very different Babylonian speculations about history being divided into great recurrent cycles of time, within each of which all events repeated themselves; and contrasting such theories with Zoroaster's teachings may well have led them to reflect much upon time and its nature. The result of their thinking was the Zurvanite heresy, a development, it seems, of the late Achaemenian period, which was to have a long history and wide influence. The Avestan word 'zurvan' means 'time'; and in a few late passages of the Younger Avesta (e.g. Y 72.10, Vd 19.13), it is used as the name of a minor divinity, hypostatizing time. This usage appears to be a very limited concession to the Zurvanites, who had come to believe that Time, Zurvan, did not merely provide the framework for events but was actually in control of them, hence a sentient being. They found their main scriptural justification for this in the great Gathic verse, Y 30.3: 'Truly there are two primal spirits, twins, renowned to be in conflict. . . .' Meditating upon this they postulated, with scholastic ingenuity, that for twins there must be a father; and this being so, they declared, the only possible father for Ahuramazda and Anra Mainyu was Zurvan, Time. Originally this was perhaps no more than intellectual speculation, but it grew into a full-blown heresy, with Zurvan being invested with power, and myths evolving around him – although all accounts of Zurvanite mythology belong to the Sasanian and post-Sasanian epochs, and only the bare existence of the heresy can be established for the Achaemenian period itself. According to one of these relatively late sources, Zurvan alone 'has always been and shall be for ever-more. . . . Yet for all the grandeur that surrounded him, there was none to call him Creator, for he had not brought forth creation' (Second Ulema-i Islam 8, ZZZ 410). So he was moved, it was said, to generate Ahuramazda and Anra Mainyu, although there were many different explanations, it was admitted, as to why he brought the latter into being. The best attested is that before Ahuramazda was born Zurvan began to doubt his own powers to beget a worthy son, and from this doubt Anra Mainyu was engendered and came first into the world, a black and hideous creature who horrified his sire. Naturally this myth gave scope for further elaboration (in whose womb, for instance, had the twins been conceived?). The heresy also opened the way for philosophical reflections on the power of time and hence on predestination. Zurvan was seen, moreover, as lord of the

Three Times, and was invoked with three cult-epithets (preserved only in a Syriac source). Then these epithets, meaning, it seems, Lord of growth, maturity and decay, became in characteristic Iranian fashion hypostatized as independent divinities, and Zurvan was accordingly invoked as a quaternity, and the number four was prominent in his cult.

This cult seems, however, to have had few, if any, observances; for Zurvan was held to be a remote first cause, who, having begotten Ahuramazda, entrusted to him as soon as he could the power over this world. He does not himself intervene in the present struggle between his 'sons', and belief in his existence produced no change, therefore, in the objects or manner of Zoroastrian worship, or in moral or spiritual goals. Moreover, the fundamental doctrine having been adopted that Zurvan created both Ahuramazda and Anra Mainyu, the Zurvanites then ascribed all subsequent acts of creation to Ahuramazda, and so could venerate him by his due title of Dadvah, 'Creator'. They were able therefore to call themselves 'Mazda-worshippers', and so could live in general harmony with the orthodox. Indeed there can be little doubt that they felt themselves to be the most truly orthodox followers of Zoroaster, who had divined the correct meaning of the prophet's words in the crucial Gathic passage.

There is even less doubt that theirs was in fact a deep and grievous heresy, which was greatly to weaken Zoroastrianism in its later struggles with Christianity and Islam; for by declaring (in the words of a later polemicist) that 'Ohrmazd and Ahriman are brothers', the Zurvanites betrayed Zoroaster's fundamental doctrine that good and evil are utterly separate and distinct by origin and nature. They also diminished the grandeur of Ahuramazda, who had been proclaimed by Zoroaster as uncreated God, the only divine Being worthy of worship who exists eternally; and they confused the clear teachings of the faith with tedious speculations and ignoble myths. Moreover, the Zurvanite preoccupation with fate, and the inexorable decrees of Time, obscured the basic Zoroastrian doctrine of the existence of free-will, and the power of each individual to shape his own destiny through the exercise of choice. Indeed, so deep is the doctrinal gulf which separates Zurvanism from Zoroastrian orthodoxy that it only seems possible to account for the tolerance shown it by assuming that it early gained influential adherents. The Sasanian royal family are known to have been Zurvanites, and they consciously maintained

Achaemenian traditions in a number of ways; so it is very possible that it was the later Achaemenians who set them an example in this, and who, won over by certain of the magi, established the heresy in western Iran. This would help to account for the enormous influence it came to exert on many Gnostic faiths (for which the concepts of the Three Times, the remote First Cause, and the lesser Creator of this world, were fundamental doctrines). Once it had been established, continuing royal favour, and devout orthopraxy, evidently ensured its survival for many centuries. Nevertheless, equally persistent rejection of the heresy by other members of the community finds expression in a passage in one of the Pahlavi books (Dk IX. 30.4), and it finally disappeared some centuries after the coming of Islam.

The Zoroastrian calendar

Since Zurvan had no place in daily worship, it is not surprising that he received no dedications in the 'Zoroastrian' calendar, which was evidently evolved during the later Achaemenian period. The early Zoroastrians had presumably continued to use variants of the traditional 360-day Old Iranian calendar, in which the twelve months were named for various festivals, or activities of the pastoral year, and the days of each month were simply numbered from one to thirty. Evidence for the existence of such calendars is provided by Old Persian inscriptions and tablets (for there are no calendar references in the Gathas or older parts of the Younger Avesta). These show that the scribes of the early Achaemenians used the Babylonian calendar, but modified it by 'translating' its month-names by their Old Persian equivalents. The Babylonian calendar was also of 360 days, and Herodotus (III. 90) states that Darius exacted annual tribute from the Cilicians of '360 white horses, one for each day of the year'. But Zoroastrian priests would hardly have been prepared to use a semi-foreign system for reckoning their own holy days, and they presumably continued to calculate these according to the local Iranian calendars – all essentially the same, but with variations in the month-names, and perhaps also in the times of intercalation (for it was necessary to intercalate a thirteenth month every six years or so to keep the 360-day calendar in harmony with the seasons). Variations in calendar usage were plainly undesirable, however, in a unified empire, and at some stage, it seems, the Persians took the lead in creating a distinctive Zoroastrian calendar, to be used everywhere

throughout the religious community. Eminent men wer
summoned from all the Iranian provinces to confer over tl
tant step, for there are features in the calendar which suggest ;
of debate and compromise.

Persian initiative appears in the fact that not only the twelve
but also the thirty days of the new calendar were each piously
cated to a yazata. The inspiration for this seems to have come
Egypt, whose practices were well known to the Persians sinc
days of Cambyses. Further, although traditionally the Iran
divided the month into two or three parts according to the phases
the moon, the new calendar had four divisions, which suggests t
influence (to which western Iran was susceptible) of the Semitic weel
This may have been reinforced by that of Zurvanite theology, witl
Zurvan being venerated under four aspects. If so, Zurvanite influence
was held in check at that point, for the division was achieved with full
orthodoxy by devoting four days in the month to Ahuramazda. The
first was dedicated to him by name ('Ahuramazda day'), and three
others by his title of Creator ('Dadvah day'). The second to the
seventh days were devoted to the six Amesha Spentas, making up the
first 'week'. The eighth was the first 'Dadvah day', and the six
following days were named for Fire, the Waters, Sun, Moon, Tiri and
Geush Urvan. That the thirteenth day was devoted to Tiri, not
Tishtrya, suggests the powerful influence of the western magi. Yet
Tiri was evidently given this particular place because Tishtrya, with
whom he is identified, is a star-yazata, and as such has associations
with both the moon and Geush Urvan.

The fifteenth day, introducing the third 'week', was the second
'Dadvah day', and the sixteenth was dedicated to Mithra, who thus
heads the dedications of the second half of the month. The next two
days were devoted to yazatas especially connected with him, Sraosha
and Rashnu. Then came dedications to the Fravashis, Verethraghna,
Raman (who was associated with Vayu and so with both death and the
wind) and finally to the other wind-yazata, Vata. The twenty-third
was the third 'Dadvah day' and ushered in the last 'week', made up
of days dedicated to three female yazatas, Daena, Ashi and Arshtat,
the pair Asman and Zam (Heaven and Earth), and finally Manthra
Spenta (the Bounteous Sacred Word) and Anaghra Raocha (the
'Endless Light' of paradise).

It is noteworthy that, although the western priests gained a place
for Tiri, neither Aredvi Sura Anahita, nor great Varuna whom she had

eclipsed, received a dedication. Possibly this represents a stalemate between the wishes of the eastern and western communities. Each, however, seems to have won a secondary victory, for on the one hand the tenth day, devoted to the female Waters, came to be regarded as Aredvi's and on the other there are three yazatas, displaced probably by the decision to name three days for the Creator, who are regularly invoked with the 'calendar' divinities at all services devoted to the pantheon, and *Varuna Apąm Napat is among them. The other two are Haoma and Dahman Afrin (who hypostatizes the prayers of the faithful). The Zoroastrian priests thus acknowledge thirty major beings as 'worthy of worship'. Neither the three 'displaced' yazatas, nor Aredvi Sura Anahita, are invoked in Yasna 16, a short section of the extended yasna which sets out, in liturgical form, the dedications of the thirty days, which coincide with the day-names except in the case of Tiri-Tishtrya.

The dedications of the months coincide with twelve of the day-dedications; but there is no passage in the Avesta which sets them out or shows how they corresponded to the natural seasons in Achaemenian times. However, the established symbolism of the Zoroastrian holy year demands that the 'New Day' should be celebrated at the spring equinox; and since the Babylonians also had a spring new year, it appears safe to assume that the Achaemenians held their 'New day' festival then, with the month in which it fell corresponding with March/April in the Gregorian calendar. There were other traditional festivals to be taken into account in naming the months in what was evidently a carefully pondered scheme. Thus the mid-winter month, equivalent to December/January, when the powers of evil were held to be at their strongest, was devoted to the Creator, so that he, with his mighty spenta powers, should be constantly invoked then. The next month was dedicated to Vohu Manah, who is always close to the supreme Lord; and five other months were duly given to the other great Amesha Spentas, though in an unusual order. Their arrangement was probably to allow the fourth month (counting from the 'New Day'), in which the feast of Tirikana took place, to be dedicated to Tiri, and the autumnal seventh month, when *Mithrakana was celebrated, to be named for Mithra. The remaining three months were devoted to Fire and the Waters, and to the Fravashis. The month of the Waters corresponded to October/November, when rains may be looked for

in Persia, and that of Fire to November/December, when the ancient fire-festival of Sada took place, celebrated one hundred days before 'New Day'. The month of 'New Day' itself, March/April, was assigned to the Fravashis, presumably because of the link between these immortal beings and the coming of Frasho-kereti, foreshadowed at that feast. Spenta Armaiti, guardian of earth, has the preceding month, when the corn is beginning to grow, while her partner, Khshathra Vairya, was given the one immediately before that of Mithra, his 'hamkar' or coadjutor. Their two months are thus exactly half a year apart. The ancient feast of the Fravashis fell on the last night of Spenta Armaiti's month, which suggests the enduring nature of the link between earth and the dead. Asha Vahishta, lord of fire, had the month of April/May, when summer heat begins to make itself felt on the Persian plateau; and Haurvatat and Ameretat received the months on each side of Tiri's, perhaps because of Tishtrya's traditional connection with rain, which nourishes their creations.

The religious importance of the calendar dedications was great, for they not only fixed the pantheon of major yazatas, but ensured that their names were continually uttered, since at every Zoroastrian act of worship the yazatas of both day and month are invoked. Further, the fact that Mithra's great feast was now celebrated on Mithra day of Mithra month, and Tiri's on Tiri day of Tiri month, set a pattern for 'name-day' feasts, so that whenever a day and month name coincided, a feast was celebrated in honour of the divinity concerned. So in the winter month devoted to the Creator (when people were mostly at home, weather-bound, and with leisure for extra observances), four new feasts were held in honour of Ahuramazda. The yazata Atar acquired a festival close to the ancient feast of Sada (but, unlike it, celebrated not in the open but mainly at the new fire temples), and the Waters and Fravashis also gained name-day feasts, as did each of the six Amesha Spentas. This increase in the number of holy days, although piously inspired, carried a threat to the effectiveness of the simple devotional year created by Zoroaster, with its chain of seven feasts in honour of the seven Amesha Spentas and their creations; for since each of the Amesha Spentas, and two of the creations, now had separate feast-days as well, there was a danger that the doctrinal significance of the holy days of obligation would become obscured, so that they would no longer remind the faithful so clearly of fundamental beliefs.

Another drawback to the increase in festivals was that, though it brought more leisure and gaiety into people's lives, it also created more work for the priests, since every holy day was celebrated with religious services; and more work for the priests meant more charges on the laity. The enormous importance gained by Sraosha, yazata of prayer, in the Zoroastrian cult may owe something to such increases in observances, although it probably largely predates the western spread of Zoroastrianism, for Sraosha was plainly beloved by Zoroaster himself. The prophet names him several times in the Gathas, and once (Y 33.5) calls him 'greatest of all', presumably as guardian of the means – prayer – through which man can approach God. It was apparently because of these words that his followers came to regard Sraosha as virtually the eighth Amesha Spenta, and Ahuramazda's vice-regent on earth, with an especial duty, therefore, to care for his creation, man. So at some stage a new hymn (preserved as Y 57) was composed in his honour. This was modelled on the Mihr Yasht, for, like Mithra, the yazata of prayer is a mighty warrior, able to defeat invisible foes.

The three world Saviours

Another development which can be assigned to the Achaemenian period concerned the belief in the world Saviour, the Saoshyant. This belief became elaborated into an expectation of three Saviours, each to be born of the prophet's seed by a virgin mother – an elaboration which appears to have been connected with a newly evolved scheme of world history, according to which 'limited time' (that is, the three periods of Creation, Mixture and Separation) was regarded as a vast 'world year', divided into segments of 1000 years each. This scheme, it is generally held, derived from Babylonian speculations about the recurrent 'great years', those spans of time which perpetually repeated themselves with all the events that had taken place in them. The texts vary as to how many millennia made up the Zoroastrian world year. Some give the figure as nine (three times three being a favoured number), others as twelve (corresponding to the months of the natural year). There are, however, grounds for thinking that the original figure was 6000 years, which was increased as priestly scholars developed the scheme. Of these 6000 years, the first 3000, it appears, were assigned to creation, the process of mixture, and the early history of mankind. Zoroaster himself was held to have been born towards the end of the third millennium, and to have received his revelation in the year 3000. A time of goodness follows, and of progress towards the ultimate goal of creation, but thereafter men will begin to forget his teachings. In the year 4000 the first Saviour, named Ukhshyat-ereta, 'He who makes righteousness grow', will renew the prophet's gospel. History will then repeat itself, with his brother, Ukhshyat-nemah, 'He who makes reverence grow', appearing towards the year 5000; and finally, towards the end of the last millennium, the greatest of the Saoshyants, Astvat-ereta himself, will appear and usher in Frasho-kereti. This doctrine of the three Saviours further allowed priestly scholastics to fuse Zoroaster's message of hope with ancient Iranian traditions of humanity's descent from a gold age – that of Yima – to the sorry present (assigned to the period of degeneracy before the coming of the first Saoshyant); and it gave them scope for elaborating patterns of recurring events. The whole scheme, of world chronology and the three Saoshyants, seems to have remained, however, a matter for the learned, while the people in general (to judge from later times) continued to look and long simply for the coming of the one Saviour foretold by Zoroaster.

Practices of the faith

As for details of the practice of the faith during Achaemenian times, little direct evidence survives. The portion of the yasna concerned with the new calendar dedications suggests a steady development of devotional usages, with the composition of new liturgies to accompany them consisting, essentially, of adaptations from older parts of the Avesta, with simple linking formulas. Herodotus, our chief informant about Iranian religion at this epoch, had presumably no access, being an infidel, to the inner ceremonies of the faith, to which he makes no reference; but he describes (I. 132) a sacrifice made to one of the divine beings by a layman in an open place: 'To pray for blessings for himself alone is not lawful for the sacrificer; rather he prays that it may be well with the king and all the Persians, for he reckons himself among them. He then cuts the victim limb from limb into portions, and having seethed the flesh spreads the softest grass, trefoil by choice, and places all of it on this. When he has so disposed of it a magus comes near and chants over it the song of the birth of the gods, as the Persian tradition relates it; for no sacrifice can be offered without a magus. Then after a little while the sacrificer carries away the flesh and uses it as he pleases.' There is a mixture here of what Zoroastrian usage suggests is accuracy (prayers for the whole community, the manner of disposal of the flesh, the presence of the priest), and inaccuracy (the sacrifice being made by a layman without previous consecration, the content of the priest's utterances); and this probably arises from Herodotus depending even for this 'outer' ceremony on a description, not fully understood, rather than his own observation. He also writes more generally (I. 131) of the sacrifices offered by Persians to 'Zeus', i.e. Ahuramazda, on the peaks of mountains, and adds that they sacrificed there also 'to the sun and moon and earth and fire and water and winds'.

With regard to the magi, Herodotus commented with surprise (I. 140) on their killing with their own hands 'every creature, save only dogs and men; they kill all alike, ants and snakes, creeping and flying things, and take much pride therein'. This was natural, since they felt themselves, in destroying such khrafstras, to be reducing the forces of Anra Mainyu. In general Herodotus observes of the Persians (I. 138) that 'they chiefly reverence rivers; they will neither make water nor spit nor wash their hands therein, nor suffer anyone to do so', while fire, he says (III. 16) they 'regard as a god'. Of social behaviour he remarks (I. 138) that 'they hold lying to be foulest of all, and next to that debt, for which they have many other reasons, but this in especial, that the debtor must needs (so they say) speak some falsehood'. 'Truth-telling' he says (I. 136) was one of the things in which the Persian nobles trained their sons.

The spread of Zoroaster's teaching

Zoroaster's doctrines thus shaped the conduct of his own followers. They also exerted a profound influence at this time throughout the Near East. There is no evidence for any proselytizing among non-Iranians under the Achaemenians, but Persian officials, with their households, were to be found in dominant positions in every province of the empire, together (in non-Iranian regions) with colonies of merchants and other settlers; and when there were Persians there were Zoroastrian priests to minister to their needs and serve at their place of worship. (The clearest evidence for this, because of Greek notices, comes from the provinces of Asia Minor.) Presumably both priests and the laity were prepared to discuss matters of religion with inquirers; and gradually many of Zoroaster's fundamental doctrines became disseminated throughout the region, from Egypt to the Black Sea: namely that there is a supreme God who is the Creator; that an evil power exists which is opposed to him, and not under his control; that he has emanated many lesser divinities to help combat this power; that he has created this world for a purpose, and that in its present state it will have an end; that this end will be heralded by the coming of a cosmic Saviour, who will help to bring it about; that meantime heaven and hell exist, with an individual judgment to decide the fate of each soul at death; that at the end of time there will be a resurrection of the dead and a Last Judgment, with annihilation of the wicked; and that thereafter the kingdom of God will come upon earth, and the righteous will enter into it as into a garden (a Persian word for which is 'paradise'), and be happy there in the presence of God for ever, immortal themselves in body as well as soul.

These doctrines all came to be adopted by various Jewish schools in the post-Exilic period, for the Jews were one of the peoples, it seems, most open to Zoroastrian influences – a tiny minority, holding staunchly to their own beliefs, but evidently admiring their Persian benefactors, and finding congenial elements in their faith. Worship of the one supreme God, and belief in the coming of a Messiah or Saviour, together with adherence to a way of life which combined moral and spiritual aspirations with a strict code of behaviour (including purity laws) were all matters in which Judaism and Zoroastrianism were in harmony; and it was this harmony, it seems, reinforced by the respect of a subject people for a great protective power, which allowed Zoroastrian doctrines to exert their influence. The extent of this influence is best attested, however, by Jewish writings of the Parthian period, when Christianity and the Gnostic faiths, as well as northern Buddhism, all likewise bore witness to the profound effect which Zoroaster's teachings had had throughout the lands of the Achaemenian empire.

CHAPTER SIX

Under the Seleucids
and Arsacids

Alexander and Iran

By the fourth century B.C. Zoroastrianism, firmly established as the Iranian religion, had thus acquired great spiritual authority as well as temporal power. Then a heavy blow fell: Alexander the Great, of Macedon, invaded Asia Minor, met and defeated Darius III in battle in 331 B.C., and in five years of campaigning conquered almost all the territories of the Achaemenian Empire. His invasion was made in pursuit of gain and glory, and had no religious impulse; and the Zoroastrian community evidently suffered more during the actual fighting than in the period of foreign domination which followed. Hence it is Alexander himself, and not his Seleucid successors, who is execrated in Zoroastrian tradition, in which he is remembered as the 'accursed' (guzastag), an epithet which he shares with Ahriman alone. In a Sogdian fragment he is set among the worst sinners of history, his wickedness being that he 'killed magi', and in one Pahlavi text (AVN I. 9) it is said that he slew 'many teachers, lawyers, herbads and mobads', in another (GBd XXXIII. 14) that he 'quenched many fires'. These crimes were presumably committed when his soldiers plundered temples and sanctuaries, whose priests may well have perished in vain attempts to defend their holy places. Little is recorded (and that only by Greek historians) of particular ravages, but the 'Fratadara' temple at Persepolis must have suffered when

Alexander sacked the capital, and another Anahita temple at Ecbatana (Hamadan) is said to have been pillaged repeatedly by the Macedonians, who stripped away even its silver roof-tiles and the gold plating from its columns. Such material damage could be made good in time; but the Zoroastrians sustained irreparable loss through the death of so many of their priests. In those days, when all religious works were handed down orally, the priests were the living books of the faith, and with mass slaughters many ancient works (the tradition holds) were lost, or only haltingly preserved. Much survived, however, and Zoroaster's own Gathas were transmitted intact, being known by heart, with the rest of the Staota Yesnya, by every working priest.

The Seleucids and Iran

Alexander ruled for seven years; and on his death his generals fought over the succession, bringing more suffering to the lands he had conquered. It was not until 312/311 that one of them, Seleucus, managed to establish his rule over a large part of the former Achaemenian Empire, including all Iran. This he governed from Babylonia, making a new capital there for himself, named Seleucia-on-the-Tigris. Alexander had founded cities across Iran, peopled by Greek soldiers and settlers, to help hold and administer the land, and the Seleucids continued this policy. Outside these foundations the Macedonians maintained much of the Achaemenian administrative system intact, with satrapies renamed as provinces, but each still with its own governor, who retained considerable powers. In the new order of things Pars or Persia proper was no longer pre-eminent, but only one among the Iranian provinces, all alike subjected to the foreigner; and this had a marked effect on the Zoroastrian community. The Macedonians had appropriated Persia's former authority in the political sphere, but they could not do so in the religious one. So when the priests of each province rallied from the carnage and destruction of the conquest, they pursued, it seems, independent courses, maintaining only fraternal links with one another. The legacy of the period of closer unity under the Achaemenians had provided them, however, with a wide range of shared observances, including the veneration of 'Anahit' and 'Tir', which continued in the east as in the west of Iran, as did the temple cults of fire and images.

One of the regions which resisted Alexander most fiercely was Bactria in the far north-east, and in consequence this satrapy, which was strategically important, was placed under a Greek governor, and several Greek cities were founded there. It was a province with old Zoroastrian traditions, and there is a suggestion that it was here that Alexander first noticed the distinctive Zoroastrian rite of exposure of the dead. After the conquest of this last area of resistance, Alexander and his generals took Iranian noblewomen in marriage (partly for political reasons); and Seleucus chose Apama, a Bactrian captive of war, who bore him a son and successor, Antiochus I. The Seleucids thus themselves had Iranian blood in their veins; and it is known that many other marriages took place between Greek soldiers and Iranian girls. Nevertheless, the two peoples, conquerors and conquered, seem to have held apart to a large extent throughout the period of Seleucid rule, with the culture of the new cities being predominantly Greek, and that of the old towns and villages remaining almost purely Iranian.

The clearest evidence for this state of affairs, and also for the regional character of Iranian life at the time, is provided by scripts. The Macedonians introduced into Iran the beautifully clear Greek alphabet, developed to represent adequately an Indo-European tongue; and the Iranian scribes had necessarily to master this, as well as at least a modicum of the Greek language, in order to communicate with the new rulers, and conform with their regulations and tax-demands. Yet for all domestic purposes they kept to the Aramaic language and script, which by this time had become the traditional means of written communication among Iranians; and because of the increased regionalism of Iranian life under the Seleucids, the Aramaic letters began slowly to develop local forms, so that in time distinctive scripts were evolved in all the main provinces. Those known from surviving documents and inscriptions are Parthian, Middle Persian, Median, Sogdian and Khwarezmian; and their existence testifies to the independence which the scribal schools of each area, and hence also their priestly colleges, enjoyed after the downfall of the Achaemenians.

The rise of the Parthians

Although the Seleucids laid claim to all lands east of Mesopotamia which had been under Achaemenian rule (that is, up to the Indus and

Jaxartes), their authority was relatively weak over areas remote from their Babylonian capital; and during either the reign of Seleucus himself (c. 312–281), or that of his son Antiochus I (c. 280–262), a tribe of nomad Iranians invaded the old Achaemenian satrapy of Parthava (Parthia), in the north-east of Iran. These presumably pagan nomads were, according to Strabo (XI. 515), the Parni, whom he identifies as kinsmen of the Scythians who lived to the north of the Black Sea. The Parni settled down and adopted the language of the Parthians, as well, evidently, as their Zoroastrian faith and the customs of their civilization, which included that of employing priestly scribes who wrote in Aramaic.

In 305 B.C. the Seleucids relinquished their Indian territories, but they maintained their authority in eastern Iran, and it was not until 246 that the Greek governor of Bactria declared his independence. At about the same time the Parthians rose in revolt, possibly also under their Greek governor; but if so, he was soon thrust aside by a Parni chieftain, one Arshak, known to the Greeks as Arsaces, founder of the Arsacid dynasty. Arshak had probably himself been born and brought up in Parthava, speaking the Parthian language; and the Arsacids are regarded as a Parthian dynasty.

Even before this the province of Pars, in the south-east, had regained a measure of independence, and local rulers were striking coins there from about 280 B.C.; but the Seleucids kept control over Media, and in about 209 brought Parthia back briefly under their rule. The Arsacids, however, maintained their dominant position there, and a few decades later Mithridates I (c. 171–138) marched westward, and in 141 entered Seleucia-on-the-Tigris as a conqueror. Under his namesake, Mithridates II (c. 123–87), the Arsacids established their rule from the frontiers of India to the western borders of Mesopotamia, and Zoroastrianism became once more the faith of a great Iranian empire. This empire was to last much longer than that of the Achaemenians, but it was never as centralized as theirs had been. The Arsacids ruled as high kings over vassal kings and great nobles, allowing the regionalism of the Seleucid period to continue to a great extent, and the Parthian priests appear to have dominated the religious community in much the same way: they exercised leadership, that is, but did not seek to impose conformity in all matters, or to practise any strict control over the affairs of the various regional priesthoods.

The Greek cities in Iran continued to thrive under the rule of early

Arsacids. From the reign of Mithradates I the Parthian kings regularly struck their own coins, which they usually had minted by Greek craftsmen; and these coins testify to a radical change in Zoroastrian iconography at this time, with the Egyptian and Mesopotamian symbols adopted by the Achaemenians yielding place to anthropomorphic representations of Hellenic type. Excavation has shown that the Greeks in Iran used to set up fine, naturalistic images of their gods in the market-places of their cities, where they would have been visible to all who came and went; and they themselves, in Iran as in Syria, Mesopotamia and wherever else they settled, identified these gods with the local divinities (being thus able prudently to propitiate both together). In this way they created a new iconography for Zoroastrianism, which the Arsacids' coinage must have helped to make generally familiar; for on the reverse of a number of their issues these kings piously placed divine figures, which (in the light of all the evidence now available) can be confidently interpreted as representing, to their Iranian subjects, yazatas in the guise of Greek gods. Among those depicted were Zeus and Apollo (representing Ahuramazda and Mithra), Herakles Kallinikos, the 'Victorious' (Verethraghna, yazata of victory), Nike and Demeter (Ashi and Spenta Armaiti).

On some later issues the Parthian kings followed Seleucid example in claiming divinity for themselves, in that they had the titles *theos*, 'god', or *theopator*, of divine descent', set in Greek letters under the royal portrait on the obverse. This practice was formerly regarded as a sign of heterodoxy; but though the claim appears indeed a startling one for Zoroastrians to make, one finds their successors, the Sasanians, likewise asserting that they were 'of the race of the gods', so that it was apparently felt (so flexible is the human mind) to be compatible with true belief. The likelihood is, moreover, that in Arsacid times it was princes and nobles, rather than priests (who would have been more concerned with doctrinal matters) who led the way in adopting Greek iconography and Greek titles; for it was necessarily they, as men of affairs, who had the most dealings with the Hellenes, and so enjoyed the greatest opportunities to see and be attracted by their art and way of life. Zoroastrian priests (apart from the scribes) probably kept as aloof as possible from the unclean infidels who had brought such harm to the faith; and many peasant farmers, working in their fields, may never have encountered the foreigners at all.

Eastern Iranian borders: the Kushans

Towards the end of the second century B.C. another group of nomads, predominantly at least Iranians, conquered the Greco-Iranian kingdom of Bactria, where they settled and (like the Parni before them) adopted much of the local culture. This included the Bactrian language, which, however, they learnt to write in Greek instead of Aramaic script. This fusion of an Iranian tongue with a Hellenic alphabet appears unique to this region, and must presumably be ascribed to the exceptionally strong Greek element there. Later – probably in the first century A.C. – the Kushans, a family of chieftains among these invaders, began (as the Arsacids had done) a campaign of conquest, and carved out a considerable realm, with territories taken from both the Parthian Empire and India, and with other lands stretching northwards into Central Asia. The Kushans traded by sea with distant Rome (by then the enemy of Parthia), and issued coins bearing the images of Zoroastrian, Buddhist and Greco-Roman divinities, most with their names written beneath in Greek script. The names of the Zoroastrian yazatas have been identified (despite problems of phonetics and orthography) as Bactrian forms of familiar Avestan ones. There are fourteen or fifteen of them, and they form by far the largest group within this early Kushan pantheon. They include Ashaeikhsho (Asha Vahishta) and Shaoreoro (Khshathra Vairya) – the two Amesha Spentas most likely to be publicly invoked by a king; Miiro (Mithra) and Orlango (Vere-thraghna), fit yazatas for the coins of a conquering dynasty; Pharro (Khvarenah), to prosper their ventures, and Lrooaspo (Druvaspa), patron divinity of the horses on which their armies depended. How the faith professed by the Kushans themselves should be defined remains uncertain, but their coinage shows that even in Greek-dominated Bactria they had found Zoroastrianism still flourishing.

A great sanctuary of the early Kushans has been excavated on a hill called Surkh Kotal, in eastern Bactria. This seems to have included a fire temple, for a building was found which contained a stone bench-altar, adorned by two great birds, and large quantities of wood-ash. Later the Kushans, growing more Indianized, abandoned both the Bactrian language and the Zoroastrian elements in their faith, and became speakers of Prakrit and noted patrons of Mahayana Buddhism. Buddhism was thus helped to spread into the Iranian borderlands and Inner Asia, where it flourished as a vigorous rival to Zoroastrianism until the coming of Islam. (Although the two faiths are utterly different in doctrine and outlook, it is held that the northern Buddhist belief in the Maitreya or future Buddha must owe something to Zoroastrian teaching about the Saoshyant.)

Western Iranian borders: Armenia

Little archaeological or literary material survives from within Iran from the Parthian period; but further evidence for the Zoroastrianism of that time comes from Armenia, on the western borders of the empire. Armenia had been subject to the Achaemenians, and as a satrapy had experienced Persian influences, including, naturally, those of Zoroastrianism. During the Seleucid period the land was divided into several virtually independent kingdoms under rulers with Persian names, who paid tribute to the Seleucids. The victory of the Roman Republic's army over Seleucid forces in 190 B.C. extended Roman influence across Asia Minor; and subsequently Armenia became a buffer state between Parthia and Rome, allied now to one, and now to the other. In 62 A.C. the Parthian king Vologeses (Valakhsh) put his younger brother Tiridates on the Armenian throne, and this cadet branch of the Arsacids ruled there into the Sasanian period. Tiridates was himself a strictly observant Zoroastrian – Roman sources even call him a magus – and there is no doubt that during the latter part of the Parthian period Armenia was a predominantly Zoroastrian land. Thereafter it embraced Christianity (partly, it seems, in defiance of the Sasanians); and it is mostly from Christian chronicles and saints' lives that information comes, through hostile allusions, about the older religion there.

These sources show that the Armenians worshipped 'Aramazd' (the Parthian form of Ahuramazda) as 'Creator of sky and earth', and 'Father of all the gods', hailing him often by the title 'Bringer of all good things'. 'Spendaramet' was honoured as protector of the earth, and the veneration of Haurvatat and Ameretat is indirectly attested through plant-names. There were temples to 'Mihr, son of Aramazd', and 'valiant Vahagn . . . bestower of courage'. 'Anahit' was much beloved, and revered as the 'noble Lady . . . Mother of all knowledge . . . daughter of the great and mighty Aramazd'. The use of the terms 'father', 'son' and 'daughter' was evidently figurative, and some of the Christian fathers in the fourth century were prepared to concede that the older faith constituted a remarkable approximation to their own monotheism. However, the Armenian Zoroastrians were orthodox dualists, and the name 'Haraman' (Anra Mainyu) occurs, as well as references to 'devs' and 'pariks' (evil female beings).

Christian chroniclers further indicate that in the temples of Zoroastrian yazatas there were statues made by Greeks, 'for no one in Armenia knew how to make images'. These were almost all destroyed when the country adopted Christianity; but a fine bronze head of a goddess has been found (indistinguishable from that of a Greek Aphrodite), which is thought to be from an image of Anahit, and a famous statue to this divinity existed at Erez, made out of solid gold, which was carried off in 36 B.C. by one of Mark Antony's soldiers.

Fire temples and image shrines

The shrines of yazatas, called, it seems, by the Parthians 'bagin' or 'place of the gods', appear to have roused the Christians' ire even more than fire temples, which are less frequently mentioned in their writings. Yet it is through Armenian that the Parthian word for a fire temple survives, namely 'aturoshan' (Armenian 'atrushan'), which is held to mean 'place of burning fire'. In the kingdom of Cappadocia in Asia Minor (also a former Achaemenian possession) Persian colonists, cut off by the Macedonian conquest from their co-religionists in Iran, continued to practise the faith of their forefathers; and there Strabo, observing them in the first century B.C., records (XV. 3.15) that these 'fire-kindlers' possessed many 'holy places of the Persian gods', as well as fire temples. The latter, he relates, were 'noteworthy enclosures; and in their midst there is an altar, on which there is a large quantity of ashes and where the magi keep the fire ever burning. And there, entering daily, they make incantations for about an hour, holding before the fire their bundle of rods, and wearing upon their heads high turbans of felt which reach down over their cheeks far enough to cover their lips.' This last detail accords both with Achaemenian representations of magi, and with the few others which survive, carved in stone, from the Seleucid and Arsacid periods.

Another account of a fire temple during the Parthian epoch is given by a Greek traveller, Pausanias (V. 27.3), who wrote of groups of Persians in Lydia, to the west of Cappadocia. They, he said, had 'sanctuaries in the cities of Hierocaesarea and Hypaepa, and in each of the sanctuaries is a chapel, and in the chapel there are ashes on an altar, but the colour of the ashes is not that of ordinary ashes. A magus, after entering the chapel and piling dry wood on the altar . . . chants an invocation of some god in a barbarous and, to a Greek, utterly unintelligible tongue. . . . Then without the application of fire the wood must needs kindle, and a bright blaze shoot up from it.' Both this account and that of Strabo are probably based on descriptions furnished to the two men by Zoroastrians, and that of Pausanias contains what appear to be simple misunderstandings (thus he says, for instance, that the priest read his invocation from a book). Nevertheless the ceremony which they describe is very close to that which still takes place daily at every minor sacred fire throughout the Zoroastrian community. Lay devotion to sacred fires in the Parthian period appears in incidents in 'Vis u Ramin', a Parthian courtly poem which survives in a later Persian rendering. Here on one occasion the King of kings lavishes lands, herds, jewels and money on a fire temple. On another, his queen visits a sacred fire in order, she says, to give thanks for her brother's restoration to health. She makes offerings to the fire itself, and liberal benefactions, and sacrifices many animals, whose flesh she distributes to the poor.

The Parthian period provides not only the oldest descriptions of tending sacred fires, but also the oldest identified remains of an actual fire temple. These are on the Kuh-i Khwaja, 'Hill of the Master', in Seistan (ancient Drangiana) in south-eastern Iran. This hill, an isolated table-mountain, rises out of a shallow depression which in winter is flooded to become a wide stretch of water; and it may well have been a holy place for the local Zoroastrians long before temples and altars were introduced to them from the west – for the hill is close to the Hamun lake (Lake Kasaoya) where the Saoshyants will one day be conceived. The fire temple there was rebuilt several times, but the oldest structure has been attributed either to the Seleucid or the early Parthian period. The ground-plan, as far as it can be traced, suggests that it consisted of a rectangular hall leading to a small square room with four central pillars, which communicated in its turn with a still smaller room which may have been the fire-sanctuary. A second temple was built on the site between, it seems, the third and second centuries B.C., and this had the same basic plan, with, however, a corridor enclosing both the small square room and the sanctuary beyond it. A stone fire altar (with pillar shaft and three-stepped top and base) has been found on the hill, which stood evidently in a third, Sasanian temple there; but the type is known from Achaemenian times, and it is very possible that it was already in use in the older edifices of the Parthian period.

As for sacred fires within Parthia proper (ancient Parthava), Isidore of Charax (who lived sometime between 66 B.C. and 77 A.C.) recorded (Parthian Stations 11) that an ever-burning fire was maintained in the town of Asaak, 'where Arsaces was first proclaimed King'. It seems probable that this was the dynastic fire of the Arsacids, established by them on the Achaemenian model, perhaps to emphasize the fact that they were heirs to the Persian Great Kings. They also (in the time, it seems, of Mithridates II) had a genealogy fashioned for themselves, which traced their descent from 'Artakhshathra, king of the Persians' (probably, that is, Artaxerxes II, who had founded the Anahita temples throughout the land, in which his name would have been daily remembered). Artaxerxes, or Artakhshathra, means 'of just dominion'; and even in Sasanian times the Arsacids were described, by a paraphrase of this name, as those 'who are known for just lordship' (GBd XXXVI. 9). Parthian priests further reshaped the story of Arsaces' rise to power to make it appear that he, like Darius the Great, had had six noble helpers; and the Arsacids, in fact, like the Achaemenians, recognized six great families in their realm, so that again the king of the Iranians had six supporters on earth, as Ahuramazda has the six Amesha Spentas in heaven. The Arsacids also revived the Achaemenian title of 'King of kings' (not used by the Seleucids); and both this, and their claim to Achaemenian descent, were probably bitterly resented in Pars, where Achaemenian tradition was kept alive, as the names of some of the local kings ('Darius' and 'Artaxerxes') show. Yet so far were the Arsacids from exercising autocratic rule that they allowed their vassal kings to establish dynastic fires of their own, which must have increased considerably the number of sacred fires in their domains.

The three greatest sacred fires of Zoroastrianism, namely Adur Burzen-Mihr, Adur Farnbag and Adur Gushnasp, if not already enthroned under the Achaemenians, must have been installed early in the Parthian period, for by Sasanian times their origins had become wrapped in mystery and legend. All three, it was said, had been brought into existence by Ahuramazda himself 'for the protection of the world' (GBd XVIII. 8); and at first they moved about freely, giving help where it was needed. Thus in the reign of the legendary king Takhmorup, it is told, people were passing one stormy night from one clime to another, riding on the mythical bull Srisok, when the brazier in which they were carrying fire was blown into the sea. Thereupon the three great fires took its place on the bull's back, and burned brightly so that there was light for the crossing. They also helped Jamshed (Yima Khshaeta) to achieve his many heroic feats (GBd XVIII. 10).

Under the Parthians Adur Burzen-Mihr was evidently especially exalted, for it was their particular fire, established on Mount Revand (probably a spur of the Nishapur mountains in Khorasan, that is, in Parthia proper). It had been placed in a temple there, the legend went, by Vishtaspa himself, after it had 'revealed many things visibly, in order to propagate the faith and to establish certainty, and to bring Vishtasp and his descendants to the faith of God' (GBd XVIII. 14). The Parthians, that is, claimed that their beloved fire had fulfilled the part earlier assigned simply to the yazata Atar in the story of Vishtaspa's conversion (Dk VII. 4.75–8). This pious legend, duly fostered no doubt by its priests, must have brought countless pilgrims to Adur Burzen-Mihr throughout the Parthian era; and the devotion of the Arsacids themselves to this sacred fire is indicated in the poem 'Vis u Ramin', where it is said that one of the kings abdicated and spent his last days in seclusion at its temple. More is known of the other two great fires from the Sasanian period (when it was their turn to enjoy imperial favour). Another exalted fire known from that later time was that of Karkoy, in Seistan, which was also probably established in the Parthian epoch.

It was in Parthian times that this region of south-eastern Iran, once known as Drangiana, acquired the name of 'Sakastan' (later Sagestan, Seistan); for in the late second century B.C. a group of nomad Sakas (an Iranian people) who had given powerful help, it seems, to Mithridates I in his campaigns, was allowed to settle – or chose to settle – there. They evidently in their turn adopted the local culture and religion, and paid reverence to the sacred fires; and in time stories of their great warrior-hero Rustam came to mingle with legends of the Kayanians, Vishtaspa's ancestors, and so entered Zoroastrian tradition.

As well as the ruins of fire temples, those of 'bagin' or image-shrines are known from the Parthian period. The 'Fratadara' temple at Persepolis appears to have been restored and used as a place of worship in Seleucid times, for a votive tablet found there is inscribed in Greek to Zeus Megistos, Apollo and Helios, Artemis and Athena. Veneration of these alien divinities probably merged into and then gave way once more, under Parthian suzerainty, to the orthodox worship of yazatas; and there is a carving in a window opening of a building nearby which shows a man in the attitude of prayer, both hands uplifted, one holding the barsom rods. It is suggested that the temple may have become the place of worship of the Fratarakas, a dynasty of vassal-rulers of part of Persia (Pars) under the Arsacids; and it is through a misreading of their name that it is now known as the 'Fratadara' temple.

A more modest testimony to the mingling of Hellenic and Zoroastrian devotions is provided by a little wayside shrine to Herakles Kallinikos cut in the rock of the Behistun mountain, near the great inscription of Darius. The shrine has an inscription in Greek, which indicates that it was made about 147 B.C.; but it also bears an unfinished one in Aramaic. Its position too suggests that it was designed for both Greek and Iranian devotees, for Herakles the Victorious (depicted reclining, bowl in hand) was identified with Verethraghna, yazata of Victory, who for Zoroastrians is the divinity who cares for travellers. So Iranians passing by on the great highway that runs beside the rock could make their offerings there and pray for his protection, while Greeks invoked the kindly strength of their own god.

A blending of cultures is also suggested by the ruins of a great temple at Kangavar in Upper Media (Kurdistan). These have Hellenic features and, according to Isidore of Charax, 'Artemis' was worshipped there. This, however, is one of the identifications of Anahita, and probably in post-Seleucid times the Kangavar temple became wholly hers. The ruins of yet another temple have been found at Susa, one of the Achaemenian capitals. It appears to have been built either in the Achaemenian period, during the reign of Artaxerxes II, or later, with stones taken from his palace there; but there is nothing to show whether this fairly modest sanctuary was a fire temple or an image shrine.

There appear to have been two Parthian words which could be used for either type of sacred building. One, again attested only from Armenian, is '*mihriyan' (Armenian 'mehean') or 'place of Mithra'. This word may well, like Old Persian 'brazmadana' have meant originally simply a place for high rituals (which, being all performed between sunrise and noon, are under the special protection of Mithra). The other word is 'ayazan' or 'place of worship', a cognate of Old Persian 'ayadana'. This occurs on ostraca from royal Nisa, the earliest capital of the Arsacids, in Parthia proper. This city, with its castles and shrines, was near the modern town of Ashkabad, in Soviet Turkmenistan; and among the objects yielded by its ruins to Russian archaelogists have been quantities of potsherds, dull records in themselves of deliveries of wine and other commodities, but containing gems of incidental information. These include two references to ayazan. One is to the 'Ayazan of the place of Nanai', which was probably an image shrine, for Nanai was an alien goddess whose veneration, known from Elam and Mesopotamia, seems to have become absorbed into the Anahita cult, and so to have spread throughout the Zoroastrian world. The other is to the 'Ayazan of Frahat'; and since Frahat (Greek Phraates) is a name borne by Parthian kings, it is thought that this temple may have held a fire consecrated for the soul of a dead ruler. This is a usage well-attested from Sasanian times. Such 'soul-fires' or 'named fires' (as they were called in Middle Persian) were regularly endowed; and the Nisa ostraca show that many of the estates round about that city were named after Arsacid kings, most probably because their produce went to support their 'soul-fires'. Thus there was the estate 'Friyapatakan', called, it seems, for Priapatius (who reigned c. 191–176 B.C.); a 'Mihradatakan', probably for Mithradates I (c. 171–138), and an 'Artabanukan' for Artabanus I (c. 211–191) or Artabanus II (c. 128–124) – for it is assumed that the endowments at Nisa were for the soul-fires of early kings of the dynasty. The tombs of the Arsacids, it is said, were near Nisa; and it is perhaps mere romantic legend that has Vis and Ramin (in the poem of that name), who are presented as a Parthian queen and king, laid in a royal sepulchre in the mountains above Adur Burzen-Mihr.

Funerary practices

Although the Arsacids maintained the Achaemenian tradition of entombing the royal dead, their subjects continued the orthodox rite of exposure. A number of rock-hewn chambers have been discovered in the mountains of western Iran, which were evidently aristocratic or priestly 'astodans' of the kind made earlier by Artimas at Limyra, that is, places to which the bones of whole families were brought after the rite of exposure. Details in the carvings at their entrances show Hellenic influence, suggesting that they should be assigned to the Seleucid or Parthian period. Only the rich could have afforded such elaborate ossuaries at any epoch, and Pompeius Trogus, writing of the Parthians in the first century A.C., recorded that 'their general mode of sepulture is rending to pieces by birds or dogs; the bare bones they at last bury in the ground'. Evidence from Central Asia in the Sasanian period suggests, however, that this 'burial in the ground' often took place in a casket or urn.

Some of the caskets recovered from later times are inscribed, for, despite the anonymity associated with the rite of exposure, many Zoroastrians evidently shared the general human desire to make some memorial to the dead. Here again the conquering Hellenes provided the Iranians with new inspiration, for it was their custom to erect commemorative statues of distinguished men, and this custom seems to have been generally adopted by the Zoroastrians as an enrichment of the fravashi cult. Two impressive buildings have been excavated at royal Nisa which, it is thought, were both devoted to this cult. One, the many-columned 'Square Hall', is held to have been built in the second century B.C., and restored again later; and it had niches all round its walls which held statues. Several small marble images have been found among its ruins, but there were the remains of many more painted figures of clay, of men and women wearing Parthian dress, some more than life-size, others quite small. These naturalistic images are thought to represent the royal and noble dead, and it is supposed that offerings for the departed were laid before them. The second building, the 'Round Hall', contained similar statues.

The use of statues in the fravashi cult spread right across Iran, and remains similar to those at Nisa have been discovered at the shrine of Shami, a village in Khuzistan, in the south-west. Here in the 1930s there came to light a splendid bronze statue, over life-size, of a nobleman wearing Parthian dress, and excavation of the mound where it had lain revealed the charred remains of an unusual shrine. This consisted of a brick platform partly roofed over, it seems, to protect a group of images – for on and near it were found fragments of other bronze and marble statues, some huge, some small, as at Nisa. Before one image-base there stood an elegant little altar, of Hellenic design, and the statues themselves appear to have been of Greek workmanship. Clearly only royal or noble families could have employed craftsmen to make individual and costly statues such as these; but ordinary people may have made use of small, stylized terracotta figurines, such as have been found in numbers at Central Asian sites. Certainly evidence from Armenia suggests that a wide variety of images was used in the fravashi cult. Agathangelos speaks of statues of the dead made there of 'gold, silver, wood, stone or bronze'; and he calls the Armenian Zoroastrians 'soul-worshippers', while St Gregory alludes to their practice of bowing down before images of the dead. A standard Middle Iranian word for image was 'uzdes', which, like Greek 'icon', meant simply a showing forth, a representation; and doubtless the orthodox and instructed regarded the statues used both in divine worship and in the fravashi cult as no more than this; but the setting up of statues always holds the danger of the icon becoming an idol, and doubtless in every generation there were some Zoroastrians who were alert to this, and who opposed the practice, wholly alien as it was to the early faith.

Developments in calendar and chronology

One innovation made by the Seleucids was the practice of dating by an era. Before their day peoples in general had dated events by the reigns of individual kings, and any sustained chronological calculations were therefore very difficult; but they took the bold and practical step of dating continuously from the year of the foundation of their dynasty (in 312/311 B.C.); and since they claimed to be the heirs of Alexander, this era became widely known as that of Alexander. In due course the Arsacids followed suit, dating their own era from 248/247 B.C. (presumably the year in which Arsaces attained power); and, as the Nisa ostraca show, they combined this, in dating events, with the Zoroastrian calendar. Their names for the months and days are Parthian equivalents of the Avestan ones used liturgically; and they differ in one or two small respects from the Middle Persian ones used by their Sasanian successors, which is another sign of the independence of the provincial priestly schools. Thus Avestan Dadvah 'Creator', a nominative, yields Middle Persian Dadv/Dai; but the Parthians called the month Datush, a form derived from the Avestan genitive Dathusho, 'Of the Creator'.

The priests of Pars or Persia proper, who under the Achaemenians had presumably taken the initiative in creating the Zoroastrian calendar, had no longer a leading part to play in the Zoroastrian community at large, and so, it may be supposed, had the greater leisure for purely scholastic pursuits; and one of the fruits of their studies was, it seems, the establishing of a 'historical' date for their prophet. Their search for this may well have been stimulated by the creation of the Seleucid era, which offered new possibilities for fixing events in time; but they were hampered by having no Zoroastrian sources on which to base any calculations. So they turned, it seems, to their Babylonian neighbours, who were long accustomed to keeping written records. From them they appear to have learnt that a great event in Persian history had taken place 228 years before the 'era of Alexander', that is, before 311 B.C. This event was the conquest of Babylon by Cyrus in 539, an occurrence of great magnitude for the Babylonians; but the Persian priests apparently re-interpreted this momentous happening as being the revelation sent to their prophet, which for them had transformed the world. Zoroaster was held to have received this revelation in his thirtieth year, and so they reached the calculation that he had been born 258 years 'before Alexander', that is, in 569 B.C. This must have seemed a very remote time to them, but in fact it falls in far too recent an epoch to be reconcilable with other data. Nevertheless the newly 'discovered' date, satisfying the contemporary interest in chronological exactitude, became accepted in learned circles in Persia and the neighbouring lands to the west; but there is no evidence that it ever gained currency among the older Zoroastrian communities of the east, where the Khwarezmians, for example, continued to assign the prophet to a much remoter epoch, in keeping with the recorded traditions of Achaemenian times.

The Avesta

Another development which, like the artificial date for Zoroaster, was to cause much perplexity to later scholars, was the appropriation by the magi of the whole Avestan tradition for their own homeland of Northern Media (the province of Atropatene, modern Azarbaijan), so that persons, places and events of north-eastern Iran were given new associations with the north-west. Such an annexation must have been relatively easy to effect at a time when geographical studies were hardly more firmly based than historical ones; and indeed partial annexations of Zoroastrian traditions had earlier been made in Drangiana (Seistan), where the Avestan 'kavis', Vishtaspa's ancestors, were associated with Lake Kạsaoya, and in Bactria, which claimed to have been the scene of Zoroaster's life and death; but the Median magi were thorough in their proceedings, placing both the kavis and the prophet in their native land, and even identifying this with Airyanem Vaejah, the legendary home of the Iranian peoples.

It may be that the magi had already evolved such traditions in Achaemenian times in order to sustain their religious authority among the Medes and Persians; or they may have felt the spur to do so in the Parthian period, as a means of re-asserting this authority then within Median borders. The tolerant Arsacids seem unlikely to have resented such developments as long as they remained unobtrusively local; but this tolerance did not arise from any indifference to the faith, as is shown by the following account of the activities of a king Valakhsh or Vologeses (a name borne by several rulers in the first and second centuries A.C.): 'Valakhsh the Arsacid commanded that a memorandum be sent to the provinces (instructing them) to preserve, in the state in which it had come down in (each) province, whatever had survived in purity of the Avesta and (its) Zand, and also every teaching deriving from it which, scattered by the havoc and disruption of Alexander, and by the pillage and looting of the Macedonians, had survived, whether written or in authoritative oral transmission' (DkM, 412. 5–11, ZZZ 8). These lines come from a general account, brought down to the sixth century A.C., of the transmission of the Zoroastrian holy texts; and one interesting point is the reference in them to writing in connection with 'teachings' derived from the Avesta, although the implication seems to be that the Avesta itself, with its commentary (Zand), was still wholly in oral transmission at that time.

One Avestan text which may possibly have been compiled from scattered traditions as a result of Valakhsh' decree is the Vendidad or 'Law against demons'. The main part of this prose work is devoted to rules about the maintenance of purity and its restoration after pollution, this being a powerful defence against the forces of evil. These rules are set out in the form of question and answer (between Zarathustra and Ahuramazda), a common way of conveying instruction in oral literature. The Vendidad contains other miscellaneous matter, however, such as might well have been added to the nucleus of purity texts as part of a deliberate effort to preserve 'whatever had survived of the Avesta'. Thus in the first chapter there is the list of the best countries in the world (all in eastern Iran), and in the second a version of the legend of Yima, while the nineteenth contains a story of the temptation of Zoroaster by the Hostile Spirit. The language is late Avestan, with the inflectional system much broken down; and a further reason for assigning the compilation to the Parthian period is that two systems of measurement are represented in it, one Iranian, the other Greco-Roman. The Vendidad also contains what appears to be the only mention in the whole Avesta of temple fires, referred to allusively as fire set 'in an appointed place' (daitya gatu, Vd VIII. 81 ff.). Further, the legend of Yima shows what seem to be Mesopotamian influences (with the story of the flood and the ark adapted to fit with the tradition of the Iranian first king); and so it seems likely that the compilation was made by magi in western Iran. There was evidently no question, though, as they piously gathered these texts together, of any deliberate additions to the Avestan originals, for the extraneous matter shows all the signs of having been unconsciously absorbed during the course of long oral transmission.

It must have been well before this time (to judge from the relative correctness of the language) that the ancient Staota Yesnya was expanded through additions such as veneration of the 'calendar' divinities, homilies on the three great prayers, and adaptations of yasht verses. This material was set evenly before and after the Staota Yesnya, so that this remained at the heart of the liturgy. Such extensions were probably begun in Achaemenian times, and continued over generations. Where or when these developments took place can never be known; but even with the regionalism tolerated by the Arsacids, it would seem probable that vital matters such as additions to the yasna liturgy must first have been discussed and agreed upon by a synod representing the religious community as a whole.

Developments in the scribal tradition

The separatism of the post-Achaemenian period was accentuated during the latter part of the Parthian epoch by the gradual abandonment of Aramaic as the common language of written communication. Very slowly this yielded place, in each of the main provinces, to the local language, written in the local variation of the Aramaic script. The beginnings of this process can be traced on the Nisa ostraca, from the end of the second century B.C.; for the brief records which these bear have a scattering of Parthian words among the Aramaic ones, and there is just enough evidence to show that the Aramaic words themselves were being used as ideograms, that is, they were no longer pronounced or thought of as Semitic words, but had become familiar shapes only, written to convey Iranian equivalents. By that stage, therefore, the earlier proceeding of translating from spoken Iranian into written Aramaic, and back into spoken Iranian, had ceased, and the thought-process was wholly Iranian. Naturally it was those Aramaic words which were most commonly used in official or business documents, or in letters, which survived as ideograms. Moreover, these words became fixed in the way in which they most frequently occurred, so that Aramaic forms meaning specifically 'the king', 'my father', 'his son', became generalized as ideograms for 'king', 'father' and 'son'. Verbal ideograms were often in origin Aramaic imperative singulars, or third plural pasts, and very slowly the system developed of adding letters to these ideograms as a 'phonetic complement' to represent the actual pronunciation of the ending of the Iranian word, and so make it possible to establish person and tense. It also became customary to mark the plural of nouns and pronouns by writing the Iranian plural ending after the ideogram. A system thus gradually developed which, though cumbersome, was fairly adequate, when used by trained scribes, for conveying a living language, but which (because it was only partly phonetic) was singularly ill adapted for recording a dead one such as Avestan, for the proper pronunciation of the holy texts would have been lost had they been set down according to this manner of writing.

The Nisa ostraca show this system just beginning to evolve for Parthian; and exactly the same system, with Middle Persian words, and in the Middle Persian development of the Aramaic script, can be traced on coins struck by the Frataraka princes of Pars at about the same time, that is, from the end of the second century B.C. It is attested also for Sogdia, Khwarezmia and Media; but in each region the forms of words used as ideograms, and sometimes the actual words themselves, tended to differ; and this, together with the distinctive scripts, meant that written communication between the Iranian regions was no longer the simple matter that it had been. Naturally Parthian, as the language of the imperial people, was the most widely used, together (for a time) with Greek. This is illustrated by the Avroman parchments – legal documents which were found in 1909 in a sealed jar in a cave near Avroman, in Persian Kurdistan. This is ancient Median territory; yet the first two documents (dated to 88 and 22/21 B.C.) are in Greek, and the third (of 58 A.C.) is in Parthian, written with ideograms in Parthian script.

Human affairs

KHVAETVADATHA

In the two Greek documents the dating formulas contain the throne-name (Arsaces) of the reigning Parthian King of kings, and the names of his chief wives. In the older one these run: 'In the reign of the King of kings, Arsaces . . . and of the Queens, Siace, his compaternal sister and wife, and Aryazate surnamed Automa, daughter of the Great King Tigranes and his wife, and of Azate, his compaternal sister and wife'. These formulas provide clear contemporary evidence that the Arsacids followed the Achaemenians in practising 'khvaetva-datha', this particular king having, like Cambyses, married two of his sisters. Other brother–sister marriages are recorded among their vassals and Zoroastrian neighbours – for example Helena and Monobazus of Adiabene, and Erato and Tigranes IV of the Artaxiad dynasty of Armenia. Tiridates I of Armenia (a notably pious ruler) describes himself as the brother of his queen on his inscription at Garni; and that the custom was not confined to princes is shown by the observation of Bardesanes, writing in the second century A.C., who cited the practice of next-of-kin marriages among the Persians of Asia Minor as an example of how people cling to ancestral customs even when dwelling in foreign parts.

ECCLESIASTICAL ORGANIZATION

The documents from Avroman further show that, even though the Parthians did not seek close control over all the Iranian regions, yet their position as the ruling power made their influence pervasive. According to Strabo (XI. 515) the Arsacid kings were advised by two councils, one consisting of men of their own royal house, the other of the lords spiritual and temporal of the realm. Probably all the prelates who took their places in this second council were Parthians; and Parthian priests must have been found all over the empire, as judges, administrators and scribes, and as the family priests of Parthian kings and nobles . It seems probable that a characteristic title of their higher ecclesiastics was 'erbad' or 'herbad' (deriving from Avestan 'aethrapati'), for under the Sasanians one finds two groups of leading clerics with virtually indistinguishable functions, namely the 'herbad' and the 'mobad' (the latter title deriving from Old Persian 'magupati'). In the Arsacid period the title 'magpat' or 'magbad' (as it appears in Parthian) may have been used mainly for the chief priest of a fire temple; and another title, 'bagnapat' or master of a 'bagin', is attested for the priest in charge of an image-shrine. All such niceties of nomenclature were lost, however, on the Greeks and Romans, to whom every Zoroastrian priest remained a magus, whatever his local origins or ecclesiastical dignity. So Pseudo-Lucian, writing towards the end of the Parthian period, describes the magi as 'an order of seers who are dedicated to the service of the gods, and who are found among the Persians, the Parthians, the Bactrians, the Chorasmians, the Areians, the Saka and the Medes'. 'They have' (he adds) 'strong constitutions and live to a great age, for their profession as magi makes it incumbent on them to observe strict rules of life.' Other classical writers of the period indicate that the concern of the magi as a body was with study and worship, with ethics, divination and prophecy, and with learning holy utterances and observing the rules of purity.

UNBELIEVERS

The Arsacids not only tolerated the existence of different ecclesiastic traditions among the Zoroastrians whom they ruled, but also showed forbearance (in the Achaemenian tradition) to unbelievers within and beyond their borders. Their empire did not reach to the full extent of that of their predecessors, yet Iranian influences continued to be felt throughout the Middle East, perhaps even more strongly than in the earlier period. One reason for this was that after the Macedonian conquest Greek became the lingua franca throughout the region, and provided a medium for the ready exchange of ideas. Another, political factor which strengthened the influence of the Parthians (and hence of their Zoroastrian faith) was their armed resistance to the remorseless and generally resented encroachments of Rome. One piece of evidence for this influence is the pervasiveness at this period of the Zoroastrian prophetic tradition. Longing for the coming of the Saoshyant must have intensified among Iranians in the dark period after Alexander's conquest, and a rich apocalyptic and prophetic literature appears to have developed then, which was widely imitated and which made the names of 'Zoroastres' and 'Hystaspes' familiar in the Greco-Roman world.

Iran continued to exert influence in other ways also on Jewish and Gnostic thought. The Arsacids had good relations with the Jews, whether as overlords (of the Babylonian community) or neighbours; and a number of Jewish works composed at this time reflect Zoroastrian ideas. So, it was out of a Judaism enriched by five centuries of contact with Zoroastrianism that Christianity arose in the Parthian period, a new religion with roots thus in two ancient faiths, one Semitic, the other Iranian. Doctrines taught perhaps a millennium and a half earlier by Zoroaster began in this way to reach fresh hearers; but again, as in Judaism, they lost some of their logic and coherence by their adoption into another creed; for the teachings of the Iranian prophet about creation, Heaven and Hell, and the Day of Judgment, were less intellectually coherent when part of a religion which proclaimed the existence of one omnipotent God, whose unrestricted rule was based not on justice but on love. They continued nevertheless, even in this new setting, to exert their powerful influence on men's strivings to be good.

Iranian beliefs also had a part, still ill-defined, in the formation of Mithraism. This strenuous faith appears to have evolved in Asia Minor during the Parthian period, and it was then adopted by the Roman legions, who carried it throughout the Roman Empire. A dearth of written records makes it difficult to trace the history or doctrines of Mithraism, which is known almost entirely from its monuments and places of worship; but the faith clearly took its name from the Iranian Mithra, who, since the eclipse of *Varuna Apąm Napat in Achaemenian times, had reigned virtually alone as the lesser Ahura, active, powerful and compassionate, though just. Personal names (notably Mithradata, 'Given by Mithra') show that his worship was popular among the Iranians of Asia Minor; but the religion called after him was evidently an eclectic one, with many non-Iranian elements in it. Its chief debt to Zoroastrianism was probably a sense of linear time, and an emphasis on personal and cosmic salvation. (The central element in Mithraic iconography is a representation of Mithra slaying a bull, apparently an act of redemptive sacrifice.) Mithraism proselytized energetically to the west, and for a time presented a formidable challenge to Christianity; but it is not yet known how far, or how effectively, it penetrated eastward. A Mithraeum has been uncovered at the Parthian fortress-town of Dura-Europos, on the Euphrates; but Zoroastrianism itself may well have been a barrier to its spread into Iran proper.

Zoroastrianism itself is the oldest of the dogmatic, proselytizing world religions; but in its case various forces had worked to limit its missionary activities and turn it into what was virtually an ethnic faith. This had enabled it to exist peaceably side by side with Hellenic polytheism, neither seeking to affect the other. But during the later centuries of Parthian rule this pattern of tolerance and self-sufficiency was threatened from two sides: in the east there was Buddhism, expanding vigorously in the Indo-Iranian border-lands, and in the west there was Christianity, ardently seeking converts. So for the first time in its long history Zoroastrianism was confronted by other faiths whose adherents attacked its tenets and sought to persuade its followers to apostatize. Even the Jews proselytized, at this period, with some success. Their activity was on a relatively small scale, however, as was the pressure from the early Christians; and it was not until the Sasanian era, when Christianity gained the support of a great temporal power, that its missionary activities became a serious vexation to the Zoroastrians. The Arsacids were able, therefore, to preserve in the main the tradition of tolerance until the end of their period of rule.

Conclusion

As for the effects of Zoroastrianism on the Parthians themselves, this has to be traced mostly through the hostile testimony of Roman historians; but even from such grudging sources it emerges that the Arsacids were in the main loyal to the leading moral precepts of their faith, with its emphasis on responsibility towards one's fellow-man and on honour and truthfulness. Thus it is acknowledged that they behaved well to captives and fugitives, treating them with kindness and respect; and that they were scrupulous in observing their given word, and remaining faithful to treaty obligations. In these regards they showed themselves loyal adherents of the Ahuric religion, and markedly superior to their inveterate enemies, the Romans. By the middle of the third century A.C. they had been champions of the Zoroastrian faith for generations, defending it against pagan armies to east and west; and the overthrow of their dynasty, even by fellow-Iranians, was an event which profoundly shook the whole religious community.

CHAPTER SEVEN

Under the early Sasanians

The rise of the Sasanians

Some obscurity surrounds the rise of the Sasanian dynasty, but according to the most likely accounts the family were hereditary guardians of a great temple to Anahid (possibly one of the Achaemenian Anahita foundations) at the city of Istakhr in Pars. At about the beginning of the third century A.C. one of its members, Papak, seized power from the local prince-governor, vassal of the Parthian King of kings, and his younger son Ardashir succeeded to his usurped position. The Arsacid Ardaban V refused to confirm Ardashir's authority, and he accordingly set out to establish himself in Pars by force of arms. So successful was he in this that Ardaban himself took the field to crush this dangerous rebel, only to be defeated by him and killed in battle, probably in 224 A.C.

This overthrow of the long-established Arsacid dynasty by an unknown adventurer caused shock and perturbation throughout Iran; but Ardashir, boundlessly ambitious, continued his victorious way. Within two years he subdued the western provinces of the empire, and had himself crowned King of kings; and later expeditions, and bitter fighting, made him master also of eastern Iran. Ardashir was not only a military genius, but a man of great shrewdness and administrative talents, who was prepared to use bloodless means as well as warlike ones to establish his rule and create a new

Persian Empire; and one of the tools which he chose for this was religious propaganda. There can be little doubt that the priests of Persia, whose forefathers had led the Zoroastrian community under the Achaemenians, felt themselves well fitted to do so again; and they plainly undertook with zeal the task of persuading their fellow-Iranians that they, together with the new dynasty to which they lent their support, were more devout and orthodox, and would be truer upholders of the faith, than their Parthian predecessors had been.

Tansar, a religious propagandist

Ardashir was fortunate in having as his chief priest a man whose abilities and energies seem to have matched his own. His name was Tansar or Tosar (the Pahlavi script is ambiguous), and he bore the title of 'herbad', which under the Parthians had presumably been that of leading ecclesiastical dignitaries. (Ordinary priests are referred to throughout Sasanian times simply as 'mog', derived from ancient 'magu'.) The task which faced Tansar as Ardashir's propagandist was a hard one; for whereas the Arsacids, at their rise to power, had had the role of champions of the faith against the pagan Seleucids, the Sasanians had to justify the overthrow of co-religionists. Fortunately we can trace how they sought to do this from a letter which survives (through various redactions and translations) written by Tansar himself to one Gushnasp, a former vassal of the Arsacids, who ruled the mountainous kingdom of Tabaristan in northern Iran. This was a difficult region to subdue by force, and Tansar wrote on Ardashir's behalf to try to persuade Gushnasp to yield voluntarily to the new régime. The existing letter is in response to one from Gushnasp, and in it Tansar answers one by one the many doubts and criticisms which the northern king had expressed. In the religious sphere, it seems, he had accused Ardashir 'of forsaking tradition; and right though this may be for the world, it is not good for the faith' (Tansar Name 36). To this Tansar replies with a double defence. First, he writes, not all the old ways were good, and Ardashir being 'more richly endowed with virtues than the ancients . . . his custom is better than the customs of old'. Second, he asserts that the faith had decayed so greatly as a result of the destruction wrought by Alexander that there had been no certain knowledge, under the Arsacids, of its ancient 'laws and ordinances', and so it 'must needs be restored by a man of true and upright judgment . . . for till religion is interpreted by understanding it has no firm foundation'. Full licence was thus claimed for Ardashir to make what changes he pleased, these being equally approved by Tansar whether he regarded them as innovations or restorations by the Persian king.

That this licence was courageously opposed by some of his co-religionists is shown by Gushnasp's further protests against 'the excessive bloodshed which he orders among those acting against his judgment and decree' (ibid. 39). To this Tansar replies that the people had become wicked, and that they were therefore to blame for the frequency of punishment and slaughter, and not the new King of kings. 'Bloodshed among people of this kind, even if of a prodigality that seems to have no bound, is recognized by us as life and health, like the rain which quickens the earth . . . for in days to come the foundations of State and Religion will be in every way strengthened through this' (ibid. 40).

The question remains, what were the religious measures which, on Tansar's admission, Ardashir waded through blood to enforce? There are a number of sources for early Sasanian history, and so it is possible to discern various ways in which Ardashir and the Persian priests must have distressed and angered their fellow-Zoroastrians. First, in place of the former fraternity of regional communities, a single Zoroastrian church was created under the direct and authoritarian control of Persia; and together with this went the establishment of a single canon of Avestan texts, approved and authorized by Tansar himself. This action is described in a Pahlavi book, the 'Dinkard', in the following words: 'His Majesty the King of kings, Ardashir son of Papak, following Tansar as his religious authority, commanded all those scattered teachings [i.e. those whose preservation had been ordered by the Arsacid Valakhsh] to be brought to court. Tansar set about his business and selected one (?) tradition and left the rest out of the canon. And he issued this decree: The interpretation of all the teachings of the Mazda-worshipping religion is our responsibility, for now there is no lack of certain knowledge concerning them' (DKM 412. 11–17, ZZZ 8). In another passage of the same work it is prophesied that no peace will come to the lands of Iran 'until they give acceptance to him, Tansar the herbad, the spiritual leader, eloquent, truthful, just. And when they give acceptance to Tansar . . . those lands, if they wish, will find healing, instead of divergence from Zoroaster's faith' (DKM 652. 9–17).

Calendar changes

Another step which affected every member of the community, and indeed still troubles its harmony today, was a reform of the Zoro-astrian calendar. Calendar changes, it is agreed, are among the most difficult measures to bring about in any society; and it is a mark of Ardashir's enormous force and energy that he managed to carry one through in the first reign of a new dynasty – although even he failed to establish it exactly as had been planned. Well before the downfall of the Arsacids the learned priests of Pars (with their interest in chronology) must have been pondering the accurate measurement of time. Since the days of the early Achaemenians the Persians had known of the Egyptian calendar, and this had 365 days, divided into twelve months of thirty days each (like those of the Iranians and their other neighbours), but with five extra days at the end of the twelfth month. During the Parthian period, in 46 B.C., the Romans under Julius Caesar adopted a 365-day calendar; and this may have prompted the Persian priests to devise a reform of the Zoroastrian one, which they were able to put into force under Ardashir. They kept exactly to the Egyptian model, merely adding, that is, five extra days to the familiar 360-day year; and these days they named the 'Gatha' or 'Gah' days, after the five groups of Zoroaster's hymns. This was a practical as well as a pious measure, since it meant that they could use the Avestan names of the five Gathas for liturgical invoca-tions on these new days, where ordinarily the yazad of the day would have been invoked. It was evidently intended that the 'Gatha' days should remain outside the religious year, and not disturb the pattern of its long-hallowed observances; but one great difficulty attended their introduction. Traditionally the fravashis were welcomed back to their old homes throughout the land at the feast of Hamaspath-maedaya, on the last night of the old year (in calendar terms, the night of 30 Spendarmad); and having spent the hours of darkness there, receiving the gifts and veneration of their descendants, they were bidden a ritual farewell at the following dawn, withdrawing before the sun rose to bring in the new year. Now this ancient custom was suddenly challenged by the insertion of five extra days between 30 Spendarmad and 1 Fravardin, and profound bewilderment and distress resulted. The new days were roundly termed the 'stolen' ones, because it was felt that they had been thieved somehow from the familiar year; and when they were first introduced they appear to

have been, as far as possible, ignored. The observance of the official
No Ruz, and all the other feast days, must have been enforced, quite
possibly on pain of death, according to the new calendar; but the
people at large evidently still kept in private what they believed to be
the true holy days, six days earlier in every case. Reckoning in this
fashion, they reached 30 Spendarmad that first year when by the
reformed calendar it was still only 25 Spendarmad; and so a whole ten
days had to elapse for them between the night when they welcomed
the fravashis and the dawn of the official No Ruz, when they were
publicly permitted to bid them farewell. Even the reformers had to
observe prolonged rites for the fravashis during the five 'Gatha' days,
which came therefore to be called also 'rozan fravardigan' or 'days of
the fravashis'. ('Fravard' is the Persian form of Avestan 'fravashi'.)
Thereafter the duplication of observances continued, with the bulk of
the population observing every festival twice, once on its official day
by the reformed calendar, once on what they reckoned to be its real
one. Evidently this practice was too widespread and general to be
suppressed, even by the most ruthless of kings; and eventually under
Ardashir's grandson, Hormizd I, the Persian reformists compro-
mised, and instituted an acceptable measure by which the new and old
holy days were linked together to form continual six-day feasts. Only
No Ruz, essentially the festival of a single day, did not lend itself to
this, and the debate as to which was the true No Ruz, 1 or 6
Farvardin, continued throughout the Sasanian period, being recorded
in the Pahlavi books. Both feasts are still celebrated, separately and
under different names, by Zoroastrians to this day.

Another intractable problem was created by the 'fravashi days',
with the reformists insisting that these were five in number, i.e. the
Gatha days themselves, and the traditionalists maintaining (in the
light of the confusions of the first year) that they had to be ten (that is,
from 25 Spendarmad to 1 Farvardin). A Muslim writer, Biruni, who
relied on Zoroastrian sources, observed (*Chronology*, 224) that the
people were much troubled over the matter, 'as this is one of the chief
institutions of their religion . . . and they wished to be careful, since
they were unable to ascertain the real facts of the case'. By observing
the longer festival they could avoid any danger of failing in their duty
to the fravashis; and so convinced were traditionalist priests of the
propriety of this that a tiny alteration was made in one verse (v. 49) of
the Farvardin Yasht, which now runs: 'We worship the good, mighty,
holy fravashis of the just, who hasten to their homes at the time of

Hamaspathmaedaya. Then they wander here for ten nights', whereas the ancient version presumably had 'for the whole night', or something similar.

Another remarkable feature of the early Sasanian calendar is that No Ruz was then celebrated, on 1 Farvardin, in autumn instead of spring. This appears to have been an inheritance from the Parthian period, and the theological implications are perplexing. The motive for the first Sasanian calendar reform seems, however, to have been practical rather than religious. Yet in the end this reform resulted, ironically, in a great extension of religious observances, while doing lasting damage, theologically, to the faith. The effectiveness of the old devotional year, with its seven holy days of obligation, had already been threatened in Achaemenian times by the founding of additional 'name-day' feasts in honour of individual Amesha Spentas; and now it became so elaborate that its dogmatic purpose was overwhelmed. From six days, the gahambars had been extended to thirty-six, and the seventh feast, No Ruz, was duplicated, and was celebrated after the new ten-day feast of the fravashis. All this gradually obscured the significance of the great obligatory feasts, and in later times the vital connection between No Ruz and the gahambars was largely lost to view.

Iconoclasm and sacred fires

As if the calendar reform alone were not enough, another hugely controversial measure was enacted by the Sasanians, apparently also from the beginning of their era: they forbade the use of images in worship, and during their epoch statues were removed from consecrated buildings, and, whenever possible, sacred fires were installed in their place. It seems that the Sasanians had been committed iconoclasts before their rise to power, for the Muslim historian Mas'udi (Les Prairies d'Or, 1403) states that although their temple in Istakhr had once contained 'idols', these had been removed in the remote past, and fire installed in their place. This fire, undoubtedly a Verethraghna one, appears to have been consecrated in the name of Anahid herself, and is referred to in a third-century Sasanian inscription as 'the fire of Anahid the Lady'. Ardashir's son and successor, Shabuhr I (who had been old enough to fight beside his father against Ardaban), named one of his daughters Adur-Anahid, in honour presumably of this fire; and this suggests that it must have been established at least under Ardashir. So the cult of images, introduced to Zoroastrianism by the Achaemenian Artakhshathra or Artaxerxes II, was finally brought to an end by measures initiated, it seems, by the Sasanian Artakhshathra or Ardashir I (the names are in origin the same); and it may have been in allusion to this that Tansar declared to Gushnasp (Tansar Name 66) that: 'In my eyes this latter Ardashir is of far greater worth than the Ardashir of old.' (This statement had all the greater propaganda value in that it was from the Achaemenian Artakhshathra that the Arsacids had spuriously claimed descent.)

The Sasanians pursued a campaign of active iconoclasm, and Ardashir's grandson, Hormidzd-Ardashir, in Armenia is said to have shattered the statues of the dead, and to have set a sacred fire (presumably in place of a statue) in the temple of Ohrmazd at Pakaran. Yet the campaign was to be long drawn out (cases involving the removal of statues still occur in the sixth-century law-book, the 'Madigan i Hazar Dadestan'), for it, like the calendar reform, must have caused great distress, and stirred up stubborn resistance. It was, however, only the use of cult-statues which the Sasanians attacked, and they themselves continued to represent the yazatas of Zoroastrianism, including Ohrmazd, in anthropomorphic fashion, according to the tradition established in the Seleucid era. One of the most striking pieces of visual propaganda on behalf of Ardashir is a great rock-carving at Naqsh-i Rustam, near the Achaemenian tombs, and not far from Istakhr. This shows the conquerer on horseback, confronting Ohrmazd himself, also mounted, with turreted crown and barsom-rods in hand, who reaches him the diadem of sovereignty. God and king are identified by inscriptions cut on their horses' flanks in three languages, Middle Persian, Parthian and Greek (Ohrmazd being duly named in the Greek version Zeus); and whereas Ohrmazd's horse treads down a snake-haired creature (probably Ahriman) beneath its hooves, Ardashir's tramples over a prostrate figure who is undoubtedly Ardaban V, equated thus in his defeat with the powers of evil. There are many other representations of divine beings in Sasanian carvings in high relief, among them Mihr with radiate crown, Ardvisur Anahid, richly-garbed, and Vahram still as a Greek Herakles, naked with lion-skin and club. There was thus no break with the iconography of the Parthian period, only a determined campaign to end the use of cult images. As one result of this campaign the Middle Persian words 'bashn' and 'bashnbad' (equivalent to Parthian 'bagin' and 'bagnapat'), meaning an image-shrine and its priest, although attested in non-Zoroastrian sources, are not to be found anywhere in the Pahlavi books.

The campaign against images went with an equally vigorous one to establish more sacred fires. This hardly seems at first sight to accord with a specific accusation made by Gushnasp that Ardashir had 'taken away fires from the fire-temples, extinguished them and blotted them out, and that no one has ever before presumed so far against religion' (Tansar Name 47). Tansar admits this grievous charge, but explains that the fires in question had been those of vassal-kings of the Arsacids, who had no ancient entitlement to them. It was, he claims, 'pure innovation, introduced by them without the authority of kings of old', and accordingly Ardashir 'razed the temples and confiscated the endowments'. The tolerant days of Arsacid rule were past, and under the Sasanians only one regnal fire might burn in Iran. This quenching of local dynastic fires must have deeply offended the pride and piety of many Zoroastrians.

The Sasanians (who in as many ways as possible, it seems, imitated their great predecessors, the Achaemenians) set great store by their own regnal fires. Ardashir placed a representation of his fire, raised on a massive pedestal, on the reverse of his coins, and this became the general practice of the dynasty. Apart from this, Ardashir is reputed to have founded many Atakhsh i Vahram (Verethraghna fires) in the province of Pars. He himself left only a few brief inscriptions behind him, made, as we have seen, in three languages, as those of Darius the Great had been; but his son, Shabuhr I, had a great inscription carved for posterity in the same three languages – Middle Persian, Parthian and Greek, with their three separate scripts – on the smooth stone walls of the Ka'ba-yi Zardusht at Naqsh-i Rustam. The first half of this inscription described Shabuhr's achievements and triumphs in campaigns against Rome (for the Persians had inherited the war with this western neighbour). The second part deals with the endowment of sacred fires and lesser benefactions in honour of members of the royal family and of others who had helped establish and strengthen Sasanian rule. The sacred fires in question are 'pad-nam adur' or 'named fires', such as the early Arsacid kings are thought to have founded at Nisa; and Shabuhr, enriched by the spoils of conquest, established five of them, one for the sake of his own soul, one for that of his Queen of queens, Adur-Anahid, and one for each of three sons who had fought with him in the Roman wars. Shabuhr further endowed a number of daily offerings to be made for the souls of other members of the royal family and the nobility. These consisted of a sacrificial sheep, bread and wine – the same offerings that Cambyses had endowed to be made daily at the tomb of Cyrus.

The rise of Kirder, the second great prelate

The founding of sacred fires is mentioned repeatedly in the inscriptions of Kirder, who was the second great prelate of the Sasanian period, and very long-lived and powerful. His eminence is shown by the fact that he alone among commoners was allowed to have inscriptions carved in royal fashion – excepting that his were in Middle Persian only. One of these was actually set – in a later reign – beneath Shabuhr's on the Ka'ba. Another was placed on the rock-face of Naqsh-i Rustam; and a third was at Naqsh-i Rajab, a rocky recess not far away across the plain. (Beside this one Kirder had his own portrait carved.) The fourth and longest is at Sar-Mashhad, now a remote and desolate place in Pars. The area was well-watered and fruitful in Sasanian times, however, and it has been surmised that he owned land there, and made this great inscription (now sadly weather-worn) as his memorial beside the resting-place of his bones, for higher up the steep rock-face where it is carved there is an ossuary niche.

The first mention of Kirder is in Shabuhr's inscription, where he, like Tansar before him, bears the title of 'herbad' (Parthian l.28, M Persian l.34). Although he was then only young, the King of kings (as Kirder's own inscriptions show) had already made him 'absolute and in authority over the order of priests at court and in every province and place throughout the empire'. (SM 3–4). Through his actions, Kirder himself says (ibid. ll. 4–6), 'religious activities were increased, many Vahram fires were founded, and many priests became happy and prosperous . . . and much benefit accrued to Ohrmazd and the yazads, and there was much harm to Ahriman and the devs.' Further, he declares (ll. 30–31) 'images were destroyed and the lurking places of devs demolished, and places and abodes of the yazads were established'. This is a way of saying that sacred fires (visited, it was held, thrice daily by the 'spenta' divine beings) were founded to replace cult statues, which the iconoclasts held were inhabited by devs, who entered the images thus impiously erected by men and misappropriated the offering laid before them. So by their destruction, and the increase in due religious observances, 'great satisfaction came in the land to the yazads and to Water and Fire and Cattle' (l. 28).

Kirder speaks of only two categories of sacred fires, 'Vahram' ones, and 'fires' without any qualifications – presumably, that is, Atakhsh i Aduran, as the ordinary local fire, equivalent to a parish church, was called; but the Sasanian law-book shows that at that epoch there was a third kind of fire which might burn in a holy place. A fire, with its constant need for fuel and attendance, costs far more to maintain than a statue; and so when an image was removed from a humble place of worship (such as a private chapel or village shrine) it might be replaced, possibly only temporarily, by a 'Little Fire', an Adurog, set there to purify the place from the evil powers attracted by image worship. Such a fire could be kindled on the spot, or formed from the embers of a hearth fire; and, like a hearth fire, it could be tended by a layman, provided he were in a state of purity. Sometimes (as a sixth-century law-suit shows) the 'Little Fire' would become as beloved as the statue it had replaced and would be maintained in perpetuity. The full name of such a fire is Adurog i pad dadgah, that is, 'Little Fire in an appointed place' (Avestan 'daitya gatu'), abbreviated in modern times to Dadgah.

Kirder won his place, it seems, in Shabuhr's inscription because he accompanied the King of kings on his Roman campaigns; and he records (SM 37 ff.) that throughout the foreign parts where these took him – Syria and Cilicia, Cappadocia and Pontus, Armenia, Georgia and Albania – he found sacred fires and priests tending them. These fires (some of which must have been those reported on by Strabo) were evidently foundations of Achaemenian times, faithfully maintained by descendants of former Persian colonists. Kirder claims to have protected the temples and their congregations from pillage, and to have established order among them. In the following century, when most of these scattered believers were back under Byzantine rule, a Christian, St Basil, seeking to proselytize among them, recorded (Collected Letters CCLVIII) that they 'practised their own peculiar customs, not mingling with other peoples; and it is altogether impossible to employ reasoning with them, inasmuch as they have been preyed upon by the devil according to his wish. For there are neither books amongst them, nor teachers of doctrine, but they are brought up in an unreasoning manner, receiving their impiety by transmission from father to son. . . . They rave after unlawful marriages, and they believe in fire as God, and other such things.'

This account, although couched in hostile terms, gives a vivid impression of the rock-like quality of these small Zoroastrian communities, and the strength of their dependence upon a living tradition, unsupported by the written word.

Kirder himself claims among his many pious achievements the encouragement of what Basil termed 'unlawful', that is 'khvaet-vadatha' marriages, in Middle Persian called 'khvedodah' (SM 45); and these were practised by the royal family, evidently even before their rise to power. Thus Ardashir, son of Papak, married Denak, daughter of Papak; and Shabuhr I made his own daughter, Adur-Anahid, his Queen of queens. Kirder not only regarded this practice, which outraged Basil, as good, but he was quite as convinced as that saint that those of other faiths had been 'preyed upon by the devil', and under later kings he took vigorous steps to reduce their ranks within Iran. 'Great blows and damage' (he says) 'came upon Ahriman and the devs, and the doctrine of Ahriman and the devs departed the land and was no more believed. And Jews and Buddhists and Brahmans and Greek and Aramaic speaking Christians and Manichaeans and Baptisers are being smitten in the land' (SM 29–30).

The prophet Mani

Of these alien religions Manichaeism had arisen with the rise of the Sasanians, and had brought its iniquity to the Persian court itself, in the person of the prophet Mani. He was an Iranian, of noble Parthian blood; but his father had joined an ascetic community (probably of Elchasaites) in Babylonia, and Mani had grown up there speaking a Semitic tongue. On reaching manhood he felt impelled to preach his own religion, which was an eclectic one, and contained a number of Zoroastrian elements; for though he had probably had no direct contact with Zoroastrianism in his youth, Mani had imbibed some of its fundamental tenets through Judaeo-Christian and Gnostic traditions. Thus he believed in God and the Devil, Heaven and Hell, the Three Times, the individual judgment at death, the final defeat of evil, the Last Judgment, and life everlasting for the blessed in the presence of the hosts of heaven. With regard to this world, however, his teachings were profoundly pessimistic; for he saw it as almost wholly evil, and held that the best course for the individual was to renounce it as fully as possible, and to lead a gentle, ascetic life, dying celibate, so that his own soul might go to heaven, and he would have had no part in perpetuating the misery of human existence on earth. Mani's doctrines were thus fundamentally opposed to the positive, practical ones of Zoroastrianism. He had nevertheless a respect for the older faith – the religion of the Arsacid Great Kings, under whose rule he had been born, and which the Sasanians were in their turn upholding; and he thought that it, and Christianity, and Buddhism, were all in origin the one true faith, distorted by human misunderstandings, which he had been sent to restore. Preaching in Persia he was very ready, therefore, to present his own religion in a Zoroastrian guise, even 'translating' the names of the many divine beings of his own pantheon by those of Zoroastrian yazatas. This approach roused deep ire among Zoroastrian priests, who labelled the Manichaeans 'zandiks' or heretics (that is, those who put their own perverse interpretations upon holy texts).

Mani was, however, kindly received by Shabuhr I, and spent many years at his court, protected during the whole of his long reign (c. 240–72) from the wrath of Kirder. He early wrote a compendium of his teachings, duly translated into Middle Persian, for the king, and fragments of this book, called the 'Shabuhragan', and other Iranian Manichaean writings, have been recovered this century from the sand-buried ruins of Manichaean monasteries in Chinese Turkestan.

Zurvanism in the early Sasanian period

These writings show that the Manichaeans rendered the name of Mani's supreme God, in Middle Persian, as Zurvan, and called his 'son', the Manichaean First Man, Ohrmazd. This is the first of many pieces of contemporary evidence which show that the Sasanians were Zurvanites (perhaps following in this also the example of the later Achaemenians). Subsequently Mani sent missionaries to Parthia, in the north-east. They duly translated his scriptures into Parthian, and rendered the names of the Manichaean gods by ones acceptable to the Zoroastrians of that region; and it is noteworthy that they made no use of that of Zurvan, but simply translated the name of Mani's supreme God literally, as 'Father of Greatness'. Zurvanism can be traced, through Buddhist sources, among the Sogdians of the far north-east – possibly carried there by Persian garrison troops in Achaemenian times – but the Parthians appear to have resisted the heresy. This was very probably the main point of difference between Parthian and Persian theology, a difference which evidently persisted, despite the efforts of the Sasanian clergy; for an Armenian writer of the fifth century A.C. refers to a Zoroastrian priest who was master of both the Persian and Parthian schools of religious thought. Kirder himself, leader of the religious community under at least four kings, must also have been a Zurvanite, as other notable Persian clerics are known to have been after him – for otherwise there could not have been that harmony which so strikingly prevailed in Sasanian times between Persian rulers and priests; but he remained undeceived by Mani's adaptations of his own doctrines to Zurvanism.

Learning and writing

How far Shabuhr himself was beguiled by Manichaeism, in its guise of a reformed Zoroastrianism, cannot be known; but the Dinkard indicates a far-ranging curiosity on the king's part in matters of intellect and faith, combined with a steady adherence to the 'Mazda-worshipping' religion. The passage in question runs as follows: 'The King of kings, Shabuhr son of Ardashir, further collected those writings from the Religion which had been dispersed [that is, theoretically, by Alexander] throughout India, the Byzantine Empire, and other lands, and which treated of medicine, astronomy, movement, time, space, substance, creation, becoming, passing away, change in quality, growth (?), and other processes and organs. These he added to (?) the Avesta and commanded that a fair copy of all of them be deposited in the royal treasury; and he examined the possibility of bringing all systems (?) into line with the Mazda-worshipping religion' (DKM 412.17–413.2, ZZZ 8). The 'Avesta' to which these foreign writings were 'added' (the precise meaning of the verb used is obscure) was plainly the Zand, that is, the Middle Persian translation with its glosses and commentaries; and the evidence of Pahlavi compilations and Arabo-Persian books shows that foreign learning did indeed penetrate the religious tradition in this way, so that, for instance, the ancient doctrine of the seven creations was sometimes contaminated by the Empedoclean theory of the four elements (of earth, air, fire and water), and Hippocratic and Indian teachings became associated with traditional Iranian medical theory. Such assimilations depended on books; and so the Zoroastrian priests became steadily more accustomed to associating writing with religious and scholastic purposes, and not merely with practical ends.

Whether any of the Zand itself was written down in the Parthian period is unknown; but it seems likely that proselytizing, first by Christians and then by the Manichaeans (who laid immense stress on the value of the written word for preserving truth) spurred the Zoroastrian priests to serious efforts to commit their own holy texts to writing. The problem of how to do this adequately for the Avesta was not solved, however, until later in the period.

The summit of Kirder's power

Shabuhr was succeeded by his son Hormizd I (272–3), one of those for whom a 'named fire' had been endowed; and he, Kirder relates (SM 9–11), increased that prelate's authority and conferred on him the new title of 'mobad of Ohrmazd'. This seems to be a reassertion of the superior dignity of western ecclesiastical titles over eastern ones, and after this the 'herbad' appears to be considered of slightly lower standing than the 'mobad', although the evidence is far from clear-cut. It was during Hormizd's brief reign that Kirder, it seems, arranged the compromise of uniting the 'old' and 'new' holy days into single prolonged feasts – a measure which must have done much, for the laity at least, to allay the bitterness and confusion following the calendar-reform. Hormizd was succeeded by his brother, Vahram I (273–6); and it was in his reign that Kirder compassed the death of Mani, prevailing on Vahram to have him tried and executed. A Parthian Manichaean fragment which relates Kirder's part in this duly refers to him as 'Kirder the magbed'.

Vahram I was followed by a young son of the same name, Vahram II (276–93), who, some think, was helped to the throne by Kirder; and it was in his reign that Kirder himself reached the summit of his dignity and power. He was given the additional honorary title of 'Kirder by whom Vahram's soul is saved' (Kirder i bokhtruwan Wahram), and was made 'mobad and judge of the whole empire'. He was also placed in authority over the sacred fires of Anahid-Ardashir and Anahid the Lady at Istakhr – that is to say, over the temple which had been in the hereditary charge of the Sasanians themselves. (The history of the fire named 'Anahid-Ardashir' is obscure.) It was under Vahram that Kirder records his own smiting of infidels. He tells also (SM 42–3) that he punished and rebuked those Zoroastrian priests whose behaviour required it, but 'made the Mazda-worshipping religion and the good priests exalted and honoured in the land'. 'And many people who were unbelievers' (he claims) 'became believers;

and many a one there was who held the doctrine of the devs, and through me gave up that doctrine' (l. 45). Dev-worship appears in fact to have persisted in certain remote regions (notably mountainous parts of Sogdia) down to the time of the Islamic conquest, so that one is not entitled to infer from these claims that the Arsacids had been unduly tolerant of unbelief, or that the early Sasanians succeeded all at once in sweeping an Augean stable clean. Iran was too vast a country, and open to too many currents of belief, for the state religion ever to obliterate all other creeds.

By this stage in his long career Kirder was naturally a man of wealth, and he states that he founded many Vahram fires at his own expense, and yearly had great numbers of rites and 'services of the yazads' performed (SM 47–8). It was also, it seems, at this point in his life that he had his inscriptions carved. By the one at Sar-Mashhad he had placed an impressive sculpture which shows Vahram II in heroic pose, thrusting a sword at a leaping lion. Behind him, tendering the empty scabbard, is a female figure who, it has been surmised, may be Anahid herself, the tutelary divinity of the Sasanian house, whose temple Vahram had put under Kirder's special care; and in the background stand two men, one perhaps the crown prince, the other Kirder himself.

In his inscriptions Kirder has little to say of doctrinal matters, being concerned rather with observances, church discipline, conversions, and the discouragement of infidels. He proclaims, however, the existence of heaven and hell, and the latter part of the inscription at Sar-Mashhad (l.57 ff.) is taken up with an account, only partly legible, of a vision of the hereafter seen by him himself. In his spirit-journey he was met, he says, by his own double, his 'hangirb', and a woman – apparently the Daena (Middle Persian Den) who greets the departed soul at the Chinvat Bridge. In their company, it appears, he saw the golden thrones of heaven, and hell full of 'owls and other khrafstras', and became assured that his own place would one day be on high, as became a true servant of the Mazda-worshipping religion. – Neither Kirder himself, nor any Sasanian king, ever refers in an inscription to Zoroaster. They are content to proclaim themselves adherents of the faith which he taught, that is, Mazda-worship, in Middle Persian 'mazdesn'. This is in marked contrast to the Pahlavi literature, which is full of the prophet's name.

Although Kirder seems to have had his inscriptions carved, and his ossuary prepared, in the reign of Vahram II, he in fact outlived that ruler also. After reigning for seventeen years Vahram was succeeded by his son Vahram III, but he was soon deposed by his great-uncle Narseh, youngest son of Shabuhr I. (His name is the Middle Persian form of Avestan 'Nairyosanha', the messenger-yazad being very popular at this epoch.) Narseh, who ruled from 293 to 302, raised a great monument in the pass of Paikuli (in modern Iraq), at a place where he was met by the Persian nobles who proclaimed him king. On its huge blocks of stone was carved a long inscription, this time in two languages only, Middle Persian and Parthian, which describes the circumstances of his attaining power; and here (Parthian l. 15) Kirder figures for the last time, appearing among the highest dignitaries with his title of 'Ohrmazd mobad'. There is little religious matter in the inscription, but Narseh proclaims himself, with formulas established by his predecessors, as the 'Mazda-worshipping King of kings', who is 'of the race of the yazads' (Middle Persian l. 1); and he piously attributes his elevation to the will of 'Ohrmazd and all the yazads, and Anahid who is called the Lady' (ibid. l. 10). He also had an investiture scene carved at Naqsh-i Rustam, where again he proclaimed his devotion to Anahid, showing himself as receiving the diadem from her, a crowned and amply robed figure.

Persian made the official language of all Iran

In his inscription Narseh names Parthian as well as Persian nobles among his supporters, thus illustrating the drawing together of the two imperial peoples, begun under his father, Shabuhr I. Nevertheless, his is the last royal inscription to have a Parthian version. A few short private inscriptions in Parthian language and script have been found on rock-faces in southern Khorasan, that is, within the territory of Parthia proper; but it is thought that none is later than the fourth century A.C. The likelihood is, therefore, that soon after the raising of the monument at Paikuli the Sasanians took the decisive step of imposing Persian as the sole official language throughout Iran, and forbade altogether the use of written Parthian. This was a step which the Achaemenians had not needed to take, because of the common use of Aramaic; and a similar imposition of Parthian would have been out of character with Arsacid rule.

This measure was one of great importance for Zoroastrianism, because it meant that all the secondary religious literature of the faith, including the Zand, was written down in Middle Persian, thereafter the only recognized living language for the state religion. In the course of its general imposition over the whole country Middle Persian came to absorb a large number of Parthian words; and so the language of the Zoroastrian books – the so-called Pahlavi literature – is a mixed koine, as can be seen by comparing it with the pure Middle Persian and Parthian of the early Sasanian inscriptions. But though Parthian thus survives as a major element in the living Persian language, the fact that the Zoroastrian secondary literature is known only in Middle Persian versions has helped to strengthen the misconception (so sedulously fostered by the Sasanians) that Parthian Zoroastrianism had been virtually non-existent, and that the faith had only truly lived through the guardianship of the southern kingdom.

Conclusion

Since the diffusion of her language marks a cultural triumph for Persia, the last-recorded royal use of Parthian under Narseh makes a fitting end to a consideration of the early Sasanian period. This was a time of conquest and innovation, which saw the vigorous imposition of a new authority in the religious, no less than in the secular, sphere. None of the religious measures of the time – iconoclasm, the promotion of the cult of temple fires, the calendar reform, the establishment of a single authorized canon of scripture – affected doctrine; and indeed (ironically, for a dynasty regularly presented as the first creators and defenders of Zoroastrian orthodoxy) the Sasanians actually weakened the faith through giving prominence to their own Zurvanite beliefs. In practical ways, however, the Zoroastrian church was evidently strengthened, becoming unified, enriched and served by an every-growing body of disciplined priests; and it also received intellectual stimulus, through encounters with foreign learning.

CHAPTER EIGHT

During the mid Sasanian period

Upholding a Zurvanite orthodoxy

Much of the fourth century was occupied by the long reign of Shabuhr II, Narseh's grandson, who succeeded as an infant in 309, and was king for seventy years. He left no inscriptions, for the later Sasanians, like the later Achaemenians, abandoned this practice; and he is known in the history of Zoroastrianism mainly from two sources. One is the Dinkard's account of the transmission of the faith, which has the following statement about him: 'The King of kings, Shabuhr son of Hormizd, summoned men from all regions to an unprejudiced (?) disputation to examine and investigate all utterances. After the triumph of Adurbad, through his tested utterance, over all those of different groups, schools (?) and sects, he made this declaration: "Now that we have seen the faith as it truly is, we shall not tolerate anyone of false religion, and we shall be exceedingly zealous". And he did even so' (DkM 413. 2–8, ZZZ 8).

Elsewhere it is told that Adurbad i Mahraspand, a Persian high priest, vindicated his interpretation of the faith by undergoing – and surviving – the ancient ordeal of having molten metal poured on his breast. Unfortunately it is nowhere said what were the doctrines which he thus valiantly upheld; but it may safely be assumed that he was a Zurvanite, like the Sasanian kings and other Persian high priests of their era – especially since clear evidence exists for the Zurvanite beliefs of Shabuhr II (who called one of his daughters Zurvandukht 'Daughter of Zurvan'). Most of this evidence comes from the other main source for his religious activities, namely Christian records, and in particular the acts of Syrian martyrs. In his reign political considerations began to intensify religious animus, for it was then that Constantine freed Christianity from oppression, and it became virtually the state religion of the Roman Empire, Iran's most constant foe. Shabuhr accordingly imposed double taxation and tribute on his Christian subjects because they could not now serve in his armies, sharing as they did 'the sentiments of Caesar our enemy'; and the Zoroastrians living under what was now Christian rule in Asia Minor also suffered. Shabuhr launched an active persecution of Christians in 322, instigated, they claimed, by the Zoroastrian chief priests, who are said to have complained to the king in these terms: 'We cannot serve the sun, nor purify the air, nor make the water clear, nor cleanse the earth, because of the Nazarenes, who scorn the sun, despise fire and do not honour water' (Braun, 1). This indictment lists the four inanimate creations of Zoroastrianism, with the sun representing, as often, fire, but with air substituted, in Greek fashion, for the sky. On hearing the complaint Shabuhr (the writer says) was filled with anger, and had two Christian bishops brought before him, and addressed them thus: 'Know you not that I am of the race of the yazads? And I pray to the sun and honour fire. . . . Who is the God who is better than Ohrmazd, or whose anger is harsher than Ahriman's? What man is wise and does not pray to the sun?' And when the bishops proved obdurate, he had them put to death. On another occasion when a Persian Christian refused to reverence sun and fire. Shabuhr is reported to have said to him (ibid. 30): 'I swear by the sun, the Judge of the whole earth [that is, Mihr], that if you force me to it, who am your friend, then I shall slay you and spare none who bears this name (of Christian).' Often persecutor and persecuted were equally resolute, and much blood flowed. Mobads or magi are frequently mentioned as haling Christians before the King, and the office of chief mobad is often referred to. Since only Christian accounts of the interrogations survive, the martyrs are always credited with the best of the exchanges; and Pusai, one of those put to death by Shabuhr, is shown (ibid. 67) making a shrewd thrust at the King's Zurvanite beliefs: 'If your Majesty says "Sun, moon and stars are the children of Ohrmazd", why, we Christians do not believe in the brother of Satan. According to what the magi say, Ohrmazd is the brother of

Satan. If we do not pray to the brother of Satan, how should we then acknowledge this brother's children?' These words illustrate how radically the Zurvanites had betrayed Zoroaster's teachings by linking together, fraternally, the good and evil which he had so clearly set apart.

Such persecutions continued intermittently through the rest of the Sasanian period, and were sometimes provoked by the intransigence of the Christians themselves. The confrontation of the two faiths brings out their striking differences in outlook and practice. Zoroaster's teachings about the 'spenta' nature of physical creation, and his vision of God's kingdom to come upon earth, kept Zoroastrianism almost as much a religion of this world as was ancient Judaism, which had no hopes for the hereafter; but the Persian Christians were ascetic, with their thoughts fixed almost exclusively upon the life to come, and they shocked the Zoroastrians by their neglect of this world and its duties as well as its joys. Celibacy, exaltation of the contemplative life, the rejection of innocent pleasures, and the embracing not only of holy poverty but also of holy dirt, were forms of religious expression wholly alien to the Zoroastrians. There were gulfs too between them and the Jews, who were also at times the victims of Sasanian persecution. One field of theological difference is illustrated by a question by a magus to a rabbi, as to why one should suppose God to have created 'vermin and creeping things'; and the rabbi's answer, that 'God created vermin and creeping things in the world as a healing for men on earth', can hardly have led to a better understanding. No record survives of any debates between Zoroastrians and Buddhists, and except in Kirder's inscriptions there are no references to persecutions of Buddhist communities, for almost all sources for Sasanian history deal with western Iran.

The long reign of Shabuhr II was followed by three brief ones; and in 399 Yazdegird I succeeded to the throne. The early part of his reign was distinguished by marked clemency towards the Christians, who hailed him as good and blessed; but in Zoroastrian tradition he is known as 'the Sinner' – perhaps, it is suggested, because of his kindness to the infidel. One of his known acts of magnanimity was to allow Christians to bury their dead – that is (in Zoroastrian eyes) to pollute the good earth. Practice in funerary matters among the Zoroastrians themselves seems to have been exactly the same as during the two earlier empires: the rite of exposure, that is, was generally practised except by the royal family, who continued to place their dead, embalmed, in mausoleums. As with the Arsacids, however, this is attested only from literary sources (Zoroastrian and Arabo-Persian), for no tomb of any Sasanian king has yet been found. (The dynasty, it is recorded, had no common funerary place for its members.)

During the latter part of Yazdegird's reign the king's forbearance towards Christians became tried by their own rash acts, and he in his turn took stern measures against them. Thus it is told how a Christian priest destroyed a fire temple that stood close to his church, and refused to rebuild it, even at the king's command; and how another boldly extinguished a sacred fire and celebrated mass in its place (Hoffmann, 34–8). It is noteworthy that even in the face of such provocation the Persians proceeded deliberately, with due processes of investigation and trial, before in the end sentence of death was pronounced. Religious zeal continued to characterize the reign of Yazdegird's son, Vahram V (421–39), of whom it is recorded (*ibid.* 39) that 'he listened to the command of the accursed Mihr-Shabuhr, chief of the magi, and dragged forth the dead who had been buried in the days of his father, and scattered them about in the sun; and he maintained this command for five years.' Theodoretus, who wrote during his reign, records, however (Sermo 9.35), that, though Persians had learnt from Zoroaster 'to expose their dead to dogs and birds', nevertheless Persian converts to Christianity 'do not now tolerate this practice, but bury their dead in the earth, disregarding the cruel laws that forbid interment, and show no fear of the cruelty of those who punish them.'

Vahram's chief minister was Mihr-Narseh, an account of whose life is given by the Arabo-Persian historian, Tabari (who relied evidently on a Sasanian source). From this it is known that he was a successful commander in the field, was appointed chief minister by Yazdegird I, and continued to hold this office under Vahram and also under his son, Yazdegird II (439–57). He is represented as enlightened, cultured, and a devout Zoroastrian; and his private life appears full of piety and charitable works. Near his birthplace, at Firuzabad in Pars, a stone bridge still stands, which bears this weather-worn inscription: 'This bridge was built by the order of Mihr-Narseh, the chief minister, for the benefit of his soul, at his own cost. Whoever has come by this road, let him invoke a blessing on Mihr-Narseh and his sons, for that he has thus bridged this crossing.' Mihr-Narseh's three sons, associated with him here, each held high office as titular head of one of the traditional estates of the realm. Thus Kardar was 'Chief of warriors'; Zurvandad, destined, Tabari says, for the church and law (a fact which raises problems about the relationship of the priesthood and nobility) held the title of 'Herbad of herbads' (Herbadan herbad); and Mah-Gushnasp was 'Chief of herdsmen'. All these archaic-sounding titles, together with that of Mobadan mobad 'High priest of high priests' for the head of the whole Zoroastrian community, appear to be creations of this epoch. Mihr-Narseh further developed four villages, with fine fields and orchards, near Firuzabad; and in one he established a sacred fire for his own soul, and in the other three 'named fires' for each of these three sons. These fires were intended, evidently, to be the centres of village worship, with the responsibility for maintaining them and appointing their priests resting with Mihr-Narseh, his sons and their heirs.

The fact that Mihr-Narseh called one of his sons Zurvandad, 'Given by Zurvan', shows that he too was a Zurvanite; and it is from his days that the only detailed documents survive about the tenets of that heresy. Yazdegird II made a determined effort to win Armenia back from Christianity, and issued a proclamation summoning its inhabitants to return to the old faith. Another document was addressed to them by Mihr-Narseh, and it is the gist of this, it seems, which has been preserved by two Armenian writers, Elishe Vartabad and Lazarus of Pharb. In it the great god Zurvan is declared to have existed before heaven and earth; and the myth is told of his twin sons, Ohrmazd and Ahriman. Thereafter Mihr-Narseh's exposition proceeds on orthodox lines. Ohrmazd, he affirms, has created heaven and earth and all that is good within them, whereas Ahriman has brought into existence miseries, sicknesses and death. 'Happiness, power, glory, honours, health of body, beauty of countenance, eloquence of tongue and length of life are the work of the Creator of good. . . . Men who say that he is the author of death, and that good and evil alike come from him, are in error.' In their answer the Armenians ignored the problem of attributing the origin of evil to God, and, like prudent polemicists, moved to the attack instead: 'We do not worship, like you, the elements, the sun, the moon, the winds and the fire. We do not make offerings to all these gods whom you name on earth and in heaven. . . . We worship . . . a single . . . God.' The Syrian Christians similarly characterized the religion of 'the followers of the wicked Zradusht' as being the 'ancient service of false gods and of the elements'; but Vahram V himself answered them by saying (Hoffman, 42) that 'he acknowledged only one God. The rest were but as courtiers of the King.'

The three great sacred fires

These contests with other, proselytizing religions, although hardly known to Zoroastrianism before the Sasanian period, can have been little more than peripheral harassments to that solidly based, immensely powerful faith, whose spiritual forces were supported by all the temporal might of the Sasanian Empire. Ecclesiastically, Zoroastrianism continued to expand and flourish, and it appears to be during this time that two great sacred fires in Pars and Media were brought into prominence to rival the glory of Adur Burzen-Mihr. The Parthian fire was itself far too holy (linked as it was in legend with the prophet and Vishtaspa) for the western priests to withhold veneration from it; but they set it now in dignity below their own fires, stating that Adur Farnbag (which burned in Pars) was the especial fire of priests, and Adur Gushnasp (in Media) that of warriors, whereas Adur Burzen-Mihr belonged to the lowliest estate, that of herdsmen and farmers. This was mere scholastic schematization; but it seems to have provided a basis for the vigorous promotion of the two western fires.

The Persian fire was presumably in origin, like the other two, a 'named fire', that of an unknown Farnbag, whose name meant 'Having a share/prospering through Farnah'. Farnah is a dialect form of Avestan Khvarenah (Middle Persian Khwarrah, Persian Khara); and in promoting the fire's fame its priests made much of this element in its name, going so far indeed as to identify their fire at times fully with divine Khvarenah itself. In the Shahname version of the story of Ardashir I (Warner, VI, 226) the founder of the Sasanian dynasty is said to have visited its temple, but this is evidently anachronistic. What appear to be reliable references to the fire all belong to the mid and later Sasanian periods. Thus Yazdegird I is represented as taking an oath by both Farnbag and Burzen-Mihr (ibid., 391); and Biruni (p. 215) records that this king's great-grandson, Peroz, prayed at the shrine of 'Adar Khara' for an end to a devastating drought. In the opening chapter of the Pahlavi work, Arda Viraz Namag, whose final redaction was made in Pars, a great assembly of priests gathers at the temple of 'the victorious Adur Farnbag' to deliberate together.

Still more is said in contemporary sources about the Median fire, Adur Gushnasp, partly because this was the nearest of the three great fires to the western boundaries of Iran, and so came to the notice of foreign observers, partly because kings belonged to the warrior-estate, and so its priests were able to promote this fire as the royal one. There is no mention of it in the early Sasanian inscriptions; and excavation suggests that it was not until the late fourth or early fifth century that it was taken to an unusually beautiful site in Azarbaijan. This, known in Muslim times as Takht-i Suleyman, 'The Throne of Solomon', is a hill whose flat top holds a lake high above the level of the surrounding countryside, making it a perfect place for Zoroastrians to venerate God and his creations of fire and water. The whole hill-top was enclosed by a massive mud-brick wall, with gateways to north and south; and from the northern one a processional way led to the temple precinct itself, surrounded on three sides by another wall, but open on the south to the lake. Here Adur Gushnasp was enthroned in an inner sanctuary, to be reached through a series of ante-chambers and pillared halls. The royal connection of this 'fire of warriors' was so successfully fostered that it became the acknowledged custom for each king, after his coronation, to make a pilgrimage there on foot (probably walking, that is, from the base of the holy hill). Royal gifts were lavished on this shrine, as by the Arsacids on Adur Burzen-Mihr, the first monarch who is mentioned in this connection being Vahram V. Tha'alibi (pp. 559–60) tells how, on his return from a triumphant campaign against the 'Turks', that is, the Chionites (yet another nomad people of the steppes), Vahram bestowed the crown of their conquered leader upon the temple, together with his queen and her slaves to be servitors there. On another occasion, according to the Shahname (Warner, VII, 138–9), this king entrusted an Indian princess, his bride, to the high priest, to undergo purification and be converted to the faith. There are also references in the epic to Vahram's visiting the shrine for the feasts of Sada and No Ruz (ibid., p. 94); and it was probably he, a devout and zealous king, who first fully acknowledged the royal link with this sacred fire, although the earliest dateable objects found in its ruins come from the reign of his grandson, Peroz (459–84). The commonalty naturally followed royal example in visiting the shrine; and in one Zoroastrian text (Saddar Bd 44.18, 21) it is enjoined that anyone praying for restoration of sight should vow to make 'an eye of gold' and send it to Adur Gushnasp; and that anyone wishing his son to be wise should send a present there. The evidence points to the great Zoroastrian sanctuaries being centres of general devotion and pilgrimage in the same way as the great shrines of Christendom, with their priests vying with one another to promote the legends and hence the sanctity of their particular fires; and ancient Iran doubtless saw in spring and autumn countless caravans of pilgrims as varied and colourful as those of medieval Europe.

Liturgical reform

Many acts of worship must have been performed at the great sanctuaries by their numerous priests; and it was possibly at this epoch that the yasna service was lengthened to increase its impressiveness. This seems to have been done by joining the Gathic Staota Yesnya (already greatly extended by the addition of Younger Avestan texts) to another liturgy with its own ritual, namely a haoma-ceremony which (though evidently old, probably pre-Zoroastrian, in origin) had a liturgy (essentially Y IX–XI) that had evolved into the Younger Avestan dialect. The present yasna service thus has two separate preparations of haoma, which differ only slightly in their rituals. By a yet further development a still longer service, called that of 'All the Masters', Visperad (Av. Vispe Ratavo) was evolved from this extended yasna, for the celebration primarily of the seven holy days of obligation. The Visperad is dedicated to Ohrmazd, as Master of all; and it consists of the rituals of the yasna, virtually unchanged, but with a liturgy extended by twenty-three short supplementary sections. These are made up in the main of formal, repetitive invocations. The extended yasna and Visperad are still reverently solemnized by Zoroastrian priests today, and there is no reason to doubt the genuineness of the piety which led to the creation of these services. Yet all such developments meant more work for priests and more expense for the laity – easily borne, no doubt, by the wealthy nobles and merchants of those imperial days, but gradually creating ever heavier pressures on the devout poor, who would have struggled, then as later, to pay for the longer ceremonies which they were taught were of greater merit and hence of more benefit to the soul.

Religious literature and royal propaganda

Another pious activity, which must have continued throughout the period, was the writing down of the Middle Persian Zand, together with much secondary Zoroastrian literature. Some of the Pahlavi texts which survive are original compositions of the Sasanian and post-Sasanian periods, but others have clearly come down from remote antiquity, and must once have existed in parallel versions in various Iranian languages. Two such works, the Drakht Asurig, 'Assyrian Tree', and Ayadgar i Zareran, 'Exploits of Zarer', bear traces in fact of having been translated from Parthian originals. Middle Persian renderings are thus often merely the final forms, fossilized in writing, of works with an immensely long oral history.

Persian priests also worked at filling out the scanty historical records of the faith; and they evolved in this connection a pseudo-genealogy for the Sasanian royal house to rival the pseudo-genealogy of the Arsacids. The Persian one was based on the fact that the father of Darius the Great was called Vishtaspa. Him they identified (quite possibly in good faith) with his Kayanian namesake. They then created a wholly fictitious blood-tie between the Sasanians them-selves and their Achaemenian predecessors, and so were able to trace the ancestry of the reigning dynasty all the way back to the first royal patron of the faith. This had a political advantage, since a claim to Kayanian blood gave these kings of the south-west an ancient title to rule also over the north-east. In this respect it exactly counter-balanced the faked genealogy whereby the Arsacids of the north-east traced their descent from the Persian Artaxerxes. The new Sasanian one had, however, the added value that, by linking these Persian kings with Kavi Vishtaspa, it made them appear as natural heirs to the khvarenah or divine grace which had accompanied him, and hence as the rightful rulers of Zoroastrians everywhere. The era of the Arsacids could thus be presented as no more than a regrettable interlude, a break in the series of legitimate sovereigns of Iran. These Iranian, Zoroastrian kings were now made indeed to seem hardly less alien and usurping than Alexander himself; and so effective has this Persian propaganda proved that it has shaped later attitudes to the Parthian epoch both within the Zoroastrian community and among modern scholars, so that the Arsacid period is regularly described as a semi-pagan one, and the true faith is presented as abiding precariously then in hiding with the Sasanians in their Persian fastness. By this means a whole glorious epoch, lasting half a millennium, was effectively blotted out of Zoroastrian history.

The faked Sasanian genealogy evidently existed in the fourth century; and it is associated with the creation of a long prose chronicle called the Khwaday Namag, 'Book of Kings'. This was essentially an account of the history of the world, narrowing to that of Iran itself, seen as the history of a series of related dynasties. The earliest the priests termed the Peshdadian (translating Avestan Paradata 'first created'). This was formed of mythical 'first men' and culture heroes, with Gayomard at their head. They were followed by the Kayanians (to whom they were linked through the hoary device of an abandoned royal infant, brought up unknown). The Achaemenians (represented by only two monarchs) were treated as part virtually of the Kayanian dynasty, which accordingly met its end through Alexander's conquest. Thereafter (it is said) there was no King of kings in Iran, but only scores of petty local rulers. A few of these are named from among the Arsacids, and include Arshak himself, and 'Ardaban the Great', prince of Shiraz and Isfahan, who (the chronicle relates) appointed Papak as governor in Istakhr. Papak, enlightened by dreams, gave his daughter in marriage to a mountain shepherd, the last of a long line of Sasans who had been in hiding since the death of their ancestor Dara, the last Achaemenian king; and from this union sprang Ardashir, who restored the faith, re-established the high kingship, and led Iran back to power and glory.

How far this distortion of history gained credence during the Sasanians' own period of rule is doubtful; but clearly for it to have any effect it had to be made widely known; and there are signs of its being proclaimed and exploited from the time of Peroz, son of Yazdegird II (459–84). As prince, Peroz had been governor of Seistan; and during his father's reign the Hephthalites, a mixed nomadic horde, had begun to menace Iran on its north-eastern frontier, thus making the Sasanians keenly aware of their need to foster loyalty among their own subjects there. Yazdegird himself moved his court for seven years into Parthian territory, the better to counter the Hephthalites; and Peroz, who had to continue the fighting against them, showed his desire to court eastern Iranian popularity by reviving the ancient title of 'Kavi', in its Middle Persian form of 'Kay', on some of his coins. (Previously this had been used only by prince-governors of north-eastern Iran.) He also called one of his sons Kavad after Kavi Kavata (the first Kayanian king), and another Zamasp after Jamaspa

(Vishtaspa's wise counsellor). This is the first time that such Avestan names appear in the Sasanian family. Peroz' son Kavad also used the title 'Kay' on his coins; and he in his turn named one son Khosrow, after Kavi Haosravah, and another Kaus, after Kavi Usan. Thereafter there was another Khosrow, grandson of the first, and a second Kavad, his son. Throughout the later Sasanian period the dynasty thus strongly affirmed, through given names, the validity of their claim to Kayanian descent.

Peroz himself was a devout Zoroastrian, and his zeal for the faith, like his father's, showed itself in the persecution of unbelievers. His harassment of Christians had an element in it of reprisal, for he complained that the Byzantines tormented the Zoroastrians under their rule, forbade them free observance of their faith and laws, and would not permit them to maintain sacred fires. Towards the end of his reign, however, he relaxed his severity towards the Christians in Persia when, as Nestorians, they were rejected by Byzantium.

Calendar reform

A matter which must have been engaging leading Zoroastrians with ever-increasing urgency during his reign was the religious calendar. Ever since this had been changed under Ardashir from a 360- to a 365-day one there had been no intercalation, and, with a quarter-day being lost annually, the holy year had slipped steadily backward until now No Ruz was being celebrated in July, remote from either equinox. The need to act led (at some uncertain date) to a great council being held of the learned men of the realm; and they evidently decided on the radical step of restoring the celebration of the 'New Day' to its Achaemenian time, in the spring. How to do this was plainly a difficult matter; and the solution found was, not to attempt to shift the calendar-months, but instead to shift No Ruz itself from the first of Farvardin to the first of whichever month was then appropriate. The actual change appears to have been made under Peroz' son Kavad I, between 507 and 511 A.C., in which years the spring equinox coincided with the first of the ninth month, Adur; and from then onwards the religious No Ruz was celebrated on 1 Adur. The six gahambars also moved their places, so as to form exactly the same chain of feasts as before in relation to No Ruz; and the fravashi days, coinciding in part with the sixth gahambar, shifted with it to the end of the eighth month, Aban. Sada too had to move with No Ruz, and so did the anniversary day of the prophet's death, calculated in relation to the first gahambar. These feasts now made up what was termed the 'moving' year – so called either because of this dramatic shift in the sixth century, or because it was intended to keep moving it by intercalating a whole month every 120 years, so that 1 Adur could never again recede more than thirty days from the spring equinox. The remaining festivals, being of far less religious importance than the seven founded by Zoroaster, were left in their former places in the calendar, to go on slipping back with it almost imperceptibly through the seasons.

The second Sasanian calendar-reform was thus devoutly intended, but in the long run its effects may well have been almost as damaging as those of the first purely practical one, for they added to the complications which it had created. Thus though the people dutifully learnt to keep the religious 'New Day' – which they called the 'No Ruz of the priests' – on 1 Adur, they could not bring themselves to abandon the traditional celebration of No Ruz on 1 Farvardin, and this remained the beginning of the secular year and the coronation day of kings. There thus came to be four celebrations of No Ruz, with the lesser and greater feasts being celebrated on 1 and 6 Adur, and on 1 and 6 Farvardin; and this must have clouded still more the general awareness of the link between that festival and the gahambars, and the doctrinal significance of seven high feasts. The celebration of all seven is repeatedly enjoined in the later Zoroastrian literature as being among the essential duties of every believer; but the festivals are named separately as 'Rapithwin' and 'the gahambars', and their observance constitutes two separate obligations.

In Pahlavi texts composed – or revised – after the second calendar reform there is much emphasis on the significance of spring in connection with thoughts of resurrection and Frashegird. So a priest writing in the ninth century declared: 'The making of Frashegird is like the year, in which at springtime the trees are made to blossom. . . . Like the resurrection of the dead, new leaves are made to shoot from dry plants and trees, and springtime is made to blossom' (Zadspram XXXIV. o.27). A sense of renewal was now characteristic of the No Ruz celebrations and new clothes were then worn, and food was of the new season. 'Among other things which it was thought propitious to begin this day with was a mouthful of pure fresh milk and fresh cheese; all the kings of Persia took it as a blessing.' The kings also ate on that morning 'white sugar with fresh

Indian nuts pared'; and it was the custom to sow for this seventh feast seven kinds of seeds, to come up fresh and green on the holy day itself. 'For the king the sight of growing barley was particularly deemed a blessing. . . . And the harvest (of these green shoots) was never gathered but with songs and music and mirth' (Ehrlich, 99–101). Music is much spoken of in connection with No Ruz, and it is said that 'Though the king's banquet was splendid, others were no less so. . . . Everyone had gone from his house to the country. . . . From every garden, field and river a different variety of music charmed the ear' (Vis u Ramin, 20).

The Mazdakite movement

Details of other Sasanian festivals show that the Zoroastrians were then as merry and devout as medieval Christians. Yet for them too the ever increasing religious observances must have had their oppressive side, with growing numbers of clergy and mounting demands for gifts and dues. Moreover, by this period the church had become a landowner on a large scale, with slaves as well as peasants to work its broad acres, and in the eyes of the lowly there may well have seemed little to choose at times between grasping prelate and greedy baron. It is against this background that one must judge the success which attended the Mazdakite movement towards the end of the fifth century. Its leader, Mazdak i Bamdad, adopted, it seems, the doctrines of an early religious teacher who had preached a faith which appears to owe much to Manichaeism. Certainly the doctrines promulgated by Mazdak had the pessimism and ascetic character of Mani's, and were similarly gentle and moral. Man should not kill, nor eat flesh, but should encourage the increase of light over darkness in this world by kindliness, tolerance and fraternal love. To further brotherliness, and reduce the causes of greed and envy, Mazdak sought to have property held in common, and in this, his detractors say, he included women. Despite Zoroastrian teachings about spiritual equality, in Sasanian law women were indeed held to belong to their nearest male relatives – father, husband, brother or son; and the Mazdakite claim to their being common property may have sprung originally from a desire among poor people to free daughters or sisters who had been taken (probably often enough by force) into the huge households of women maintained by kings and nobles. A general longing by peasants and artisans for justice and some lightening of their financial burdens (for they were the chief payers of taxes, priests and nobles being exempt) would account for much of the popular support for Mazdak; and among the well-to-do there seems to have been a current at this time drifting some towards asceticism in place of the robuster Zoroastrian ethic. Moreover, Mazdak himself was evidently a persuasive preacher, and just as Mani had gained a hearing from Shabuhr I, so he won the ear of Peroz's son, Kavad I.

Peroz himself lost his life in 484, fighting against the Hephthalites; and in 488 Kavad succeeded to the throne. He had earlier spent two years as a hostage among the Hephthalites, and it has been suggested that this experience of a semi-nomadic society, with the relative independence and equality of its members, may have inclined him to look favourably on Mazdak's proposals for social reform within Iran, as perhaps lending the empire strength to resist its formidable foes. Most nobles and leading clerics inevitably opposed the new movement fiercely, and Mazdak figures as the arch-heretic in the Pahlavi books. His teachings nevertheless gained sufficient support to convulse the whole land, with the seizure of property and abduction (or freeing) of women; but the forces of established power rallied, the movement was largely put down, and Kavad was himself deposed in 494 in favour of his brother Zamasp. He fled to the Hephthalites, who helped him to regain the throne; but he then abandoned his support for Mazdak, and named as his heir not his eldest son Kaus, who had adhered to the new faith, but his third son, Khosrow, who was to earn himself the title Anoshirvan, 'of immortal soul', through his rigorous upholding of the state religion. Towards the end of his reign, in 528, Kavad allowed Khosrow to arrange what purported to be a banquet in honour of Mazdak, which ended in the slaughter of that prophet and many of his followers. The movement was thus virtually extinguished, though influences from it lived on to nourish various strange sects at the coming of Islam.

CHAPTER NINE

Under the later Sasanians

Khosrow 'the Just'

Khosrow Anoshirvan, who succeeded to the throne in 531 and occupied it for nearly half a century, is the best known of the Sasanian kings. There are a number of reasons for this. He was a strong ruler, and his reign, coming late in the period, is relatively well documented; and because of the Mazdakite movement and its upheavals, he found it necessary to enact an unusual number of measures, for which he is remembered. Moreover, it was while he was king that Muhammad was born – a dire event for Zoroastrianism, but one that gave him a special interest for Muslim historians. Among the Arabic writings concerning him there survives a translation of a little work called the 'Karnamag i Anoshiravan', which purports to be a record of his thoughts and acts; and this shows how he came to earn his second by-name of 'the Just', for it contains a declaration of the principles on which he acted: 'I give thanks unto God . . . for all the favours which he has shown me. . . . Many benefits require in return a deep sense of obligation. . . . And since I hold that gratitude should express itself in both word and deed, I have sought the course of action most pleasing to God, and have found that it consists in that whereby sky and earth continue to exist, the mountains remain immovable, the rivers flow, and the earth is kept pure: that is to say, in equity and justice' (Karnamag, transl. Grignaschi, 26). If for the last two Arabic words one substitutes Avestan 'asha', it becomes plain how truly Zoroastrian this utterance is, with its affirmation of man's duty to uphold that great cosmic and moral principle, and thereby to help sustain all the good creations of Ahura Mazda. In spirit the words are, indeed, Gathic; and in their dignity and scope they match those of Darius the Great, engraved a thousand years earlier.

Justice, however, for a Sasanian king had nothing to do with social equality, and Khosrow restored the old rigid structure of society, thrusting rebels and malcontents firmly back into what he believed were their divinely appointed places. But he tried thereafter to protect the peasants and artisans from illegal exactions, entrusting the oversight of this (according to his Karnamag) to the Mobadan mobad, the head of the Zoroastrian community. Throughout his reign Khosrow worked closely with the clergy; and his religious convictions, and energetic support of established ways, assured him an honoured place in the Dinkard's history of the faith. The long passage devoted to him there, which derives from a contemporary source, runs in part as follows: 'His present Majesty, the King of kings, Khosrow son of Kavad, after he had put down heresy and irreligion with the fullest opposition, according to the revelation of the religion in the matter of all heresy, greatly strengthened recognition of the four estates. . . . And at an assembly of the provinces he issued the following declaration: "The truth of the Mazda-worshipping religion has been recognized. Wise men can with confidence establish its reality through discussion. But effective and progressive propaganda should be, essentially, not through discussion, but through good thoughts, words and acts, and the inspiration of the best spirit, and worship of the yazads, paid purely in conformity to the holy word. What the chief priests of Ohrmazd have proclaimed, do we proclaim, for among us they have been shown to possess spiritual insight. . . . The realm of Iran has gone forward relying on the doctrine of the Mazda-worshipping religion, which is the synthesis of the accumulated knowledge of those who have gone before us, (intended) for the whole world. We have no dispute with those who have other convictions, for we possess so much (truth) in the Avestan language by pure oral tradition, and by written records, by books and memoranda, and also in the common tongue by way of exegesis – in short the whole original wisdom of the Mazda-worshipping religion" ' (DkM 413.9–414.6, ZZZ 8–9).

The tolerant spirit of these words suggests that they were uttered late in Khosrow's reign, when re-established security for the state religion had allowed him to abandon earlier harshness, as shown to the Mazdakites. Relative leniency is also displayed in the following passage from his Karnamag: 'The Mobadan mobad submitted to our attention [the case] of several persons whom he named and who belonged to the nobility. . . . The religion of these persons was contrary to that which we inherited from our Prophet and the learned men of our faith. [The Mobadan mobad warned us] that those persons were proselytizing in secret for their religion and inviting people to adopt it. . . . I gave orders to have these heretics brought into my presence, and to dispute with them. . . . Thereafter I commanded that they should be banished from my capital, my country and my empire, and that all those who shared their beliefs should follow them' (Grignaschi, 18–19).

In another episode described in the Karnamag (Grignaschi, 19–20), Khosrow tells how, when campaigning against Khazars in the Caucasian region (for it was Turks who now constituted the nomad threat from the north), he received the voluntary submission of a number of the invaders. These he settled within his own borders, entrusting them with the defence of the area. And then, he says: 'I gave orders for the building of a temple by our priests. I gave them the mission of instructing the Turks who had put themselves under our authority in the immediate advantages which obedience to kings brings in this world, and the reward which follows in the life hereafter. I ordered them to inculcate in the Turks the duty to love us, to be just and faithful, and to combat our enemies; and [I bade them] teach the young people our beliefs and rituals.' Though this order was primarily political in motive, there was plainly no reluctance to accept these non-Iranians into the Zoroastrian fold, provided they were instructed and willing converts.

The written Avesta

In the Dinkard passage there is reference to the Avesta in both oral and written transmission, for by this time an unknown genius among the Zoroastrian priests had solved the problem of how to set down the holy texts by inventing the 'Avestan' alphabet. This, an elegant one of great distinction, is based on the Pahlavi alphabet as it was written in the mid-Sasanian period; but instead of fewer than twenty letters it has forty-six, the new ones having been created through modifica-

tions of Pahlavi characters. The Avestan alphabet permi
rendering of every vowel and consonant, in fact it has been co
for accuracy with the modern 'international phonetic alphab(
great practical objection to writing down the Avesta, that
impossible to render its sacred sounds adequately, had thus
been overcome.

With this splendid new tool, the Persian priests set about reco
every surviving Avestan text, doing this, evidently, at the dictati(
other Persian priests, for since the time of Tansar it was they
were the appointed guardians of the scriptural canon. They u.
naturally, the ecclesiastical pronunciation of Avestan accepted in I
in their day, which must have differed slightly from that of otl
regions; but considering the immense expanse of time and pl.
which separated Middle Persian itself not only from the Gathas, b\
even from the Younger Avesta, it is a matter for admiration ho\
faithfully on the whole the sacred language had been preserved.

It is of course impossible to know if any Avestan texts existed
anywhere in the sixth century which were left out of the Sasanian
canon; but this seems unlikely, since Zoroastrian scholars were more
inclined to collect and conflate than to exclude. How long it took to
write everything down is not known; but in a ninth-century book it is
said that 'at the council of Khosrow Anoshiravan, King of kings, son
of Kavad' the Mobadan mobad, one Veh-Shabuhr, 'published the
twenty-one divisions, so that it was agreed to, as it had been decreed'
(Bailey, 173). The great Sasanian Avesta was compiled in twenty-one
'nasks' or divisions to correspond with the twenty-one words of the
Ahunvar prayer; and the nasks were then sub-divided into three
groups of seven. The first group contained the Gathas and all the texts
associated with them, the second, works of scholastic learning, and
the third, treatises of instruction for priests (such as the Vendidad),
law-books, and various miscellanea, including the yashts, which,
though they had been quarried for material to extend the yasna, had
no place themselves in the daily priestly services. (The longest and
best preserved of them are the Farvardin Yasht, recited at every death
and funerary observance, and those of Mihr and Anahid. Not surprisingly the hymn to 'Ardvisur Anahid', the beloved yazad of the
Sasanian dynasty, shows signs of having been extended as much as
possible, through the use of 'floating' verses, found in more than one
yasht, and through borrowings from hymns to other yazads, notably
Ashi.)

The passage which alludes to the publishing in council of the 'Great Avesta' of the twenty-one nasks seems to imply that copies of this massive work were sent to leading priests in the provinces, so that possibly there were at one time at least four in existence, in Pars and Media, Parthia and Seistan. Each would have been placed, presumably, in the library of some great fire temple, to be studied there by scholar-priests; but clearly the written Avesta had little immediate impact on the ordinary family priest, let alone the laity; and as a community the Zoroastrians continued to worship and pray with words which they learnt by heart, passed down from father to son, without need or knowledge of a written text.

The Pahlavi literature

Scholar-priests seem to have availed themselves eagerly, however, of the rich new possibilities offered by the possession of written texts. The Great Avesta was accompanied by its Middle Persian Zand, now likewise wholly written down (though still in the defective Pahlavi script, with its ideograms); and among other activities they made extracts and compilations from this Zand on specific themes, for the enlightment of their fellows, and probably also of noble laymen. The most important of such works is the Bundahishn, 'Creation', also called Zand-Agahih, 'Knowledge from the Zand', which was added to and re-edited for generations, so that in the end it was a lengthy work with three main themes: creation, the nature of earthly creatures, and the Kayanians – those putative ancestors of the Sasanian dynasty.

The spread of literacy meant that many other slighter works of religious (and secular) instruction were composed in the late Sasanian period, most now known by their titles only. Collections of gnomic utterances were popular, attributed to famous sages from the remote past, or from the Sasanian period itself. Some of the gnomes contain worldly wisdom, others moral instruction; and their Middle Persian name was 'andarz' or 'precept'. An important work, probably composed in the sixth century, which seems to have evolved from this ancient type of literature, is the Dadistan i Menog i Khrad, the 'Judgments of the Spirit of Wisdom'. Here an inquirer seeks to establish the truth of Zoroastrianism, and receives instruction from the Spirit of Wisdom himself, who declares (LVII. 4–5): 'From first I, who am innate Wisdom, was with Ohrmazd. And the Cr

Ohrmazd created, and preserves and guides, the yazads of the creations of heaven and earth, and all other created things, through the strength . . . of innate Wisdom.' The Spirit then enlightens the seeker about the basic doctrines of the faith, indicates the moral principles which should direct his life, and provides brief summaries of traditional knowledge in certain fields, drawn from the Avesta. Throughout there is firm emphasis on dualism. 'The yazads give nothing but good to mankind, Ahriman and the devs nothing but evil' (LII.15). Among the essential duties of the faithful it is enjoined that they should pray thrice daily 'facing the Sun and Mihr as they proceed together', celebrate the gahambars, practise 'khvedodah', and worship the yazads, while abstaining from the veneration of images (LIII. 3, IV. 5, II. 93). These things they should do from means created by their own diligent labours, from which they should also shelter the wanderer, help the poor, and show benevolence to all good people (IV. 6–8, II. 42–4).

This book, written in plain and simple language, is addressed explicitly to the laity; and there is evidence from other sources of the existence of an educated laity in the late Sasanian period, and of their well-grounded interest in religious matters. In a little text called Khosrow ud Redag, 'Khosrow and the Page', Khosrow is represented as questioning a youth of good family (his father a noble, his mother a high priest's daughter) about his attainments, in order to test his fitness to be his page. The boy's answers, which show him to be a judge of food and wines, music and poetry, scents, flowers, women and horses, vividly evoke a world of refined luxury and delights; but he also claims the fruits of a sound religious education. 'At the due time I was sent to school (frahangestan) and was very diligent in my studies. I learnt the Yasna and Hadokht, the Yashts and Vendidad by heart like a priest, and passage by passage I listened to the Zand. And my scribesmanship is such that I am a good writer and a swift writer, with a fine knowledge of the art' (Bailey, 160). The 'frahangestan' was presumably a general school ('frahang' means simply 'education'), as distinct from the specialized 'herbadestan' and 'dibirestan' of priest and scribe; and a parallel to these claims by the fictitious page comes from the actual life of Mihram-Gushnasp, a Persian noble who apostatized to Christianity and, as St Giwargis, was martyred in 614 under Khosrow II. On his father's side Mihram-Gushnasp was related to the Sasanian royal family, and his mother, again, was the daughter of a high priest. Orphaned young, he was brought up by his paternal grandfather, who, though a layman, had him trained from early years (so his Christian biographer relates) 'in Persian literature and the religion of the magi, so that already as a seven-year-old boy he could recite the yasna and hold the barsom . . . in such a manner that report of his ability prompted the King of kings Hormazd [son of Khosrow I] to invite him to court and to command him to recite something from the religion of the magi. He straightway did so.' The king was pleased, and appointed him as page; and later he piously contracted a 'khwedodah' marriage, taking his sister to wife (Hoffmann, 93–5).

Religious observances

It is unlikely that Mihram-Gushnasp's sister would have had nearly so good an education as he, or that women were allowed access to the prized art of writing; but probably well-to-do ladies listened not only to minstrel-poetry and amusing tales, but also to edifying works read aloud by the family priest. In general the sources suggest that the nobles and leading clergy had much in common in religious matters, the former having the leisure to learn holy texts and to practise observances which were part also of the professional equipment and obligations of the latter. Almost nothing is known of the middle classes – merchants and tradesmen and petty squires; but the poor figure occasionally in literature; and it is plain that their religious lives, though devout and instructed up to a point, were lived more simply. They, for instance, never apparently used the barsom, which kings and nobles held to be essential for some of the private acts of worship which they performed. It was emphasized, however, that the merit of their devotional acts might nevertheless be as great, if not greater. Thus the story is told (Rivayats, Dhabhar, 325) of how Khosrow Anoshiravan celebrated the sixth gahambar one year most magnificently, inviting all his subjects, high and low, to his feast; but it was shown him in a dream that even more merit had accrued to a poor man who, unable to attend his banquet, had sold a leaf of his house-door to acquire the means, and had then 'celebrated the gahambar as best he could', depriving himself (as the king had not needed to do) in order to honour God.

One religious observance which was practised by all, with varying degrees of elaboration, was the distinctive one of 'taking the vaj'. 'Vaj' (Persian 'baj') simply means 'word' or 'utterance', and the practice involved saying Avestan manthras before engaging in a variety of daily activities, such as eating, sleeping and bathing, as well as before various religious rites. The vaj would then be 'held' by performing the action in silence, after which it would be 'given up' with the recital of another manthra. The purpose was to surround the action with a secure shield of holy words, whose efficacy would have been broken by the interruption of ordinary speech. The action concerned might be almost sacramental (like eating and drinking), or one which put the doer at risk from the evil powers. The self-discipline required for 'holding the vaj' was severe, but there is abundant evidence that the observance was rigorously carried out by kings as well as commoners, and even in the direst circumstances – in flight for life, or with assassins lurking. As a Zoroastrian explained to a Byzantine emperor, unless one of the faithful had 'taken the vaj', he would not be willing to drink a drop of water, even if tormented by thirst (Shahname, Warner, IX, 34), and when a Byzantine prince once tried to trick Khosrow II into compromising his religion, that king is represented as crying out: 'God forbid that I should abandon the faith of my fathers, chosen and pure lords of the earth, and go over to the faith of Christ – not take the vaj while eating, and become a Christian!' (ibid. VIII, 310).

The purity laws were also generally observed, it is evident, by high and low, although only scraps of evidence (outside the Pahlavi literature itself) come down to us. We have seen how Vahram V entrusted his Indian bride to the high priest of Adur Gushnasp, so that she might undergo purification (including undoubtedly the barashnom) before entering his household. The Sasanians had many foreign women among their queens and concubines, including Jews, Christians and pagan Turks; and though there seems to have been no objection to these women practising their own faiths, they must all have had, like the Hindu princess, to accept and keep the Zoroastrian purity laws, to avoid diminishing the King's own purity. The Christians commented that in the 'religion of the magi' the greatest weight was laid on this, that during their periods women should keep apart, and not even look on fire or candle; and when the sister-wife of Mihram-Gushnasp embraced Christianity in her turn, she signalized her rejection of her ancestral faith by picking up a brazier of fire while in her monthly courses, flinging it to the ground, and trampling the embers underfoot – a double and deadly sin for a Zoroastrian (Braun, 99).

The reasons for this lady's conversion were neither intellectual nor spiritual. She happened to fall ill, offered libations and prayers in vain to the yazads, decided to fast like a Christian, and was both cured and converted. Mihram-Gushnasp himself was a Christian by conviction, however, and proved an energetic and hard-hitting opponent of his old faith. The following purports to be a record of a discussion between him and a magus (Braun, 109). The magus declared: 'We in no way hold fire to be God, but only pray to God through fire, as you do through the cross.' Mihram-Gushnasp: 'But we do not say, as you do to the fire, "We pray to you, Cross, God." ' Magus: 'That is not so.' The well-trained Mihram-Gushnasp then cited texts, saying 'So you have it in your Avesta that it is a god.' The magus, driven into a corner, abandoned his first position and said: 'We reverence fire because it is of the same nature as Ohrmazd.' M.-G. 'Does Ohrmazd have everything which fire has?' M. 'Yes.' M.-G. 'Fire consumes dung and horse-droppings and in brief whatever comes to it. Since Ohrmazd is of the same nature, does he also consume everything like it?' And he asked further: 'Why do you not worship the fire while it remains hidden in stones, wood and other things? First you bring it out and then you pray to it. Meanwhile you have first made it worthy to be worshipped, and without you it is not so. Yet all that makes no difference; for it cannot distinguish between the magus who makes it offerings, and a man who does not venerate it, but burns for both alike indifferently.' The magus is represented as silenced by this attack; but temporal power was on his side, and in the end Mihram-Gushnasp was put to death by order of the king.

For the faithful themselves the Zoroastrian church, supported by the crown, governed almost all aspects of their lives; and the fact that the clergy both interpreted and administered the law gave them enormous influence. Some cases are recorded in the law-book, the Madigan i Hazar Dadestan, which suggest an unscrupulous use of their powers at the expense of the laity. In one (MHD, ed. Modi, 31) a man had left all his property to his wife and children, but subsequently – persuaded, perhaps, on his death-bed by a zealous priest – made another will, leaving everything instead to endowing a sacred fire, so that his family would only enjoy, as its trustees, the residual income. He died, however, before he could sign this second will, and the wife and children inherited. Some person or body, possibly the Divan i Kirdagan (the Sasanian ministry concerned with pious foundations) took the matter to court, however, and the judgment was given that 'Since the maintenance of the sacred fire is essential, the property should be taken back from the wife and children, and given to the sacred fire. . . . (Although the will) is not sealed, the judgment is not in fact against it.' Although there is no reason to suppose that the priest-lawyers of Sasanian Persia did not strive to be just and fair, a case like this illustrates the difficulty which the laity must sometimes have felt of getting an objective hearing in an ecclesiastical court, where instinct would be to give preference to the sacred over the profane.

The sacred fire in this lawsuit was an Adurog, a 'Little Fire', which could be maintained with comparatively small expense; But major fires, the Atash i Vahram, not only needed much attendance, but were great devourers of fuel, for they were kept blazing brightly throughout the twenty-fours hours. In a Jewish text of the period a rabbi is reproached by a co-religionist for having sold a forest which he owned to a fire temple; and there is no doubt that by the end of the Sasanian period the ancient state religion, with its many major shrines, its elaborate rites and observances, its chantry-endowments and demands for sacrifices and offerings, had become in this and other ways a mighty consumer of the wealth of the land.

The last years of Zoroastrian Iran

Sasanian Persia was still enormously rich, however, despite exhausting wars. Khosrow Anoshiravan himself spent many years under arms, and though he achieved peace on other frontiers, making an end at last of the Hephthalite troubles, he died in the field against the Byzantines. His son Hormizd IV (579–90) is said to have been an even juster ruler than his father, and he showed a broad tolerance to his infidel subjects. The following is from a letter said to have been written by him to the Zoroastrian priests, when they urged him to persecute the Christians: 'Even as our royal throne cannot stand upon its two front legs without the back ones, so also our government cannot stand and be secure, if we incense the Christians and the adherents of other religions, who are not of our faith. Cease therefore to harass the Christians, but exert yourselves diligently in doing good works, so that the Christians and the adherents of other religions, seeing that, may praise you for it and feel themselves drawn to our religion' (Nöldeke, 268). For all his equity, however, Hormizd angered one of his most powerful generals, Vahram Choben, of the great Parthian family of Mihran. Vahram rebelled successfully, and Hormizd was put to death. Another faction set Hormizd's son Khosrow II on the throne; but the house of Mihran claimed Arsacid descent, and on this score Vahram asserted his own hereditary right to rule. (This development, in the last half-century of Sasanian power, shows how sturdy a resistance Iran had put up to Persian propaganda about the 'illegitimacy' of the Arsacids.) Vahram received considerable support, and a year's fighting ensued before Khosrow, with the support of the Byzantine Emperor Maurice, was able to defeat him and secure the throne. His reign, from 591 to 628, was the last long, stable one of the dynasty, and was distinguished by great splendour and luxury, with lavish benefactions to the faith. The means for these were partly secured by a long succession of successful wars against Byzantium (engaged on by Khosrow after the assassination of his friend Maurice in 602), which also earned the king his by-name of Parvez, the 'Victorious'.

In a grotto at Taq-i Bustan, near Kermanshah, Khosrow II had made the last Sasanian carving of an investiture scene. He is again shown receiving the diadem of sovereignty from Ohrmazd, and behind him stands Anahid, to the end the patron yazad of the dynasty, symbolically pouring the waters of the world out from a little jug. Khosrow was famed for his piety and his zeal in founding sacred fires, and he also (it was later said) appointed 12,000 priests to pray at fire temples throughout his realm. A number of his other acts of piety are recorded in the Shahname; and he is known to have been devoted to Adur Gushnasp, carrying (it seems) embers from that sacred fire as a palladium before his victorious army. In the year 623 he spent many days in prayer at its shrine; but even while he did so, fortune turned against him. The Emperor Heraclius invaded Iran and in the course of a devastating campaign seized and sacked the temple of Adur Gushnasp itself. The priests had evidently managed to carry off the sacred fire to safety, but the invaders gutted its sanctuary, and filled the lake there with the corpses of all that moved and breathed upon the hill — men, women, children and animals.

Iran rallied, and the shrine of Adur Gushnasp was restored; and it was probably then that a massive stone wall was built round the very rim of its hill, fifty feet high and ten feet thick, with thirty-eight towers along it, strung out within bowshot of one another, for the better protection of the re-enthroned fire. The cost must have been enormous; and the crumbling remains still testify today to the wealth and power of the Zoroastrian church in the seventh century, and the devotion to it of the last great Sasanian king.

Khosrow died in 628, the victim of a revolt by his own generals; and the Shahname (Warner, IX, 34) tells how the King, divining that the hour of his assassination was at hand, bathed, put on fresh garments, 'took the vaj', and uttered a formal confession, so that he met his death clean in body and in a state of spiritual grace. His favourite wife, Shirin, a Christian, is said to have disposed of all her wealth for his soul's sake, with rich donations to the fire temples (ibid. 40). Khosrow was succeeded by his son Kavad II, who ruled a bare six months; and thereafter one short reign followed another with claimant and counter-claimant, murders, assassinations and internal strife. Two princesses were among those who briefly occupied the throne; and in 632 the crown was set on the head of a young prince, Yazdegird III. His reign began promisingly, but was to see the greatest of all disasters for Zoroastrianism, the Arab conquest of Iran.

Conclusion

Much has been written by Western scholars about the supposed aridity of Zoroastrianism at this time, and the impression is often given that by the seventh century this ancient faith had become so mummified by ritual and formality that it needed only the thrust of a conquering sword to crumble into nothingness. Such interpretations owe much, however, to preconceptions engendered by the ultimate victory of Islam; and similar analyses of medieval Christianity would undoubtedly have been offered if Saracen and Turk had succeeded in subduing Europe. In general the testimony of native and foreign sources shows Zoroastrianism at this epoch to have been the strong religion of a mighty state, able to command the allegiance of both rich and poor, and providing its adherents, in direct and vivid terms, with a purpose in life and clear prescriptions for achieving it. Its teachings gave hope and strength; and it offered not only rules for conduct, but also a full devotional life, which included many joyous observances to temper the strictness of its demands for discipline. It was a life-enhancing, not a world-denying faith. True, it suffered under the burden of its immense age, which meant a heritage of archaic doctrine and usages that set its scholars and theologians grave intellectual problems; but these would hardly have affected the mass of the faithful, who are more likely to have been troubled, if at all, by priestly exactions. Undoubtedly by the end of the Sasanian epoch Iran was priest-ridden, like Europe before the reformation; and every man, whether rich or poor, could be subjected to pressures to pay for religious services, purification rites and penitentiary observances, all designed to help save his soul. The subsequent history of the faith shows that many of the laity accepted such dues and obligations as a part of their share in fighting the good fight; but there must have been others who, encountering greedy or unscrupulous priests, longed, like numbers of medieval Christians, to get the clergy off their backs. After the many ecclesiastical and ritual developments of the period Zoroastrianism was ripe for reform, and a return to the simpler usages of earlier days, when each man's hope of salvation lay more measurably within his own grasp; but what in fact sprang up for the faith was not the reviving breeze of reformation, to give new life and strength, but instead the withering tempest of militant Islam.

CHAPTER TEN

Under the Caliphs

The Arab conquest of Iran

Even before Yazdegird III was set upon the throne, the Muslim Arabs, driven by poverty and religious fervour, had begun to attack the rich lands bordering their deserts. In 636 they overran the Byzantine province of Syria, and soon afterwards crossed into Mesopotamia and met the Iranian imperial army at Qadisiya. A bitter battle was fought with wavering fortunes for several days, but in the end the Arabs were the victors, and could seize the fabled Sasanian capital at Ctesiphon. Two more hard-fought battles opened the way for them up onto the Iranian plateau, and shattered imperial resistance. Yazdegird fled from place to place before the slow advance, over years, of the Arab forces, while meantime individual provinces and cities fought, were conquered, rose again, were once more savagely subdued, and finally capitulated. By the time Yazdegird met his death in Merv, in the far north-east, in 652, the Arabs were masters of most of Iran, though there was fighting in remoter areas until the beginning of the eighth century.

This conquest, utterly different from that of Alexander, was carried out in the spirit of Surah 9.29 of the Quran: 'Fight those who believe not in God and the Last Day and do not forbid what Allah and his Messenger have forbidden – such men as practise not the religion of truth, being people of the book – until they pay tribute out of hand and have been humbled.' It was not, that is, undertaken so much to convert the unbeliever as to subject him, and so extend the sphere of Islam's might. By 'people of the book' also called 'people of the covenant' or 'dhimmis', Muhammad is thought to have meant Jews, Christians and Sabians, who had adherents among the Arabs. To them the Muslim armies presented three choices – death, Islam, or the payment of tribute. To other infidels, in theory, only two were offered – death or Islam; but because of sheer numbers, the conquered Zoroastrians had to be treated as dhimmis (despite doubts that persisted down the centuries). So in the main, once the conquest was over, with its slaughter, enslavement, looting and destruction, local terms were agreed on, as in the following treaty: '500,000 dirhams were given [the Arab commander] on account of the people of Ray and Qumis on condition that he should not kill nor enslave any of them, nor raze any of their fire temples, and that they should be the same in regard to their tax as the people of Nihavand' (Baladhuri, II. 4). The Arabs took over the Sasanian tax-system, with its land-tax and poll-tax (called by them 'jizya'); and it was the latter which was made the special tax on unbelievers, and the means of duly humbling them. 'In a guide to the duties of a civil servant, the following instructions for the collection of poll-tax are given. . . . The dhimmi . . . has to stand while paying and the officer who receives it sits. The dhimmi has to be made to feel that he is an inferior person when he pays. . . . He goes on a fixed day in person to the emir appointed to receive the poll-tax. He sits on a high throne. The dhimmi appears before him, offering the poll-tax on his open palm. The emir takes it so that his hand is on top and the dhimmi's below. Then the emir gives him a blow on the neck, and one who stands before the emir drives him roughly away . . . The public is admitted to see this show' (Tritton, 227).

A number of laws and restrictions governing the lives of dhimmis were gradually evolved to emphasize their wholly inferior status; but under the early orthodox caliphs, if they paid their taxes and conformed to these laws, they were sometimes left very largely to themselves. Thus Abu Bakr enjoined: 'if a province or people receive you, make an agreement with them and keep your promise. Let them be governed by their laws and established customs, and take tribute from them as is agreed between you. Leave them in their religion and their land' (Tritton, op. cit. 137). The jurists said further that since only a Muslim could be perfectly moral, unbelievers might as well be left to their iniquities, so long as these did not vex their overlords.

Each subject community was required to choose its own representatives, with whom Muslim officials could deal; and in a huge country like Iran there must have been many such local leaders. As far as the Zoroastrians as a whole were concerned, however, it seems that the Sasanians had done their work well, and that the system of one supreme head residing in Pars survived the conquest. Thus under later caliphs the title is attested of Hudinan peshobay 'Leader of those of the Good Religion' – to the Arabs presumably simply the 'Leader of the majus' or (more contemptuously) 'the gabragan'. ('Gabr', meaning probably 'infidel', was a word which in Iran came to be applied especially to Zoroastrians.)

Inducements and barriers to conversion

Many Zoroastrians, though subjected and harassed, were thus able, once the horrors of conquest were over, to continue in their former ways; but events had already weighted the odds in the encounter of their ancient religion with Islam. Power and worldly advantage lay now with the victorious worshippers of Allah, and there was evidently a steady stream of converts, some willing, some enforced, to the new faith – for though the official policy was one of aloof contempt, there were individual Muslims eager to proselytize, and ready to use all sorts of means to do so. Thus after the conquest of Bukhara, it is recorded, the Arab commander, Qutaiba, thrice converted its citizens to Islam 'but they (repeatedly) apostatized and became infidels. The fourth time he made war he seized the city and established Islam there after much difficulty. He instilled Islam in their hearts and made (their religion) difficult for them in every way. . . . Qutaiba thought it proper to order the people of Bukhara to give one-half of their homes to the Arabs so that the Arabs might be with them and informed of their sentiments. Then they would be obliged to be Muslims. . . . He built mosques and eradicated traces of unbelief and the precepts of the fire-worshippers. He built a grand mosque, and ordered the people to perform the Friday prayer there. . . . That place had been a temple. . . . He had it proclaimed: "Whosoever is present at the Friday prayer, I shall give him two dirhams" ' (Narshakhi, 10–11). The cities, where Arab governors took up their quarters, were especially vulnerable to such pressures, and one by one the great urban fire temples were turned into mosques, and the citizens were forced to conform or flee.

One common inducement to convert was to give his freedom to a slave who became Muslim (and many Persians had been enslaved by the Arabs). The humiliations of the poll-tax drove others to renounce the old faith – to the indignation sometimes of tax-gatherers. 'I have learned' (one Arab governor wrote to a local official) 'that the people of Sogdia . . . have not become Muslims sincerely. They have accepted Islam only to escape the poll-tax. Investigate this matter and discover who is circumcised, performs the required acts of devotion, is sincere in his conversion to Islam, and can read a verse of the Quran. Relieve that man of his tax.' As a result of this inquiry, it is said, 7000 Sogdians abandoned their superficial profession of Islam (Dennett, 120–1). Once a man was nominally a Muslim to recant could be dangerous, however, for the lawyers were agreed that death was the penalty for apostasy from Islam. A case put to a Hudinan peshobay in the ninth century begins: 'A man who has put off the kusti repents within a year. But he cannot tie the kusti again for fear of his life. . .'. (Rivayat of Adurfarnbag, LII). The kusti was the obvious outward sign of adherence to the old faith; and Tabari records that Arab tax-collectors in the eighth century would mistreat Zoroastrians, tearing off the sacred girdle and hanging it round their necks in derision.

Though many conversions were reluctant, or dictated by self-interest, yet the children of such converts grew up within Islam, trained from infancy to say Arabic instead of Avestan prayers; and each generation saw an increase in the number of Iranians who knew no other faith. Among the converts there were moreover some who became in their turn ardent proselytizers, either to obtain the comfortable support of greater numbers, or out of true missionary zeal; for not all who adopted Islam did so for worldly motives, or under coercion. A number were convinced that the success of Muslim arms proved the truth of Muslim doctrine; and yet others must have been persuaded by the preaching of religiously-minded Arabs. The doctrines of early Islam were attractively simple; and some of the most important – such as belief in Heaven and Hell, the end of the world and the Day of Judgment – derived ultimately from Zoroastrianism, and so were disarmingly familiar, as were certain Muslim practices: the five times of daily prayer (also adopted from Zoroastrianism), the rejection of images, and the injunction to give alms. And all this went with a devotional life of striking simplicity, which needed no priests. By accepting Islam a Zoroastrian freed himself at a stroke from the many rites and obligations which bound him to his own priests from cradle to grave; and for a thinking man there was the further attraction that as a new religion Islam had yet to create its own hard shell of scholastic dogmatism, and so laid few constraints on independent thought. Women too, though in the long run losers under Islam, experienced an immediate benefit on conversion through freedom from those laws of purity which pressed so heavily on them in their daily lives.

Yet there was much too to hold the Iranians back from the Semitic faith. At the simplest level there was usage, familiarity, loyalty to the religion of their ancestors, which in essential doctrines and their moral consequences yielded nothing in nobility to the new creed. Islam was alien, imposed by harsh conquerors, with scriptures in a foreign tongue; and it brought customs strange to the Iranians: circumcision, arbitrary rules about clean and unclean meats, abstention from wine, veneration of a distant sacred stone, the Ka'ba. At a deeper level conversion meant change from a dualistic faith, with veneration of a wise Being whose actions were held to be wholly just and accessible to reason, to one which demanded submission to an inscrutable, all-powerful God, whose decrees and purposes were regarded as beyond man's understanding. This radical difference in theology is expressed by the different ways of praying, with the Zoroastrian standing erect in the presence of his beneficent Lord, the Muslim kneeling before the Omnipotent, his forehead in the dust. Doctrinally Zoroastrianism, with its explanation for the woes of the world, and its solid basis for belief in the individual and last judgments, had its great strengths, and its learned priests were able to confront Muslims with the same firmness with which they had earlier met proselytizing Christians; but now it was Islam which was supported by the secular power, and which could end argument with sudden death.

Even for the humblest Zoroastrian, to whom familiar rituals would have meant more than theology, there was much to lose in relinquishing the ancient faith. The many kindly yazads to whom he had turned for help had to be renounced and their shrines neglected; and instead of the celebration of their holy days, with many joyful observances, there were Friday prayers and sermons at the mosque, confronting a stone 'qibla' instead of a bright leaping flame. It is not surprising, therefore, that Iran remained predominantly Zoroastrian under the four orthodox caliphs (632–61). Thereafter rule of the Muslim world was seized by the Umayyads (661–750), who made their capital in Syria. Their epoch has been called one of Arab imperialism, and there was little serious pressure then on the subject peoples to adopt Islam, except in the brief reign of the devout ʿUmar II (717–20). However, one striking instance of oppression is recorded during their epoch by an Arab governor of Iraq, who appointed a commissioner to supervise the destruction of fire temples throughout Iran, regardless of treaty obligations. The commissioner, acting on instructions, left unharmed all those sacred fires whose congregations could buy him off with a sufficient sum: and thus he is said to have extorted forty million dirhams, a testimony to the number of fire temples still standing, and the devotion of those who worshipped in them.

Islam takes root in Iran

An unpremeditated blow to the old faith was struck under the Umayyads when in the government ministries the use of Middle Persian, written in Pahlavi script, was abandoned for Arabic in Arabic script. The change, imposed about 700, emphasized the permanence of the Arab presence in the land, and enforced a widespread knowledge of Arabic, the holy tongue of Islam; and as its use spread, this created a further barrier between Iranian Muslims, who learned their sacred language willingly, and Zoroastrians, who abhorred all things Islamic. Soon Arabic became the language of polite letters also, and a number of Middle Persian works were rendered into it. The most famous labourer in this field was Rozbeh son of Dadoy, nicknamed the 'Mutilated' (al-Muqaffaʿ), an unenthusiastic convert to Islam, who worked in the government tax-office at Basra. One of the books which he translated into elegant Arabic was the great Sasanian chronicle, the 'Khwaday Namag', which Muslim historians then used, selectively, as a basis for constructing their own accounts of world history. The ancient myths and heroic traditions preserved by Zoroastrian priests were thereby divested of their religious associations, so that noble Iranian families, turned Muslim, could still claim descent from figures in their country's annals without making their attachment to the new faith suspect. Thus another defence of Zoroastrianism – the uniqueness of its links with Iran's glorious past – was undermined.

A further blow came when Iranian Muslims succeeded in shaping a tradition which made Islam appear as a partly Iranian religion (which indeed by remote origin it is), so that national pride was disarmed. One element in this was the historical figure of Salman al-Farisi, the Persian who, having abandoned Zoroastrianism for Christianity, eventually attached himself to Muhammad and became a member of his household. The extent of his influence could be made much of by Iranian Muslims. The other main element was the legend that Husayn, son of ʿAli (the fourth orthodox caliph) and grandson of Muhammad by his daughter Fatima, had married a captive Sasanian princess called Shahrbanu, the 'Lady of the Land'. This wholly fictitious figure, whose name appears to derive from a cult-epithet of Ardvisur Anahid, was held to have borne Husayn a son, the historical fourth Shiʿa Imam; for the Shiʿa or 'Party' of ʿAli claimed that the caliphate belonged rightly to him and his descendants, and had been unlawfully wrested from them by the Umayyads. Many Iranian converts espoused the Shiʿite cause, which enabled them to oppose the Umayyads with their harsh exactions and narrow Arab nationalism, and to uphold the claims of the heirs, through the princess Shahrbanu, of the Sasanian royal house; and so it was no longer the Zoroastrians alone who stood for patriotism and loyalty to the past.

The Shiʿite movement grew steadily through the eighth century, fostered by propagandists for the house of ʿAbbas, rivals of the Umayyads; and in the end there was open rebellion, which led to an ʿAbbasid victory in 750. The new caliphs, having relied largely on Iranian supporters, showed marked favour to Iranians in their regime; and at their capital in Baghdad they revived the traditions of the Sasanian court and reigned in royal splendour, their dynasty lasting, nominally at least, until 1258. Persians occupied many posts in the new government; and with the gates of worldly advancement now opened wide to Iranian Muslims, the disadvantages of remaining a Zoroastrian became ever more apparent. Moreover, as antagonism between Arab and non-Arab disappeared, so that between Muslim and non-Muslim grew sharper. (Nevertheless the early idiom persists for centuries in the Zoroastrian books, that to adopt Islam was 'to become a non-Iranian(anēr)', a damning indictment.)

The ʿAbbasids not only revived the magnificence of the Sasanian court, but imitated Sasanian authoritarianism in religious matters. (In this and associated developments one can only guess at the part played by Zoroastrian priests turned Muslim.) They began their rule by persecuting heretics; and though their zeal was naturally directed against Muslim sectarians rather than the despised dhimmis, a harsher climate was created for the unbeliever also. Yet the Zoroastrians were still numerous enough for the Hudinan peshobay to be a figure of dignity and some consequence; and later in the epoch we find one holder of this office taking part in a religious debate at the Caliph's court. This was during the reign of the latitudinarian al-Ma'mun, who earned himself the ironic title of 'Commander of the Unfaithful'. Yet even he actively encouraged the general spread of Islam, ordering his commanders in Khorasan, for instance, to make raids beyond their borders on those people who had not yet accepted the faith. Because of their harshness towards unbelievers, and their lavish patronage of Persian Muslims, the 'Abbasids proved deadly foes of Zoroastrianism, and it was during their epoch that Islam took root and came to flourish everywhere in Iranian soil. In the process it grew steadily more Zoroastrianized, with adaptations of funerary rites and purity laws, and a cult of saints springing up in place of the veneration of yazads. The Shi'i also found a figure to replace, in their hopes and longings, that of the Saoshyant. Bitterly disillusioned by the failure of the 'Abbasids to restore the caliphate to the descendants of 'Ali, they continued to regard the latter as the true imams or leaders, attributing to them by virtue of their lineage an especial divine grace, like the royal Khvarenah. Of the nine imams descended from Husayn (supposedly through Shahrbanu), eight died violent deaths; but the last was held to have disappeared miraculously, in 878. He is the 'hidden', or 'expected' imam, who will, like the Saoshyant, appear at the end of time, restore the faith, and fill the earth with justice. All such developments and adaptations built bridges for apostasy, making it easier for Iranians to embrace the Semitic faith.

Zoroastrians in ninth-century Iran

Yet in the ninth century – some seven generations after the conquest -- Zoroastrians still formed a substantial minority of the population, and a certain amount was written about them then by Muslims, chiefly 'Abbasid officials. So Abu Zaid al-Balkhi recorded of the province of Fars (ancient Pars): 'The Zoroastrians have preserved the books, the fire temples and the customs of the era of their kings, thanks to an uninterrupted succession; they retain their ancient usages and conform to them in their religion. There is no country where the Zoroastrians are more numerous than in Fars, because that country is the centre of their power, rites and religious books' (Nyberg, 9). Neighbouring Kerman, to the east, first became predominantly Muslim under the Saffarids (869–903), and in the late tenth century there were still many Zoroastrians in the province of Jibal. Further north in the mountains of Tabaristan (where Gushnasp had once held out against Ardashir) a local dynasty upheld the old faith down to the mid ninth century, when the prince Mazyar led a rebellion in a last desperate attempt to restore it and the ancient ways. This was crushed, and in 854 another prince of Tabaristan finally yielded to the Caliph's summons to 'break his Zoroastrian girdle and embrace Islam' (Ibn Isfandiyar, 157).

At that time there were still imposing fire temples to be seen, in which the sacred fires continued to burn. In the north-west Adur Gushnasp was tended in its hill-top sanctuary down to at least the middle of the tenth century; and in the south-east, the sacred fire of Karkoy was maintained until the thirteenth century. The geographer Qazwini has left a description of its temple then with its twin domes, bearing horns like those of a great bull; and he wrote of the many servitors of the ever-burning fire, which was fed reverently with dry tamarisk wood by its priests, who used silver tongs for the purpose, their mouths being covered.

There are also Zoroastrian sources for the history of the community in the ninth century, for much of the surviving Pahlavi literature consists of works which were composed or re-edited at that time – the last century under Islamic rule when the Zoroastrians still had the means and energy to engage in creative work on any scale. The Hudinan peshobays were themselves leaders in this activity, so that it is possible to identify from their writings the members of a family who held this office for over a hundred and fifty years. The first one known is Adurfarnbag Farrokhzadan, a pious and distinguished man who lived at the time of Ma'mun (813–33), and ably defended the Zoroastrian faith in debate at his court. He was succeeded by his second son Zardusht, who is suspected of having brought sorrow to the community by apostatizing in the reign of Mutawakkil (847–61), and becoming one of the intimates of that caliph. If this is so, his son Vahramshad remained unshaken, for he is twice cited as an authority in matters of Zoroastrian law; and the office of Hudinan peshobay passed to his son Goshnjam. Goshnjam himself had four distinguished sons, one of whom, Manushchihr (fl. c. 881) succeeded him in office.

Three letters survive written by Manushchihr (unfortunately in a difficult, involved style), and also a book, the 'Dadestan i dinig', or 'Religious Judgments', which deals with questions put to him by laymen on points of faith and practice. This sheds some light on the difficulties and struggles of the community in his time. Thus Manushchihr is asked why so much evil should have come upon the faithful, so that it is the good who suffer; how grievous is the sin of those who desert the Mazda-worshipping religion for 'foreignness and evil religion'; and whether it is permissible to buy and sell with 'non-Iranian' infidels. The increasing poverty of the community is evident, and the difficulties of finding enough fully-trained priests, and recompensing them adequately. Manushchihr instructs, adjudicates, and exhorts the faithful to hold firmly by the laws of the religion as expounded by the authorities of old. He felt deeply that Zoroastrianism could only survive and fulfil its mission as the bearer of God's revelation if it strictly maintained its traditions and avoided any changes or accommodations; and this appears very clearly in his letters, which were occasioned by his younger brother Zadspram seeking to shorten the barashnom purification. Manushchihr's basic and uncompromising objection to this innovation was that it lacked authority and that the cleansing thus administered was therefore invalid. He was also shocked by Zadspram's presumption in introducing such a change on his own initiative. Nothing, he insisted, could be altered in the rituals of the faith without the approval not only of himself but also of other leading Zoroastrians of the time. There must be consultation and agreement between 'the priests who are the leaders and heads of the community . . . members of the assemblies of the different provinces' (Ep Man I. iv. 12, 14) – a striking indication of how the Zoroastrians still held together. The different regional communities clearly looked, however, for leadership to the Persian high priest; and Manushchihr exerted himself courageously for them, striving to ward off 'penalties and disasters', and to prevent the unlawful seizure of fire temples for conversion into mosques – a process which was evidently continuing remorselessly.

Zadspram's deviation from tradition appears limited to this single act. He was a diligent scholar, and his one work to survive shows him in the main thoroughly conservative. This is his 'Selections' (Wizidagiha), culled mostly from the Zand, and dealing with four subjects: cosmogony and cosmology; the life of Zoroaster; the physiology and psychology of men; and eschatology. In making his excerpts he tended to draw on those parts of his sources where Greek science had been adduced, and attempts made to reconcile this with Zoroastrian scholastic tradition. This distinguishes his cosmographic section from the corresponding part of the Bundahishn, the lengthy compilation from the Zand which was re-edited and enlarged by Zadspram's nephew, Farnbag Ashavahisht. Comparison of both these works with ninth-century writings by Muslim geographers shows how the heritage of ancient myth and learning trammelled Zoroastrian scholarship.

Most other surviving books of the ninth century are mainly practical (concerned with ritual, the purity code, law or daily observances), or attempt some response to the troubles and problems of the time. So there are a number of short, popular works for the laity which embody simple statements of belief, or deal with such things as the symbolism of the kusti, or the efficacy and importance of various religious services; and again and again in these the priests admonish the faithful to say: 'I must be without doubt regarding . . .', trying to stiffen them against proselytizers. All these works were in Middle Persian (free from Arabic words), and in the difficult Pahlavi script; but if read aloud, they would have been easily understood by the laity.

Some of the laity themselves still wrote and read Pahlavi; and one of them, Mardanfarrokh, produced in the ninth century a carefully reasoned book in defence of the faith. In this, the 'Doubt-dispelling Exposition' (Shkand-gumanig Vizar) he explains that he set out to compare the teachings of Zoroastrianism with those of other faiths, and became convinced of the fundamental truth of Zoroaster's revelation, since this summons man to worship a Creator who cherishes all the seven creations he has brought into being. It is not he who enfeebles or inflicts suffering on them, a part which, it seemed to Mardanfarrokh, Jews, Christians and Muslims must ascribe to an omnipotent God. He rejected also the pessimistic dualism of Manichaeism, concluding that the tenets of Zoroastrianism were the only ones acceptable to just and rational men. Doctrinal arguments are also presented in the Dinkard or 'Acts of the Religion', the longest extant Pahlavi work. This great compilation (written unfortunately for the most part in a style as difficult as Manushchihr's) was begun by the first known Hudinan peshobay, Adurfarnbag Farrokhzadan, and was re-edited and enlarged by his descendant Adurbad Emedan, who probably held the same office at the end of the ninth century. It contains a great variety of matter, and includes at the end a summary of the contents of nineteen books of the Great Avesta, and a detailed analysis of three of them.

The Sasanian Avesta contained twenty-one books; but Adurbad states that by his day one of these had been wholly lost – that is, the Avesta and its Zand – while of another only the Avesta survived, of which he offers no summary. One can only speculate as to how such a loss came about; but the Persian copy of the Great Avesta was presumably kept in the library of some great religious foundation in Pars, most probably that of Adur-Anahid in royal Istakhr; and Istakhr had suffered dreadfully at the conquest, succumbing to the Arabs only after 'fierce fighting, casting with siege engines and killing therewith 40,000 of the Persians and wiping out most of the noble families together with the chiefs of chivalry who had taken refuge there' (Baladhuri, II, 389). The city thereafter was laid waste and deserted, and Mas'udi (Prairies d'Or, 1403), visiting it in the ninth century, described the ruins of its magnificent fire temple, with its great pillars, walls, and carvings. The sacred fire (he says) had been carried away by the Zoroastrians; and if they had also had to rescue their holy books, there is small wonder if these then suffered damage.

Among the twenty surviving books of the Avesta was the Vendidad; and a curious development now took place with regard to this work, which was that the reading of it in its entirety was made part of a night celebration of the yasna. This service was solemnized (notably after a death) in order to exorcize the powers of darkness; and adding to it the Avestan 'Law against demons' was presumably felt to be a strengthening of its efficacy. This is the only occasion when the use of a written text is permitted to a priest – all parts of every other service must be known by heart; and it seems possible that the practice was introduced to help substantiate the Zoroastrians' claim to be a 'people of the book', and so to be less mercilessly harried. This long night-office came to be known simply as a 'service of the Vendidad', or more briefly, a 'Vendidad'.

Zoroastrians in tenth-century Iran

What shows that this development was a late one, and initiated in Pars, is that when the founding fathers of the Parsi community (who came from Khorasan, that is, ancient Parthia) left Iran early in the tenth century, they do not seem to have taken a manuscript of the

Vendidad with them, and it was only later that they were supplied with copies from Iran. Our knowledge of the events which drove this small group of Zoroastrians to quit their native land, and seek freedom of worship elsewhere, is slight; but they seem to have made their resolve during the times, additionally hard for Zoroastrians, when local Iranian dynasties, all vigorously Muslim, were emerging as largely independent vassals of the Caliphs. Among them were the Samanids of Khorasan (874–999), who claimed descent from Vahram Choben. (Saman himself is said to have abandoned Zoroastrianism for Islam towards the end of the eighth century, at the persuasion of the ʿAbbasid governor of Khorasan.) It seems to have been under their rule that a band of Zoroastrians, originally from the little town of Sanjan in south-western Khorasan, despaired of finding peace or justice, and made their way south to the port of Hormuzd on the Persian Gulf, where eventually they secured a ship to take them overseas. According to Parsi tradition, the migrants – men, women and children – spent nineteen years on the island of Div before making their final landfall on the coast of Gujarat in 936 A.C.

There was to be sporadic contact down the centuries between these migrant 'Parsis' or Persians (as the Gujaratis, from long tradition, called anyone from Iran), and the Zoroastrians who held out in the mother country. Yet clearly most of what the two communities have in common stems from what was general usage for all Zoroastrians in Iran at the time when the Parsis left. Thus the religious vocabulary of both (with regard to ritual vessels, sacred precincts, etc.) shows an admixture of Arabic words, witness to the pervasive influence of Arabic on spoken Persian after two and a half centuries of domination. In both communities the word 'fereshte' or 'angel' is commonly substituted for 'yazad', the result no doubt of trying to counter Muslim accusations of polytheism. Both communities too have abandoned the simple term 'mog' for a priest, and call any priest in minor orders – qualified, that is, to perform the basic religious ceremonies – a 'herbad' (Parsi 'ervad'). The title 'mobad' is used for one who has proceeded to higher qualifications, while a high priest is called a 'dastur', that is, one with authority.

Both communities also erect stone-surfaced towers on which to expose their dead, which they call by the old word 'dakhma'. The first allusion to a structure of this kind comes in a letter written in about 830 by the Hudinan peshobay, Adurfarnbag Farrokhzadan, to the Zoroastrians of Samarkand, who had asked how they should act while a new dakhma was being built, the old one having been damaged. He answered 'Until a new dakhma has been completed, when a person dies, small stones should be arranged on the surface of the old dakhma, in a corner, and the body laid on them with (proper) rites' (Dhabhar, 104–5). The practice of erecting funerary towers was thus clearly widespread by that time, but was probably not older than the Islamic period, since there seems to have been no established tradition governing their use. Erecting a tower prevented corpses being seen and so avoided a possible vexation to Muslims (which had always to be an object for dhimmis); and at the same time a high building shielded the dead from risk of violation. The early towers in Iran and India were simple, solid structures, round, with a high parapet to screen the stone platform from view. There was no stairway, ladders being used for each funeral, to limit ease of access. In Iran some communities who lived near mountains simply enclosed a ridge of hill with a high, blank, mud-brick wall.

In the tenth century a wealthy Zoroastrian of Ray built a dakhma on a hill-top with much trouble and expense; but the day it was finished a Muslim official contrived to get up into it and cry the call to prayer from its walls, and this was made a pretext to annex the building (Siyasat Name, 172). The Muslims had no use for it, but 'gabr-baiting' was a popular sport, which was to go on down the centuries, and was indulged in by Caliphs and high officials as well as by the uneducated. Thus there was a noted Zoroastrian sanctuary in Khorasan where a huge cypress grew, planted, according to Parthian tradition, by Zoroaster himself; and this deeply venerated tree the Caliph Mutawakkil had felled in 861, despite desperate appeals by Zoroastrians, in order to obtain timber for a new palace he was building. But by the time the camel-caravans had wound their slow way with it to Iraq, Mutawakkil was dead, murdered by his own son – a fitting retribution in Zoroastrian eyes.

Another means of distressing Zoroastrians was to torment dogs. Primitive Islam knew nothing of the now pervasive Muslim hostility to the dog as an unclean animal, and this, it seems, was deliberately fostered in Iran because of the remarkable Zoroastrian respect for dogs. Probably maltreating a dog (like discarding the kusti, or spitting in a fire) was a distinctive outward sign of true conversion; and the amount of suffering since inflicted on these animals by Muslims down the centuries is a sad instance of the cruelty that religious rivalry can bring about.

By the tenth century the composing of Middle Persian works, written in the Pahlavi script, had virtually ceased; and after that date the Zoroastrians wrote in the contemporary vernacular, that is New Persian, with its admixture of Arabic, and used the Arabic script. These later works are in the main derivative (consisting of re-statements of instructive or devotional matter), for with the remorseless erosion of its numbers the community was losing resources of both wealth and intellect. (The harsh decree had by then been enacted that if one member of a Zoroastrian family turned Muslim, he inherited all its property, to the exclusion of his brethren.) Yet the Zoroastrians enjoyed a last brief period of relative tranquillity when the Buyids established control over much of Iran. This Iranian dynasty claimed descent from the Sasanian Vahram V, and had some kindness for the old religion. The Buyid ʿAdad ad-Dawla is said at one time to have had a magus as his secretary, and an Arabic inscription, cut in the stones of Persepolis, tells how in 955 this ruler visited the ruins there and caused Marasfand, mobad of Kazerun in Fars, to read him the Pahlavi inscriptions. Kazerun was then still strongly Zoroastrian, and in the early eleventh century it even had a Zoroastrian governor, named Khorshed. There was never any abiding security for Zoroastrians under Islam, however, and in 979 there was fighting in Shiraz between Muslims and the magians, 'in which many of the latter were killed and their houses burnt' (Tritton, 131).

It was in the tenth century that an Iranian noble in Khorasan (probably, from the names in his genealogy, the great-grandson of a Zoroastrian) brought together four learned Zoroastrian priests to transcribe a version of the 'Khwaday Namag' out of Pahlavi into Arabic script, a task which they completed in 957. This transcribed text was to become the basis for Firdausi's 'Shahname', which gained enormous popularity and made the old heroic traditions live for Zoroastrian and Muslim alike. As a result, Sasanian propaganda finally gained currency throughout the Zoroastrian community, so that the Parsis (whose ancestors came from what had been ancient Parthia) learnt to think like the Iranis (who are mainly of Persian stock) that the Arsacids had usurped the kingship and neglected the faith, which owed its survival to the 'legitimate' and 'orthodox' Sasanians.

It was during the time of respite under the Buyids that the community found energy to deal with calendar matters again. The religious No Ruz was still being celebrated on the first of Adur; but the intercalation of a month to keep that date at the spring equinox, which should have been carried out under Khosrow Parvez, had been neglected during the wars and upheavals of his reign, and Adur had accordingly receded steadily, to become by the tenth century a winter month. This recession meant that in 1006 the first day of Farvardin actually coincided once more with the spring equinox; and so in that year the religious No Ruz was celebrated again on that date, with the five 'Gatha' days being shifted back to stand at the end of Spendarmad month, and all the gahambars moving accordingly. The Parsis made the same change, having, it seems, contact at the time by land with the Zoroastrians in Seistan. For the Irani community, this was the last calendar change to be made until the twentieth century.

A little earlier, a formidable Muslim scholar of the tenth century, the Persian ʿAbd al-Jabbar (chief judge at the Buyid capital of Ray) had thought it desirable to devote a part of his energies to attacking the old faith; and though in doing so he alluded briefly to orthodox Zoroastrian thought, he directed his main polemic against the Zurvanites, who with their weak theology presented the easier target – for if, as he says (Monnot, 267) it is admissible to say that God (i.e. Zurvan) created him who is the principle of all evil (i.e. Ahriman), why is it not admissible to say that God, as the omnipotent author of all, created evil directly? – this being his own stand as a Muslim. The position of Zurvanism in the post-conquest years is in general perplexing. There is not a trace of this heresy in the writings of Manushchihr or his brother Zadspram, and indeed it needs special pleading to identify it in the works of any of their family; and this suggests that the leadership of the community was taken over by Persian prelates who rejected the heresy upheld by the Sasanian kings and high priests. The layman Mardanfarrokh also wholly ignores Zurvanism. Yet Zurvanite theology is vigorously propounded in the 'Kitab-i Ulama-i Islam', the 'Book of the Muslim scholars'. This treatise, written in New Persian, was composed, it seems, early in the twelfth century; and it represents an exposition, in fairly abstruse and speculative terms, of Zoroastrian doctrine for the benefit of certain learned Muslims by the Mobadan mobad of the day. There are two versions of the work, and in both Time, called Zaman, is represented as the original principle by which 'both Ormazd and Ahriman have been produced' (Dhabhar, 452). Yet the Mobadan mobad admits that there were many different opinions among Zoroastrians themselves on this matter; and presumably in the harsh centuries that lay ahead such speculative theology was abandoned, and the community clung again, in unity, to the fundamental, orthodox doctrine of the utter separation of good and evil. Zurvanism seems to have been unknown among the Parsis (as one might expect from their origins in the Parthian north-east); and it is barely alluded to in later Irani writings, though one Persian priest attempted to end the matter for good with the following definition: 'Zoroaster asked Ohrmazd: "When the world was created, what (already) existed?" Ohrmazd said: "At that time, I existed and the Ahunvar". The Ahunvar has been called Zurvan' (Dhabhar, 438).

Turkish and Mongol invasions of Iran

The Ulama-i Islam was composed at a time of dire new trouble, and before the breaking of an even worse storm. The ninth and tenth centuries have been called the Persian intermezzo, 'between the Arabs and the Turks'. Early in the eleventh century the Seljuk Turks swept into Khorasan from Central Asia, and swarmed over the whole of Iran, exterminating every local dynasty; and once established there, they embraced Islam with fervour. Little is known directly of the Zoroastrians under their rule (1037–1157), but many must have died in the wars of conquest, or have been forcibly converted during those harsh times when 'all paths were closed save the path of Muhammad'. Thereafter came the even more dreadful Mongol invasions, which made an end both of the Seljuks and of the ʿAbbasid caliphate, propped up by them in Baghdad. The Mongol hordes rolled relentlessly over everything which came in their way, and the slaughter of Muslim, Zoroastrian, Jew and Christian was impartial and in places almost complete, a catastrophe 'whereof the sparks flew far and wide, and the hurt was universal'. Of the Mongol devastation a modern scholar has written: 'The loss suffered by Muslim learning, which never again reached its former level, defies description and almost surpasses imagination: not only were thousands of priceless books utterly annihilated, but, owing to the number of men of learning who perished or barely escaped with their lives, the very tradition of accurate scholarship . . . was almost destroyed' (Browne, II, 463). The Zoroastrians suffered no less grievously, and it must have been then that the last great collections of their holy books – including every copy of the Sasanian Avesta – were destroyed. Every major fire temple which still survived, such as Karkoy in Seistan, must also have been demolished at that time.

Within half a century of the conquest Ghazan Khan (1295–1304) had become a Muslim, and Mongol converts were again swelling the ranks of Islam, which their grandfathers had so cruelly reduced. For the Zoroastrians, already a dwindling minority when the tempest struck, no such increase came to repair their losses, but only fresh sufferings from the zeal of the newly converted. Most fortunately Fars, by timely submission to the Mongols, had escaped the worst of the actual slaughter; and it was around the oasis cities to the north of this province, namely Yazd and Kerman, that the Zoroastrians now grouped themselves, finding here the last bastions where they could hold out, in poverty and protective obscurity.

CHAPTER ELEVEN

Under Il-Khans, Rajahs and Sultans

Zoroastrian survival

Under the Mongol Il-Khans the best hope of survival for the unbeliever was to be inconspicuous; and it was probably in the late thirteenth or early fourteenth century that the Mobadan mobad sought refuge with his priests in as remote a place as possible – a tiny village known as Turkabad in the north-west corner of the plain of Yazd. This was the furthest point in that inhospitable, mountain-locked region from the city of Yazd itself, with its Muslim governor; and in the hills nearby there was a shrine to the 'Lady of Pars' – Ardvisur Anahid – which may have helped determine the choice of this particular place. Further, two Atash Bahrams were brought to the neighbouring village of Sharifabad, where they were installed in small mud-brick houses indistinguishable from ordinary village homes. (From that time all sacred fires, however exalted, were necessarily kept in this unobtrusive way; lofty domes, from then on, belonged only to the mosques of Islam.) One of these two fires is known to this day as Adur Khara, a New Persian form of Adur Farnbag; and there is no reason to doubt that this is indeed one of the three great fires of ancient Iran. The other, called simply 'the' Atash Bahram, was even more beloved and reverenced, and so this is probably Adur-Anahid, rescued (as Mas'udi states) from its temple at Istakhr, and brought finally to this obscure haven. In the third century this fire had been put into the care of Kirder, and it may well have remained thereafter in the hereditary charge of the Sasanian high priests, so that it would have been natural to bring it near the chosen refuge of the Mobadan mobad (now known to the faithful, as his worldly dignity declined, by the still more respectful title of Dastur dastur). These two fires (now conjoined) are the oldest surviving Zoroastrian sacred fires, and have probably been burning continually for well over 2000 years.

Thereafter the villages of Turkabad and Sharifabad together formed the ecclesiastical centre of the Zoroastrians in Iran; and it is evidently of them that the French merchant Chardin wrote in the seventeenth century (II, 183): 'Their chief temple is near Yazd. . . . This is their great fire-temple . . . and also their oracle and academy. It is there that they communicate their religion, their maxims and their hopes. Their high pontiff lives there always, and without quitting it. He is called the Dastur dasturan. This pontiff has with him several priests and several students who form a kind of seminary. The Mahometans allow it because it is inconspicuous, and generous presents are given to them.' These 'presents' were evidently made possible by the devotion of the Zoroastrian community as a whole; and it was recorded later that 'pilgrimage to Yazd is a strict obligation, and none among them can dispense with making it at least once in his life. They then bring presents to the high priest' (Drouville, II, 210). Partly, no doubt, to meet the needs of pilgrims two great shrines to yazads (great in the sense of their sanctity) were also established in Sharifabad. One, in the vicinity of the sacred fires, was devoted to Mihr, lord of fire and protector of the cult; and the other, out in the fields, was dedicated to Teshtar (Tishtrya), yazad of the rain so sorely needed in most years. These were empty shrines, Sasanian iconoclasm having won its battle before the coming of the Arabs. An annual pilgrimage was also made, at a fixed time, to the shrine of the 'Lady of Pars' (Banu-Pars). This consisted of a sacred rock by the bed of a mountain torrent, with a perpetual spring close by. Here sacrifices and prayers were offered in the ancient tradition of worship in high places, as described by Herodotus in the fifth century B.C. There were four other holy places in the mountains around Yazd, each the goal of annual pilgrimage.

The villages of the region must still have been predominantly Zoroastrian when the Dasturan dastur took up his residence there. There was a strong concentration of Zoroastrians too in and around the oasis city of Kerman, some 150 miles to the east, in a region only a little less isolated by mountain and desert than that of Yazd. The Kermani community had its own Dasturan dastur, who acknowledged the supremacy of the high priest of Yazd. Beyond Kerman again there were Zoroastrians in Seistan, but the subsequent extinction of the community there means that none of its records survive. Even more remarkably, there were also still Zoroastrians in Khorasan, that gateway of invasion and slaughter; but no more is heard after the tenth century of any of the old faith in Azarbaijan, in the north-west, and the community there may well have met its end under Ghazan Khan, who made his capital at Tabriz.

Manuscript copying and preservation

All such historical details are necessarily a matter of deduction for this period, for from this time on Muslim historians ignore the Zoroastrians, their numbers having been reduced to a point where they no longer had any political or social importance; and their own records are largely blank for the Mongol period, the chief source of information being the colophons of manuscripts. The priests who retreated to Turkabad and Sharifabad evidently took with them all the books which they could save, and once there they kept diligently copying them, while their brethren in Kerman did the like. Of the Avesta itself they had managed to preserve little more than the liturgical parts – in constant use in the religious services – together with (in almost every instance) the Pahlavi translation and commentary. These liturgical texts now included the whole Vendidad; and the oldest surviving Avestan manuscript is in fact a copy of this work written at the Parsi stronghold of Cambay in Gujarat, in 1324; and this was made from a copy written in Seistan in 1205 – before the Mongol onslaught, that is – especially for a visiting Parsi priest. One of the oldest and most important groups of yasna manuscripts with Pahlavi translation derives from a copy made by Hoshang Siyavakhsh of Sharifabad in 1495, who (if the colophon is rightly interpreted) copied it from a manuscript written in 1280; and the Avestan text of this manuscript can be traced back (again through the obscurities of Pahlavi colophons) to a manuscript written by one Dadag Mahyar Farrokhzadan – probably, it is thought, a nephew of the ninth-century Hudinan peshobay. Such manuscripts were evidently handed down within families, and so escaped the general destruction that must have befallen temple libraries. Pahlavi texts were similarly preserved. Thus one Rustam Mihraban copied the Arda Viraz Namag in 1269, and this and others of his manuscripts were re-copied by his great-great-nephew Mihraban Kay Khosrow in the fourteenth century. Both these priests visited the Parsis in India, so that mention of their names gives good occasion to turn from the Iranis, surviving as best they could in harsh times, to consider the happier fortunes of their migrant brethren.

The Parsi founding fathers

Parsi tradition is that the founding fathers of their community landed on the coast of Gujarat in western India on Bahman day of Tir month, Vikram Samvat 992, which is 936 A.C. (Hodivala, 70–84). In the local script of the tenth and eleventh centuries the number 'nine' could be written with a sign very much like the modern one for 'seven'; and so this date came to be read as V.S. 772 = 716 A.C., with resulting confusion for Parsi chronology. (The wrong date is still very generally reproduced.) The Parsis had already spent nearly two decades on the island of Div, where Gujarati was spoken, and so were able to present their case to the local rajah, one of the Silhara dynasty, who were famed for their tolerance and encouragement to foreigners to trade and settle. He allowed them to make a home by the seashore where they had landed; and there they founded a settlement which they called Sanjan after their home-town in Khorasan. The main source for the history of the little community is the 'Qissa-i Sanjan', a narrative poem composed largely from oral traditions by a Parsi priest, Bahman, in 1600 A.C. (transl. by Hodivala, 94–117). This tells how, some time after the landing, they were able to establish an Atash Bahram. They sent back messengers by land to Khorasan to fetch the necessary ritual objects for the ceremonies of consecration – notably consecrated 'nirang', and ash from an existing Atash Bahram – and these gave their new fire a link with the sacred fires of the mother country. The Qissa states that the priests who had been among the original settlers were the better able to perform their task because 'several parties of priests and laymen of righteous life had also arrived at that spot' (Hodivala, 106); and there is no doubt that the Sanjan settlement attracted other Zoroastrians, probably both from Iran and from those who had already as individuals sought refuge in India. The Sanjana Atash Bahram remained the only sacred fire among the Parsis for the next eight hundred years or so, and in the main priests and laity said their prayers and performed their rites before their own hearth fires, as their forefathers had done in earlier days before the temple cult of fire was introduced. This may be attributed partly to poverty, and partly perhaps to a Khorasani tradition, in which local sacred fires may have had little or no part, in contrast to the usage of western Iran.

'Three hundred years, more or less' then passed, according to the brisk treatment of the Qissa. During this time the Parsis learned to speak Gujarati as their mother-tongue, and adopted Indian dress, though with small differences. (Their priests still dressed all in white, and had white turbans, and laymen too wore white for religious occasions. The women took to the coloured sari, but kept their hair covered by a kerchief worn beneath it, indoors as well as out.) Gradually, as the Sanjan settlement prospered, groups of laymen left it to make new homes for themselves at ports and small towns elsewhere, mainly along the coast. The tradition names Vankaner, Broach, Variav, Anklesar, Cambay and Navsari as their main centres. When they prospered, they sent back to Sanjan asking for a priest to come to minister to them. When the priests who followed them throve and grew numerous in their turn, they divided the work among themselves, each priest taking a group of lay families to minister to. This group was called his 'panthak', he their 'panthaki', and the association tended to become hereditary. The Gujarati terms were new, but the system, with its individual bond between priests and the laity, was essentially the traditional one. Then as the priests consolidated their local associations, they agreed, some time in the thirteenth century, to divide Gujarat ecclesiastically into five groups or 'panths'. From south to north there were the Sanjanas, in the original area of settlement; the Bhagarias or 'sharers', based on the little port of Navsari (first settled in by Parsis, it seems, in 1142 A.C.); the Godavras, who served a large rural area, including the small town of Anklesar; the Bharuchas of the more famous port of Broach; and the Khambattas of Khambat or Cambay, which like Broach was an ancient and wealthy port. Each priestly 'panth' had its own council and administered its own affairs; but all were linked to the mother-settlement at Sanjan through the presence there of the Atash Bahram, whose ashes were needed for rites of purification, and which must itself have been, from the earliest days, a goal of regular pilgrimage.

The unity of the Parsis during these obscure centuries is shown by the fact that at some stage, very probably during the years 1129–31, when the spring equinox had come (through recession) to correspond to the first day of the second calendar month, they intercalated a thirteenth month in order to restore the first day of Farvardin to this position. They called this thirteenth month simply Second Spendarmad. This reform would have been made just over 120 years after the one initiated by the Iranis under Buyid rule, in 1006 A.C.; and it is the only attested instance of the actual intercalation of an extra month after the first, disastrous Sasanian calendar reform under Ardashir (although both Zoroastrian and Arabo-Persian learned works exist which give calculations based on the theory of such intercalation having taken place). That it could be carried out in twelfth-century Gujarat is a testimony to both the intelligence and authority of the Parsi priesthood then, and to the cohesion of the community. The measure was never repeated, so thereafter the Parsi and Irani calendars both receded against the natural year, but with the Parsi one now a month behind the other.

Parsis in the twelfth to fourteenth centuries

That there were learned Parsi priests in the twelfth century is borne out by the writings of Neryosang Dhaval, a Sanjana priest who is thought to have flourished at the end of the eleventh or early in the twelfth century. With the community speaking Gujarati, Sanskrit was fairly readily accessible to its scholars; and Hindu kindliness meant that the Parsis felt none of the aversion for this language which the Iranis felt for Arabic. Accordingly Neryosang addressed himself to the task of translating Zoroastrian religious texts into Sanskrit, working from the Middle Persian versions. For the yasna he used a manuscript which descended from the same original as that written by Hoshang Siyavakhsh in the fifteenth century (Geldner, xxxiii–iv); but how he acquired his copy of this rare work is unknown. (The Parsis on their migration seem to have taken with them only the 'sade' or simple Avestan texts (without Zand) of the yasna, Visperad and Khorda Avesta – those works which were essential for worship and private prayer; and all other scriptures were preserved by the Iranis, and gradually transmitted by them to their brethren in India.) Neryosang's Sanskrit rendering of the yasna is incomplete; but he also translated some of the Khorda Avesta as well as the Pahlavi Menog i Khrad, and Mardanfarrokh's Shkand Gumanig Vizar. He further transcribed the original Middle Persian into the clear Avestan alphabet, for the ambiguous Pahlavi script had become additionally difficult for Parsis to read, because the Middle Persian language which it enshrined, though still readily comprehensible to speakers of New Persian, was a dead church language now for them. Since this re-writing in Avestan characters was a form of interpretation, it came to be referred to as 'pa-zand' that is, 'by interpretation', and then simply as Pazand.

Neryosang's Sanskrit was naturally provincial; and working as a priest rather than a man of letters he kept his renderings literal (retaining also a number of special Zoroastrian terms). Nevertheless, his work shows him to have had an admirably extensive knowledge of both Sanskrit and Middle Persian, and it marks one of the peaks in Parsi scholarship. Thereafter there came a decline in Sanskrit studies, which seems to have coincided with the arrival of Muslim forces. In 1206 a Muslim sultanate had been established in Delhi, and in 1297 an army was despatched from there to conquer Gujarat. The region was ravaged and Cambay, its wealthiest port, suffered greatly. 'The citizens were taken unawares and there was a terrible panic. The Muslims began to kill and slaughter on the right and left unmercifully, and blood flowed in torrents' (Commissariat, I, 3). The little Parsi community there, too small to be mentioned, must have suffered with the rest.

Thereafter Gujarat was ruled by governors appointed from Delhi; and a period of religious intolerance began, with the jizya being imposed, and used by the more zealous sultans as an instrument for conversion. The Parsis themselves were nevertheless better off than their co-religionists in Iran, in that they formed only a tiny group in a huge population of 'infidels', who were able to put up considerable resistance to their rulers through sheer numbers. A complicating factor was that the conquerors brought with them an Arabo-Persian culture, and the Parsis, althou,h now thoroughly acclimatized in their chosen land, were still intensely proud of their Persian lineage and traditions, and regarded the Persian language as part of their own inheritance. Its spread through Gujarat as a learned tongue at this time probably contributed therefore to a decline in Sanskrit studies among the Parsi priests. Moreover, they began at this period to make Gujarati versions of Avestan and Pahlavi texts, basing these on the existing Sanskrit renderings; and these readily comprehensible texts in the vernacular gradually replaced all others for general study, as earlier in Iran the Middle Persian translations had come to be relied upon in place of the more difficult Avestan originals.

Parsi concern for the writings of their faith continued through the troubles of this time. Just before the Muslim conquest of Gujarat the Irani priest, Rustam Mihraban, who in 1269 had copied the Arda Viraz Namag in his native land, visited India; and a manuscript of the Visperad still exists written by him in 1278 'at Ankalesar in the land of the Indians'. Rustam returned, evidently, to Iran; and other manuscripts which he had copied for his own use descended in his family, coming finally into the possession of his great-great-nephew, Mihraban Kay Khosrow, the most famous of all priestly copyists. Mihraban was, it seems, invited in his turn to go to India (taking with him precious manuscripts) by a layman called Chahil, a pious merchant of Cambay. The first codex which Mihraban copied there is unique, a miscellaneous collection of Pahlavi texts popularly known as the 'Pahlavi Shahname', because it includes the heroic poem, Ayadgar i Zareran, and the prose romance, the Karnamag i Ardashir. This manuscript, the colophons state, Mihraban wrote in 1321 at the port of Thana, 'the Parsi merchant Chahil having given much respect, an honorarium for copying, and paper'. Thence he travelled north to Navsari, and then on to Cambay, where his scribal activity can be traced over the next thirty years.

.It was while Mihraban was still at work, in about 1350, that a Christian traveller, the Dominican friar Jordanus, halted in Gujarat on his way to the Malabar coast, and there noticed the Parsis, of whom he wrote (p. 21): 'There be also other pagan-folk in this India who worship fire; they bury not their dead, neither do they burn them, but cast them into the midst of a certain roofless tower, and there expose them totally uncovered to the fowls of heaven. These believe in two First Principles, to wit, of Evil and Good, of Darkness and Light, matters which at present I do not purpose to discuss.'

Not long after this the Delhi sultanate began to break up, and received its death blow from the Tatar Timur Leng (Tamburlaine). Timur, a professed Muslim, had invaded Iran in 1381, conquering first Khorasan, and thereafter ravaging the whole land. Of Seistan, which he devastated in 1383, it was said; 'Whatever was in that country, from potsherds to royal pearls, and from the finest fabrics to the very nails in the doors and walls, was swept away by the winds of spoliation' (Browne, III, 187). Among the sufferers must have been the Zoroastrians who were still holding out there, and Timur's campaigns, tradition holds, drove more of them overseas as fugitives to Gujarat. This region fortunately lay too far south to suffer directly when in 1398 Timur turned his attention to India. He occupied Delhi, devastated the land, and withdrew laden with booty. Thereafter, in 1401, the Muslim governor of Gujarat, Muzaffar Shah, declared his independence, and there was a period of local strife while he and his successors fought to establish their authority. It was perhaps at this time (the date is uncertain) that the Parsis of Variav, a village in the Godavra district, were slaughtered by the local Hindu rajah, according to one account because they refused to pay exorbitant taxes. A ceremony for the souls of the slain – men, women and children – is still solemnized annually.

During the troubled early Muzzaffarid period two well-known Parsi scribes, Ram Kamdin and his son Peshotan, managed to pursue their quiet labours. The latter wrote a famous codex at Broach in 1397; and in 1410 his father copied a manuscript which contains the Pazand and Sanskrit versions of the Arda Viraz Namag. Five years later he transcribed a codex of miscellaneous Pazand texts, some accompanied by Sanskrit and Old Gujarati renderings. Ram does not show much grasp of Middle Persian, and these works suggest a steady erosion of knowledge of this now foreign tongue through the use of the local vernacular.

Parsis in the fifteenth century

Hindu resistance to the Muzzaffarid continued sporadically into the mid fifteenth century, when Sultan Mahmud Begada (1458–1511) came to the throne. In 1465 he sent an army to reduce some stubborn areas of resistance, and it is thought to be during this campaign that Sanjan was sacked and destroyed. The story of the Parsis' valiant part in the battle, fighting side by side with their Hindu benefactors, is told in epic fashion in the Qissa-i Sanjan (Hodivala, 108–13). Many lost their lives; but the priests managed to rescue the Atash Bahram, and carried it safely to a cave on 'a hill named Bahrot', an isolated peak some fourteen miles away. Here, protected by jungle and sea, they are said to have guarded it for the next twelve years; and then, when conditions were quieter, they took it to Bansda, a little town some fifty miles inland, still within the Sanjana 'panth', where the small Parsi community welcomed it with reverence and joy. Here it remained for two years, with Zoroastrians coming on pilgrimage 'from every district in which there were people of that pure creed. Just as before men used to go . . . to far-famed Sanjan, so now the Parsis came to Bansda . . . with numerous offerings' (Hodivala, 113).

Among the pilgrims was one of the great men of Parsi history, Changa Asa, a wealthy layman of Navsari. The author of the Qissa gives him the ancient Iranian title of 'dahyuvad' or 'lord of the land', thus translating evidently the Gujarati term 'desai' (as it were 'squire'). He also calls him 'davar', that is, 'magistrate' or 'judge'. He states that 'he would not suffer the faith to fall into neglect. . . . He gave money from his own wealth to those who had no sudra or kusti.' Changa Asa made the pilgrimage to Bansda in the rainy season, when the ways there through the jungle were difficult; and soon after he called a meeting of the Navsari Anjoman (the local assembly of all adult Zoroastrian men) and proposed that they should invite the Sanjana priests to bring the sacred fire to Navsari, on the coast. (Communications then by sea were easier than by land.) The Sanjanas accepted, the Bhagaria priests of Navsari prepared a 'fine house' for the fire, and it was safely installed there; and with this event Bahman (himself the great-great-great-great-grandson of one of the Sanjana priests who had guarded the sacred fire) concludes the Qissa-i Sanjan.

The Atash Bahram had thus been some fourteen years or more without a fixed abode; and it seems to have been kept during this time in a metal vessel, one of the 'afrinagans' used ordinarily to hold glowing embers during acts of worship. The tradition of enthroning a sacred fire on a stone pillar-altar was thus broken, and instead a huge metal container, shaped like the little 'afrinagan', was made to hold the Atash Bahram in its new temple in Navsari. This created a precedent, which was followed for all the sacred fires which the Parsis established subsequently.

Navsari now became the centre of Parsi religious life, with the community's one sacred fire established there, and the leading priests of the two oldest 'panths' living together in the town, while the affairs of the community prospered under the guidance of Changa Asa. He was a man who cared greatly, it is clear, about the proper maintenance of tradition; and he persuaded his co-religionists to send a messenger to Iran to consult the priests there about certain details of ritual and observance, over which there was uncertainty. This brave envoy, Nariman Hoshang, sailed from Broach to the Persian Gulf, and thence made his way inland to Yazd, from where he was taken to the Dasturan dastur in Turkabad. He was warmly welcomed; but because of the language barrier (he spoke very little Persian), he had to live for a year in Yazd, supporting himself by petty trade, before he knew enough to receive instruction (Dhabhar, 593). In 1478 he returned, bearing two Pazand manuscripts copied especially for 'the priests, leaders and chief men of Hindustan' by two Sharifabadi priests, and a long letter for the Parsis. His was the first of a number of such missions down the years, and fortunately the Parsis of Navsari not only preserved the manuscripts, received then and thereafter, but also collected the letters and all the treatises or Rivayats of instruction which the Persian priests wrote out for them. The signatures to the letters, as well as their contents, shed light on the conditions of the two communities from the fifteenth to the seventeenth centuries, while the Rivayats themselves show that both Parsis and Iranis remained thoroughly orthodox, and deeply concerned to maintain with the utmost fidelity the religion which both had suffered so much to preserve.

No differences in doctrine existed between the two communities, and the advice asked for and given is on matters of observance, such as the exact rituals for solemnizing the elaborate ceremony of Nirangdin, consecrating a dakhma, or administering the barashnom. Much attention too is devoted to details of the purity laws. Probably the Parsi priests studied these writings partly in order to find confirmation there for their own practices, and added authority for their exhortations to the laity. Yet they clearly also derived benefit from the description of details of observances which had become neglected in the hard circumstances of their forefathers' migration; and they continued to send messengers with inquiries, despite the perilous conditions – all laymen, for the priests were not prepared themselves to undergo the loss of purity entailed in travelling by sea in infidel ships. (The Iranis administered the barashnom to the messengers on their arrival.)

In one or two respects the Parsis' residence in India had forced changes on them in observance. Thus they had no access to the 'hom'-plant – the ephedra which grew so thickly on the Persian mountains – and what they had been using as substitute we are not told. (The Iranis now began to send them supplies of 'hom' whenever they could.) Then, while the Irani Zoroastrians had naturally maintained all the old rites of sacrifice (since blood sacrifice is a part of Muslim observance also, this was one point where there was no clash with their conquerors), the Parsis, while continuing the sacrifice of goats, had had to give up that of cows and bulls on settling among Hindus, and now, several centuries later, must have been shocked to be urged by their Irani brethren to offer this on occasion. It was presumably the influence of Hindu reverence for the cow which led them to evolve the custom of keeping a sacred bull to provide the tail-hairs which, when consecrated, are used in the 'varas' or sieve for straining the 'hom'-juice. The bull, called the 'varasya', had to be pure white, unblemished, with pink muzzle and tongue. He was also used for procuring 'nirang'. The custom was unknown in Iran, where of old the tail-hairs were obtained, it seems, from a sacrificial bull, and 'nirang' was taken from any healthy animal, who would be fed on pure food beforehand, and thereafter returned to the fields.

The coining of the name 'varasya' was part of a steady divergence in terminology between Parsis and Iranis. The former kept a number of Persian and Arabo-Persian words, and understood even more, through literary sources; but in ordinary life they naturally adopted more and more Gujarati words, and also applied a few old terms differently from the Iranis. Thus the latter call the initiation of a priest 'nozud', whereas the Parsis term this 'navar', and use 'nozud' ('naojot' in their pronunciation) for the initiation of a child, which the Iranis call 'sedra-pushun' or 'putting on the sacred shirt'. Nevertheless, the two communities continued to understand each other very well, on the basis of common beliefs and practices.

Yet cow-sacrifice was not the only point of difference now in outlook. Another was the question of making converts. The Parsis had come to be regarded more or less as a caste within Hindu society, and this, together with their pride in their Iranian lineage, led them to regard religion as a hereditary matter. To be a Zoroastrian one must be born of Iranian blood. This way of thinking was, as we have seen, a tendency in the whole Zoroastrian community from early times, but it had never been made a rigid principle; and when the Parsis consulted the Iranis as to whether, for example, they should allow their Hindu servants who wished it to enter the religion, they received the answer that 'if servant boys and girls have faith in the Good Religion, then it is proper that they should tie the kusti, and when they become instructed, attentive to religion, and steadfast, the barashnom should be administered to them' (Dhabhar, 276).

Another matter which troubled the Parsis was that of 'khvedodah' marriages, for the Hindus disapproved of unions even between cousins; and so Nariman informed the Iranis that the Parsis 'do not contract marriages among relatives but put many questions concerning it' (Dhabhar, op. cit. 294). The Iranis replied that 'the marriage of a Mazdayasnian . . . among his relatives is a meritorious deed and let this be known, that it is approved by Ormazd.' A case of a brother-sister betrothal (broken off before marriage) is recorded in a Pahlavi text of the eleventh century (Rivayat of Adurfarnbag CXLIII); but all that the fourteenth-century priests urged was that 'efforts should be made that the son of one brother should be given in marriage to the daughter of a brother'. This, they pointed out, should be easier now that the Parsis were under Muslim rule (for this was a favoured form of marriage among Arabs); and certainly from the time that records of Parsi marriages exist (that is, from the eighteenth century) this was the most popular form of union for them also.

Irani Zoroastrians in the sixteenth century

In their first letter the priests of Yazd had lamented to the Parsis that from the time of Gayomard – that is, from the beginning of human history – no period, not even that of Alexander, had been more grievous or troublesome for the faithful than this 'millennium of the demon of Wrath' (Dhabhar, 598). They were then living under the rule of Turkmans, who had wrested power from Timur's son; but in 1499 Shah Isma'il, the first of the Safavids, defeated them, and was crowned king of Iran. He and his descendants, who were to rule until 1722, were Shi'i, and by remorseless pressure they brought almost all the Muslims of Iran to adhere to this branch of their faith. The Shi'i were more Zoroastrianized, in their purity laws and other ways, than the Sunni; but this merely made them more conscious of the uncleanness of the infidel, and life under Safavid rule was hard for those of the old religion.

Parsis in the sixteenth century

Meanwhile a new trouble had come upon the Gujaratis in the shape of the Portuguese who, having rounded the Cape of Good Hope, were searching for trading bases in the east. Mahmud Begada died in 1511, and no Muzzaffarid ruler of like ability followed him to confront this menace. Nevertheless for a quarter of a century the Sultans held off the hovering Portuguese, who, partly to instil terror, partly for loot, raided up and down the coast. Then in 1534 the Mughal emperor

Humayun, now ruling Delhi, invaded Gujarat, and in despair its Sultan made a treaty with the Portuguese, conceding them, in return for help, the port of Bassein and its islands (including the tiny, insignificant one of Bombay), and agreeing that all vessels leaving Gujarati ports should pay dues to them. The Portuguese gave the Sultan little actual aid in return for this munificent concession, and the troubles of Gujarat continued. Humayun overran the north of the land, and Broach and Surat, with their Parsi colonies, were among the places which he sacked. In 1547 the Portuguese attacked Broach again, putting its inhabitants to the sword. They also won from the Sultan more territorial concessions, including the 'district of Sanjan'; and wherever they established themselves they made vigorous efforts to convert the inhabitants to Roman Catholicism. A Portuguese doctor, named Garcia d'Orta, noticed Parsis in Cambay and Bassein, and described them as merchants and shopkeepers, who came originally from Persia.

In 1572 the emperor Akbar, Humayun's son, invaded Gujarat and within a year made himself master of the land, putting an end to its independence. During the siege of Surat (then developing into its chief port) he met some Parsis and dealt with them graciously. The rule of the Mughals began therefore auspiciously for their community, and was indeed to mark the beginning of their rise to prosperity, while that of the Safavids was to see their Irani brethren thrust down into ever greater poverty and deprivation.

CHAPTER TWELVE

Under the Safavids
and Mughals

Irani Zoroastrians under Shah ʿAbbas: their beliefs and practices

From the sixteenth to eighteenth centuries there survive increasingly abundant records by Zoroastrians themselves, and notices by foreign observers. In Iran Shah ʿAbbas the Great, the most famous of the Safavids, came to the throne in 1587, to rule until 1628; and his brilliant court at Isfahan attracted European ambassadors, merchants and even Christian missionaries, some of whom became interested in the Zoroastrian community nearby. This was there because in 1608 Shah ʿAbbas had 'a very great number of Gaurs' (the then current form of the insulting term 'gabr') brought from Yazd and Kerman to work as labourers in and around his capital. They were settled in a suburb containing some 3000 houses, all 'low, single-storeyed, without any adornment, suited to the poverty of those who inhabit them' (Pietro della Valle, II, 104); and there they toiled as fullers, weavers and carpet-makers, or went into the city (being careful not to jostle Muslims) to work as grooms or gardeners, or hired themselves out on the farms and vineyards round about. 'They regard agriculture', wrote Chardin (II, 186), 'not only as a good and innocent calling, but also as meritorious and noble, and they believe that it is the first of all vocations, that which the "Sovereign God" and the "lesser gods", as they say, approve of most and which they reward most generously.'

'These ancient Persians' (he continues) 'have gentle and simple ways, and live very peaceably under the guidance of their elders, from among whom they elect their magistrates, who are confirmed in their office by the Persian government. They drink wine, and eat all kinds of flesh . . . but otherwise they are very particular, and hardly mix at all with other people, especially not with Mahometans.' 'Their women', another traveller commented, 'far from avoiding us as other Persian women did, were very pleased to see and talk with us' (Daulier-Deslandes, 28). They were distinguished from their Muslim sisters by being unveiled; but their dress was very modest – long full trousers reaching to the ankle, a long, full-sleeved tunic, and a series of head-cloths, the inner one covering the hair entirely, like a nun's coif. Their garments were gaily coloured, mostly in greens and reds. The men dressed like other labourers in trousers and tunic, but had to leave the cloth (of homespun wool or cotton) undyed, and this marked them out wherever they went.

Although friendly, the Zoroastrians were reticent about religious matters, and one inquirer observed: 'There are no men in the world so scrupulous of discovering the mysteries of their religion as the Gaurs' (Tavernier, 163). This was plainly because they set as blank a wall as they could between themselves and the Muslims (who used mockery as a sharp weapon), and the foreigners might betray confidences to their Muslim hosts. Some Europeans were misled therefore into thinking that the Zoroastrians were actually ignorant, 'a simple people, who had lived for so many centuries in servitude, they had forgotten all their other ceremonies, keeping only veneration of the sun at its rising, care for the fire, which they call eternal, and their former fashion of disposing of the dead' (Figueroa, 177). This was said, however, at the time when the priests of Yazd and Kerman were writing the Rivayats for their Parsi brethren, full of minute instructions concerning a whole variety of ancient observances and rituals. One especial barrier which the Zoroastrians had raised in self-protection, and upon which Western observers commented, was linguistic. In their rural fastnesses they had adopted a local dialect, incomprehensible to speakers of standard Persian, which they called 'Dari', the Muslims 'Gabri'; and this was spoken (though almost never written) by all Zoroastrians among themselves.

Chardin, however, a man of immense intellectual curiosity, managed by sheer persistence to penetrate some way into the 'mysteries' of the Zoroastrians' faith. Of their doctrines he wrote (II, 182): 'They suppose that there are two principles of things, it not being possible that there should be only one, because all things are of two kinds, or of two natures, that is, good or bad. . . . These two principles are of Light, which they call Ormous . . . and Darkness, which they call Ariman. . . . They hold that there are angels, whom they call lesser gods ('dieux subalternes'), assigned to protect the inanimate creatures, each according to his own province.' He further records that they held feasts in honour of the 'elements', a clear reference to the gahambars. He does not speak of the kusti, so he could never have seen Zoroastrians at prayer; but he learned (II, 183) that each family prayed five times a day in the presence of their own hearth fire, which was kept always alight and pure. Tavernier, who visited the Zoroastrians of Kerman, tried in vain to see their temple fire. They justified their refusal by telling him how the Muslim governor had forced them to let him into its presence. 'He, it seems, expected some extraordinary brightness; but when he saw no more than what he might have seen in a kitchen or a chamber fire, fell a-swearing and spitting upon it as if he had been mad' (p. 167). The Rivayats contain instructions for purifying a sacred fire, should it become necessary through incidents such as this; and by the seventeenth century the Iranians were adopting the practice of concealing each sacred fire in a tiny, hidden chamber within its mud-brick temple, windowless, with a little cupboard-like door, to be entered only by the attendant priests. Elsewhere, in a bigger room, there would be an empty pillar-altar on which embers could be placed for private prayers or public festivities. The laity thus denied themselves the joy of seeing their beloved sacred fires in the hope of better protecting them.

In the open, the Europeans (like Herodotus before them) noticed Zoroastrians waging war on 'khrafstras'. 'Above all', wrote della Valle (p. 107), 'they have a horror of frogs, tortoises, crayfish, and other creatures which they think trouble and pollute the water; so much so, that they kill as many of them as they find.' Tavernier (p. 166) noted that 'there is one day in the year when all the women of every city and village meet together to kill all the frogs they can find in the fields', and he further observed (p. 168): 'There are some beasts that the Gaurs do mightily respect, and to which they give a great deal of honour. There are others which they as much abhor, and which they endeavour to destroy as much as in them lies, believing that they were not created by God, but that they came out of the body of the Devil, whose ill nature they retain'.

The Europeans were also interested, like all others who came into contact with Zoroastrians, by their method of disposing of their dead. Poor though they were, the Isfahani 'Gaurs' built an impressive round tower in a lonely place outside the town 'from large dressed stones . . . about 35 feet high and 90 feet in diameter, with no door or entrance', lest any seek 'to profane a place for which they have much more respect than either the Mahometans or the Christians show for the tombs of their dead' (Chardin, II, 186). They laid their dead fully clad in this tower instead of naked in the traditional way, doubtless because of Muslim intrusions. About fifty feet away, Chardin relates, there was a little mud-brick building, where fire would have been kept burning to comfort the souls of the departed. This custom was common to the Iranis and Parsis.

Another practice which caught Tavernier's eye concerned the purity laws. He wrote (p. 166): 'So soon as women or maids perceive the custom of nature upon them, they presently leave their houses, and stay alone in the fields in little huts made of hurdles or wattlings, with a cloth at the entering in, which serves as a door. While they are in that condition, they have food and drink brought them every day; and when they are free, they send, according to their quality, a goat, or a hen, or a pigeon, for an offering; after which they go to the bath, and then invite some few of their kindred to some small collation.' This cramped and solitary confinement, in summer heat and winter cold, must have been very hard on the women; and in time it evidently also became dangerous, for by the nineteenth century places for their withdrawal were made in the greater safety of house-yards or stables. Ending the ordeal with friends and a 'small collation' displays, however, the Zoroastrian instinct to seize on every possible occasion for merry-making; and Tavernier records (p. 167) of the 'Gaurs' in general that 'they love to feast, and to eat and drink well'. He also mentions (p. 166) that 'the day of the birth of their Prophet is celebrated with an extraordinary pomp, besides that they then bestow large alms'. This day was the Greater No Ruz, on 6 Farvardin (which has as much true claim to be Zoroaster's birthday as 25 December has to be that of Christ). In Kerman there were evidently still some Zoroastrians of substance able to give generously in charity; and an elegantly carved marble stone survives there which records the building of a 'House of Mihr' (Khane-i Mihr) in the reign of Shah 'Abbas by one Rustam Bundar. (A 'House of Mihr', usually Dar-i Mihr or Bar-i Mihr, is the regular term at this late period for a place of worship or fire temple.)

It was probably men of some means, like Rustam Bundar, who were the 'magistrates' or 'davars' of the local community (like Changa Asa in Navsari). Ordinarily they probably had little difficulty in guiding its affairs; but if two of its members were in dispute, and the elders could not decide the merits of the case, then it is laid down in the Rivayats (Dhabhar, 39 ff.) that they might require the accused man to take a solemn oath at the fire temple, with ritual drinking of sulphur (a form of the ancient ordeal by fire). After recitation of the Khorshed-Mihr Niyayesh, whereby the sun and Mihr were called upon as witnesses, the man testifying was to invoke the seven Amahraspands and their creations, and then make a formal asseveration, concluding with these words: 'If I perjure myself, then every good deed I have done I confer on you (the accuser), and for every crime done by you, I draw upon myself the penalty of it on the Chinvat Bridge. Mihr, Srosh and the just Rashn know that I speak the truth. . . .' The Zoroastrians were convinced that anyone who perjured himself would soon be smitten by God; but the community were urged to see that things seldom reached this point, but that honesty prevailed, since he who breaks an agreement has already come into 'the jurisdiction of Ahriman and the demons' (Dhabhar, 41).

Honest, peaceable, hard-working, living as much as possible to themselves, the Zoroastrians still could not escape tyranny. Shah ʿAbbas, Chardin relates (II, 179), had heard tell of the marvellous contents of the books of the 'Gaurs', and in particular of one rumoured to have been written by Abraham, containing prophecies of all events to come until the end of time. This he sought persistently, forcing the Zoroastrians to bring him their manuscripts. Chardin heard of twenty-six volumes lodged in the royal library at Isfahan; but naturally the imaginary book of Abraham could not be produced, and in the end the king in his frustration had the Dasturan dastur put to death with several others. In a letter to the Parsis dated 1635 the Irani priests speak sorrowfully of these events. Their sadness at this time was intensified by disappointment. They had come to believe that the tenth millennium of the 'world year' had begun with the reign of Yazdegird III; and so they expected its glorious end, with the coming of the Saoshyant, a thousand years later, that is, in 1630 A.C. Four years previously they wrote to the Parsis: 'The millennium of Ahriman is ended, and the millennium of Ormazd is at hand, and we look to see the face of the glorious King of Victory, and Hushedar and

Peshotan will come without doubt' (Dhabhar, 593–4). The uneventful passing of that longed-for year was a cruel blow, and though they never ceased to hope for the Saoshyant's coming, their expectations thereafter were more vague. Chardin noted, however (II, 184), that 'one of their most constant traditions is that their religion will again be paramount . . . and that empire will once more be theirs. They sustain themselves and their children with this hope.'

After Shah ʿAbbas matters grew only worse for them. ʿAbbas II (1642–67) moved the Isfahani 'Gaurs' to a new suburb (wanting the old one for a pleasure resort); and here under the last Safavid king, Sultan Husayn (1694–1722), they suffered terribly, for soon after his accession he signed a decree for their forcible conversion. A Christian archbishop witnessed the violent measures taken to enforce this; the Zoroastrian temple was demolished, large numbers of the 'Gaurs' were compelled at sword-point to accept Islam, and the bodies of those who refused stained the river with their blood. A few escaped, and there are still families in the Yazdi region who trace descent from such fugitives.

Parsis in the sixteenth and seventeenth centuries

The story of the Parsis meantime is a happier one, for they were making a modest rise in wealth and consequence. The emperor Akbar was interested in religions, and when he questioned the Parsis of Surat in 1573, they fetched a learned Bhagaria priest, Meherji Rana, from Navsari to expound their beliefs to him. Five years later Meherji was summoned to a discussion at the Mughal court between the adherents of various religions, an event recorded by a Muslim historian in the following words: 'Fire-worshippers also have come from Navsari in Gujarat and proved to his Majesty the truth of Zoroaster's doctrines: they called fire-worship the great worship, and impressed the Emperor so favourably that he learned from them the religious terms and rites of the Parsis, and ordered . . . that the sacred fire should be kept burning at court by day and night, according to the custom of the ancient Persian kings' (Commissariat, II, 222). In his tolerance and eclecticism Akbar abolished the jizya and granted freedom of worship to all; and the Parsis of Navsari, sharing in the general rejoicing, conferred on Meherji Rana and his descendants the office of their high priest or Great Dastur in perpetuity. (To this day the Bhagarias are led by a Dastur Meherji Rana.)

Later – probably on Parsi advice – Akbar asked Shah ʿAbbas to send him a learned Zoroastrian to help in compiling a Persian dictionary; and Dastur Ardashir Noshiravan of Kerman spent 1597 at his court. Two other Parsi priests were accorded the title of 'mulla' by the emperor for their religious learning, and they, like Dastur Meherji Rana, received grants of land, the deeds of which survive. From this time on, Parsi written records become steadily more extensive, and include legal documents, registers of religious ceremonies and dues, lists of priestly ordinations, agreements between priests and the laity, and lists of benefactions. All such documents, together with inscriptions on dakhmas and fire temples, were drawn on by a nineteenth-century Parsi scholar, Bamanji Byramji Patel, for a work in Gujarati called 'Parsi Prakash' ('Parsi Lustre'), which is an invaluable source for the history of the community.

There are a number of notices about the Parsis in the seventeenth century from Europeans, rivals in trade of the Portuguese, some of whom already knew the 'Gaurs' from visits to Isfahan. Most Parsis at this time, they record, were, like the Iranis, 'rather husbandmen than merchants, not caring to stir abroad' (Fryer, II, 295); and though most of them lived along the coast, ancient respect for the creations made them reluctant to sail the waters. 'And if at any time they go a voyage, will not exonerate in the sea, or on the water, but have jars on purpose; if their houses be on fire, they quench them not with water, rather choosing to load them with dust or sand' (Streynsham Master, II, cccxv). These houses were humble dwellings, single-storeyed, small and dark, like those of the 'Gaurs' of Isfahan; and they were kept as fortresses of the faith, no unbelievers being invited in. Their inhabitants were 'very industrious, and diligent, and careful to train up their children to arts and labour. They are the principal men at the loom in all the country, and most of the silks and stuffs at Surat are made by their hands' (Ovington, 219). Yet they had not lost their Zoroastrian zest for enjoyment, and had become great 'toddy' drinkers, subsisting this fermented palm-juice for the wine of their mother country.

When the Europeans (by leave of the Mughals) established trading factories in Gujarat, Hindus and Parsis readily entered their employment; and in 1620 a Parsi clerk at the English factory in Surat interpreted between a priest of his faith and an inquiring English chaplain there, one Henry Lord, who wrote down what he thus learnt (pp. 29 ff.). The Parsi priest, describing the community, said that the layman, 'being by secular occasions drawn from the services of religion, had therefore a less difficult injunction laid upon him', but should always fear lest he lose heaven, and 'whensoever they are to do anything, to think whether the thing be good or bad that they go about'. The ordinary priest 'called their herbood' must know 'in what manner to pray to God, observing the rites prescribed in the "Zundavastaw", for God is best pleased with that form of prayer, that he hath given in his own book.' He is to be strict in self-discipline, truthful, and 'known only in his own business, and not to enquire after the things of the world, it belongeth only to him to teach others what God would have them do. Therefore the behdin . . . shall see that he want nothing needful, but shall afford it him, and he shall seek nothing superfluous.' Lastly he is 'to keep himself pure and undefiled . . . for God is pure, whose servant he is, and it is expected he should be such.' As for the high priest, 'as he is above the rest in dignity, so he is enjoined to be above the rest in sanctity. . . . He must never touch any of a strange caste or sect . . . nor any layman of his own religion, but he must wash himself. . . . He must do everything that belongeth to himself with his own hand . . . the better to preserve his purity. . . . He must use no pomp or superfluity, so of that great revenue that cometh yearly to him he must leave nothing over-plus at the year's end, that must not be bestowed in good uses, either in charitable contributions to the poor, or in building of the temples of God. . . . That his house be near adjoining to the church, where he must keep and make his abiding. . . . That the Dastur be acquainted with all the learning contained in the "Zunda-vastaw". . . . That he stand in fear of nobody but God, nor fear anything but sin . . . that . . . when any man sinneth, he may tell him of it, be he never so great.'

With regard to observances, Lord learnt (pp. 46–7) that some time after birth the parents would take a child to the temple where the priest would give it some 'hom'-juice, 'uttering this prayer, that God would cleanse it from the uncleanness of his father and the menstruous pollutions of his mother'. At the age of about seven (thus reduced from the traditional fifteen, doubtless under Brahman influence) the priest teaches the child 'to say some prayers and instructs it in religion'. Then he is given a ritual bath, and the priest puts on him the sacred shirt and girdle, 'which he ever weareth about him, and is woven . . . by the preacher's own hand'. As for festivals,

Lord learnt (pp. 41–2) only of the gahambars, 'celebrated for five days together, each of them according to the six works of creation'. (All the gahambars had been reduced to five days each, on the pattern of the five 'Gatha' days, early in the Islamic period). A successor of Lord's, John Ovington, observed, in 1689, that 'at their solemn festivals, whither a hundred or two sometimes resort, each man according to his fancy and ability, brings with him his victuals, which is equally distributed, and eat in common by all those present' (p. 218). Lord further says (p. 40) that 'their law alloweth them great liberty in meats and drinks. . . . Whensoever they eat of any fowl or flesh, they carry some part of it to the "agiary" or temple, as an offering to appease God, that for the sustenance of man they are forced to take away the life of his creatures.' This is clearly a reference to the 'atash-zohr'.

A young German nobleman, de Mandelslo, visiting Surat in 1638, has been credited with learning a fair amount from the Parsis about their doctrines. He records (pp. 59–60) that they believed in 'but one God, Preserver of the Universe', but had also a 'great veneration' for the 'seven servants of God', who have 'only an inferior administration'. Besides these 'subalternate spirits . . . whose dignity is very great, God hath twenty-six other servants, who have all their particular functions'; and he lists the calendar Yazads by name. The Parsis believed, he says, that these beings 'have an absolute power over things whereof God hath entrusted them with the administration, whence it comes, that they make no difficulty to worship them.' It is thus clear, on the testimony of independent witnesses, that the beliefs of Parsis and Iranis at this time were identical and orthodox.

Lord describes two dakhmas built near Surat on land granted to the Parsis by Akbar, 'of a round form, a pretty height from the ground, sufficiently capacious and large; within they are paved with stone'. A number of old towers have been examined by Parsi scholars, who have been able to trace gradual refinements such as a stone outside staircase, and the dividing of the stone platform within into three concentric circles with separate partitions. It was difficult in fertile Gujarat to find barren places for the towers, but the Parsis did their best by using rising ground remote from houses or roads.

Early in the seventeenth century the Parsi colony at Cambay was extinguished, possibly in 1606, when the last Muzaffarid sultan made a stand there. Surat had already taken over the trade and prosperity of the older port, and during the next century and a half it became the largest centre of Zoroastrian population in the world. In 1774 a Dutch sea-captain, Stavorinus, estimated the number of Parsis there at about 100,000 souls (one-fifth of the population) and (he said) 'they increase in numbers from day to day, and have built and inhabit many entire wards in the suburbs' (II, 494). They were in general on excellent terms with the Hindus; but Akbar's policy of tolerance had not outlasted his own reign. His successor re-imposed the jizya, and thereafter Muslims were 'allowed a precedence to all the rest, because of their religion' (Ovington, 139). This led at times to violence, and one famous instance for the Parsis is that of a weaver of Broach, one Kama Homa, whom a Muslim called a 'kafir' or unbeliever. Kama retorted with spirit that it was he who was the 'kafir'. The Muslim carried this insult to the local magistrate, who ruled that no infidel could so insult a worshipper of Allah, and therefore Kama must himself become a Muslim or die. He chose death, and was beheaded in 1702.

Despite such evidence of inner fire and courage, the travellers' accounts in general give the same sort of picture of the Parsis as of the Iranis, showing them to be a gentle, quiet, industrious race. They lived, it was said, 'in great harmony among themselves, make common contribution for the aid of their poor, and suffer none of their number to ask alms from people of a different religion' (Niebuhr, II, 429). 'Their universal kindness, either in employing such as are needy and able to work, or bestowing a seasonable bounteous charity to such as are infirm and miserable, leave no man destitute of relief' (Ovington, 218). Such communal care required some organization, and the Parsis, like the Iranis, were governed by their own elders or magistrates, the position being generally hereditary. These 'great ones' or 'akabir' might be laymen, or men of priestly stock pursuing secular callings. Priests did not concern themselves directly with worldly matters (as the 'herbood' explained to Lord), but had their own associations to control their separate affairs. (This was so also in Iran.) They co-operated, however, with the elders in supervising morals. The usual means by which the latter enforced their authority was that 'when a Parsi behaves ill, he is expelled from their community' (Niebuhr, II, 428), that is, he was cut off from all religious rites and communal benefits. The priests would not minister to him, and he could not enter a fire temple, nor would his body be carried to a dakhma when he died. He was in fact made 'out caste'. Occasionally more direct penalties were imposed. Stavorinus notes (II, 496) that 'adultery and fornication they punish among themselves, and even by death; but they must, however, give cognizance of any capital punishment to the Moorish [i.e. Muslim] government; the execution is performed in secret, either by lapidation, drowning in the river, or beating to death and sometimes poison'. 'Such heavy crimes' (he adds) 'I was told, are very seldom heard of among them.' This sternness in punishing may seem at variance with the gentle nature attributed to the Parsis in most reports; but it is clear that the Zoroastrians of Iran and India could not have maintained their religion and way of life against all odds without having a granite streak in their characters.

Parsi spirit was shown also in daily life, and the Qissa-i Rustam Manek celebrates the bravery as well as goodness of an 'elder' of Surat. Rustam Manek, a prosperous factor and merchant, fought valiantly in the troubles which broke out in the late seventeenth century when the Hindu Marathas of the Deccan began a series of campaigns against the Mughals, during which Gujarat was repeatedly ravaged. The Qissa also celebrates his benevolent activities: building roads and bridges, making public wells, and paying the jizya on behalf of poor Hindus as well as Parsis, to save them from the tax-gatherers' harsh treatment.

The growing prosperity of such prominent Parsis meant that they mingled more with people of other communities, and employed more Hindu servants. Their houses were thus less secure strongholds of Zoroastrian purity; and perhaps because of this, perhaps also because of the urgings of their co-religionists in Iran, they began to found lesser sacred fires locally. The first of these was probably established in Surat, but (because Surat was so often destroyed by fire and flood) the fullest records come from what was to be the rival port of Bombay. This had become a British possession in 1661, and was entrusted to the East India Company to administer from Surat. The Company set out to make it 'the flourishingest port in India', and as one means of achieving this proclaimed complete religious freedom there. This brought a steady flow to the island of Hindu and Parsi settlers, eager to escape harassment by Mughal and Portuguese. In 1671 Hirji Vaccha built a Dar-i Mihr there, and soon afterwards a dakhma; and in 1709 an Atash-i Adaran was consecrated. From this time on, records usually distinguish between three types of Parsi sacred foundations: the Dar-i Mihr without an ever-burning fire (into which fire was brought, usually from a priest's house, for rituals); the Dar-i Mihr with a Dadgah fire; and the Dar-i Mihr with an Adaran. In common parlance, however, all three might be referred to by the

Gujarati term 'agiary' or 'place of fire'. During the eighteenth and nineteenth centuries more and more sacred fires were thus founded by individuals, both in new places of Parsi settlement, and in the old centres in Gujarat. The oldest village Adaran appears to be that of Siganpur, not far from Surat; this was the birthplace of Lowji Nassarwanji, the 'Wadia' or shipbuilder, who moved to Bombay in 1735, and there played a leading part in developing its great dock-yards. He thus became wealthy, and not only endowed this sacred fire, but also established a annual gahambar-celebration for his soul's sake. The new fire temples of the Parsis, like those of the Iranis, were indistinguishable from ordinary houses in the streets where they stood, for outside Bombay the times were still dangerous. Thus Streynsham Master (p. ccxv) records that the Parsis had a fire temple in Surat, but that in 1672 'the tumultuous rabble of the zealot Moors destroyed and took it from them.'

Eighteenth-century Parsi religious disputes

There was during all this while still only one Parsi Atash Bahram, the Sanjana fire in Navsari. For several generations the Sanjana priests had lived harmoniously among the Bhagarias there, supporting them-selves from the offerings made to their fire; but as their numbers grew, they began to encroach on the Bhagarias' rights to perform all other religious work in the town. Friction increased during the seventeenth century, and led to a law-suit before a Hindu court, and a decree that the Sanjanas must keep to their original agreement to serve the fire only. They decided that they would rather leave Navsari, and in 1741 did so, taking the Atash Bahram with them. A year later they installed it in a new temple at the village of Udwada, on the coast a little to the south of Sanjan, where it burns to this day.

The removal of the sacred fire distressed the Bhagarias, and they resolved to consecrate an Atash Bahram of their own. Leading priests consulted 'Pazand, Pahlavi and Persian manuscripts' to discover the appropriate rituals for so great an undertaking, and other Parsi communities gave help, in particular Surat. A hundred priests who 'knew well the Avesta', purified and consecrated the many lesser fires which were needed, and in 1765 the new 'King of fires' was enthroned. The Sanjanas were naturally a little jealous of this rival to their own 800-year-old fire, and must have feared that fewer pilgrims would now come to remote Udwada; and they evolved a legend to enhance its dignity. Previously, in its uniqueness, it had been referred to in documents simply as 'the' Atash Bahram, or 'Shri Atash Saheb'; but now the name 'Iranshah' was used for it, and the story was put about that the first Parsi settlers had brought it with them from Iran, and that it was somehow linked to the khvarenah of the Persian kings of old. This legend is widely believed among the Parsis, who continue loyally to make the pilgrimage to its shrine.

Other causes of friction between different groups of priests arose in Bombay, which was outside the old territorial divisions into 'panths'. Surat was in Bhagaria territory; but when the Parsi community there prospered so greatly, its priests, becoming numerous, had broken away from Navsari to form an independent self-governing group, the Suratyas. But Bombay, whose growth was being artificially fostered, attracted Parsis from every part of Gujarat, so priests from all the different 'panths' followed the lay settlers there, to minister to them and to serve in the fire temples which they founded. There was therefore no one ecclesiastical authority at the southern port.

It was in Surat, however, that a serious element of discord first arose in the now thriving community. Controversies developed there about whether the 'padan' or mouth-veil should be tied over the faces of the dead, and whether the dead should be laid out with legs extended, or crossed; and in 1720 the Suratyas invited a learned priest from Kerman, Dastur Jamasp 'Vilayati' ('of the mother land') to pronounce on these matters. He gave his opinion that 'padan' should be used, and the legs crossed, in the Irani manner; and he then turned to other matters. He had brought with him some manuscripts, including a Vendidad, and he invited three young priests (Darab Kumana from Surat, Jamasp Asa from Navsari, and a third from Broach) to study the Avesta with him through the Pahlavi translation (then neglected by the Parsis, in favour of the Gujarati rendering). After a little while Dastur Jamasp returned home, leaving the Parsis still fiercely debating, not only over funerary practices, but also about the calendar. The letters between India and Iran had long since made the priests of the two communities aware of the month's difference between their reckonings, but, not being able to explain this, they had simply accepted it; but in 1746 a group of priests and laymen in Surat decided to adopt the Irani calendar, regarding it as the 'qadimi' or 'ancient' one. Thus the Kadmi movement was born, which in general gave preference to Irani over Parsi usages, on the assumption that these represented an older (rather than a slightly different) tradition.

Most Parsis, however, held stoutly to the calendar and ways of their forefathers, calling themselves Rasimis ('traditionalists') or, more popularly, Sharshais or Shenshais (a word of disputed origin, sometimes mistakenly rendered later as Shahanshahis, 'royalists').

The controversy between these groups became very bitter, and remained so for at least a century. Some wealthy laymen adhered to the small Kadmi party, and one of them enabled the leading Kadmi priest of Broach, 'Mulla' Kaus, to visit Iran in search of decisive evidence in its support. He was away for twelve years, and returned in 1780 laden with Arabo-Persian manuscripts and papers. The Shenshais meantime had been searching through works available to them in India, so the dispute stimulated a concern with the writings of the faith among laymen as well as priests – for the laity, through their involvement with commerce, were beginning to share in the literacy which till then had been a priestly prerogative.

Demand grew therefore in the eighteenth century for Gujarati translations of the daily Avestan prayers, and of such popular works as the Menog i Khrad and Arda Viraz Namag; and copies of these were provided by priests, who also continued their traditional labour of transcribing Avestan and Pahlavi manuscripts. Most surviving Zoroastrian manuscripts date from this time. About thirty copies of the Vendidad are known to have been made in the eighteenth century by one Bhagaria priest alone; and the yashts were also transcribed from a unique codex written in Navsari in 1591, presumably from a lost Iranian manuscript.

At its height the dispute between Shenshais and Kadmis produced so deep a schism that it necessitated the founding of separate places of worship. In 1783 a wealthy philanthropist, Dady Seth, had a Kadmi Atash Bahram consecrated in Bombay, with Mulla Kaus as its first high priest, and also founded an Adaran there, to be served by visiting Irani priests; and in 1823 two rival Atash Bahrams, one Shenshai and one Kadmi, were installed in Surat. One consequence of the schism was that some of the angry feelings of the Shenshais were directed against the Iranis, whose usages the Kadmis championed; and after this time the majority of Parsis ceased to look to the Iranis for counsel in matters of the faith.

Irani Zoroastrians in the eighteenth century

This change in attitude (of which the Iranis, in their own deep troubles, were probably unaware) was encouraged by the changing circumstances of the two communities, with the Parsis thriving while the Iranis struggled to survive. In 1719 their country was invaded by Afghans, who marched through Seistan and fell unexpectedly on Kerman. The Zoroastrian quarter, the Gabr-Mahalle, was outside the city walls, and its inhabitants – men, women and children – were almost all slaughtered. The Dasturan dastur and other leading men lived near the Atash Bahram within the town, under the eye of the Muslim authorities, and so they survived; but so few were the living that they could do no more for the dead than bring the bodies together on the plain and surround them with an earthen wall. This makeshift dakhma can still be seen some way from the ruins of the Gabr-Mahalle, which was never rebuilt.

The Afghans overthrew the Safavids, but were driven out after seven years by the Qajars (a Turkish tribe of northern Iran, who claimed descent from Timur Leng), and a mercenary leader, Nadir Kuli, who in 1736 was proclaimed Shah. Two years later Nadir invaded India, defeated the Mughal army, and sacked Delhi, but victories seemed only to make him more cruel and covetous, and under him Iran itself was a ravaged land. He was assassinated in 1747, and power passed to one of his captains, Karim Khan Zand, who reigned from 1750 to 1779, with Shiraz as his capital. It was during his kindly and just rule that Mulla Kaus visited Iran. He found the Dasturan dastur removed from Turkabad to Yazd (leaving the two ancient Atash Bahrams still in Sharifabad) – doubtless so that he too could be under closer Muslim surveillance. A general assembly of Zoroastrians was called to meet Kaus in Yazd, and he put to them seventy-eight questions. Their answers constitute the Ittoter ('Seventy-eight') Rivayat, which is the last of the Rivayats from Iran. It was treasured by the Kadmis, but naturally regarded with suspicion by the Shenshais. Kaus then went on to study astronomy and other matters in Kerman, where he found the Zoroastrians struggling under a crushing burden of tax, because the same amount of jizya was being wrung from the survivors as had been exacted before the Afghan massacre. Kaus was able to help bring their plight to the notice of Karim Khan, who granted them instant relief.

The Zand dynasty was not long lived, and in 1796 its last representative was besieged in Kerman by the Qajar Agh.. Muhammad, who took the city and exacted a terrible vengeance on its inhabitants for sheltering his enemy. Agha Muhammad was crowned in that year as Shah, and from then until 1925 the Qajars ruled Iran from their northern capital, Tehran; and the early part of their epoch saw the fortunes of the Irani Zoroastrians sink to their lowest ebb.

The Parsi Panchayat of Bombay

Meantime in India, Nadir Shah having dealt its death blow to the Mughal Empire, Gujarat was being fought over by Muslim nobles, Maratha princes and European merchants. In 1759 the East India Company emerged as master of Surat, but, the countryside being still in turmoil, it continued to encourage the shift of trade and population to its safer island-possession of Bombay. As a mercantile venture the Company was glad to devote as little time as possible to governing, and so encouraged the different 'nations' there to choose their own representatives to manage their internal affairs. The Hindus being hugely in the majority, the English called such representatives by their term, 'panchayat'. A 'Parsi Panchayat' seems to have been constituted in 1728, which despite its new name was essentially the traditional Zoroastrian council of elders, and so had no working priests among its first nine members; but since in Bombay there was no corresponding priestly body to manage the ecclesiastical affairs of the community, matters which in Navsari, for instance, would come under the jurisdiction of the Bhagarsath Anjoman (such as upkeep of the dakhmas) were dealt with in Bombay by this lay Panchayat. Even the fire temples there, endowed by wealthy laymen, were in the control of lay trustees, mostly of the founder's family, who appointed the priests, whereas the older Sanjana and Bhagaria fires were in the charge of the priests themselves. Priestly responsibility, and therefore authority, was thus weaker in Bombay than anywhere else.

Much of the work of the Bombay Panchayat was the same as that of the elders of earlier days, though theirs was a harder task, trying to maintain the strict morality of former times in a jostling, expanding, cosmopolitan city, where the Parsis no longer lived in separate wards, as in Surat, and where the growing diversity of their employment and interests eroded the old sense of communal solidarity. It was on this solidarity that the ultimate sanction of the Panchayat rested, that of making an offender 'out caste'; and without it (and being forbidden by the English to inflict physical punishment) they could do little more than admonish and fine, and hope that the fines would be paid. In these circumstances, it is a tribute to the calibre of its members that the Panchayat exerted a considerable authority not only in the eighteenth but throughout the nineteenth century, and indeed even today its approval is still sought for any major Parsi undertaking.

In social matters, the eighteenth-century Panchayat tried to uphold the stability of marriage and to regulate divorce (which they permitted, though reluctantly, in a fairly wide range of circumstances). Bigamy they only countenanced, on stringent conditions, if a first marriage were barren. In the religious sphere, they sought to discourage any visiting of Hindu shrines, and to support the institutions of their own faith, notably the celebration of the gahambars; but they tried to curb extravagance in their observance, and in the ceremonies for the dead, lest new wealth should lead people to vie with one another in lavishness. (This was a largely unavailing struggle.) They also maintained the purity laws; and as late as 1857 a man and his daughter were forbidden to enter any place of worship until they had undergone barashnom, because they had eaten a meal cooked by a Muslim. In seeking to keep the community separate and untainted, the Panchayat set itself resolutely against proselytizing or accepting 'juddins' (those of another religion) into the faith, taking their stand on a statement attributed to the first settlers at Sanjan, that they were those 'in whose caste men of different religion are never accepted'. They also opposed investing with the kusti the children of Parsi fathers and Hindu mothers.

Another side of the Panchayat's work was administrative and charitable (which again was in the tradition of the former 'akabir'). They had considerable funds at their disposal (from fees for weddings and funerals, fines and charitable bequests), and in 1823 they appointed four of their members as Trustees to administer these. With them they maintained the dakhmas, organized gahambar feasts, (still attended by rich and poor alike), and provided for the sick, destitute, widowed and orphaned. They also established a special fund to pay for the funerals and soul-ceremonies of the needy.

For nearly forty years Bombay had only the one Kadmi Atash Bahram; but soon after the two Atash Bahrams were established at Surat, three brothers of the Wadia family installed a Shenshai fire in Bombay. The consecration was performed in 1830 by Bhagarias, and the first high priest was Dastur Edalji Sanjana (despite his surname, a Bhagaria priest). The high priest of the Kadmi Atash Bahram was then Mulla Firoze, son of Mulla Kaus; and both men were to play active parts in the controversies which lay ahead in the days of British India.

Eighteenth-century European studies of Zoroastrian beliefs

An external factor which aggravated these controversies was Western contribution to the interpreting of Zoroastrian doctrine. The travellers' reports had awoken scholarly interest in Europe in the religion of Zoroaster, and in 1700 the first fruits appeared in Thomas Hyde's 'Veterum Persarum et Parthorum et Medorum religionis historia'. An Oxford Orientalist, Hyde not only ransacked Greek and Latin authors for data about Iranian religion, but made use of Arabic writings, and such Persian Zoroastrian texts as he could lay hands on. His great respect for Zoroastrianism led him, as a seventeenth-century divine, to seek in it resemblances to his own Christian faith. He was misled, moreover, by the undue prominence given in his sources to Zurvan, and also by a misapprehension on the part of Chardin (whose reports from Isfahan he had read) that the God worshipped by the 'Gaurs' was distinct from 'Ormous', the principle of light. So he concluded that Zoroaster had been a strict monotheist, sent by God to repeat the work of Abraham among the ancient Iranians; and he supposed that his teachings had been misinterpreted by the polytheistic Greeks, and later by those who, acquainted with the dualistic heresies of Manichaeism and Mazdakism, had wrongly attributed these to the older Iranian religion. Hyde's pioneer work was in many ways admirable, and it held the field for three-quarters of a century, during which time his Judaeo-Christian interpretation of Zoroastrianism established itself so firmly in the academic world that it was with difficulty shaken by the subsequent discovery of the actual doctrines of the faith.

In the mid eighteenth century a young French scholar, Anquetil du Perron, travelled to India with the hope of acquiring Zoroastrian manuscripts and learning more about the religion. He spent the years 1759 to 1761 in Surat, where he persuaded Darab Kumana (the former pupil of Jamasp Vilayati, by then a leading Kadmi priest) to translate the Avesta to him. Darab must have based his exposition largely on Gujarati and Pahlavi renderings, but he succeeded in giving Anquetil a very fair idea of the contents of the whole work (although defective, inevitably, for the Gathas). This action of his was censured as a betrayal by the rest of the community. Anquetil also acquired Avestan and Pahlavi manuscripts from Darab; and on his return with these to Europe he published a complete French translation of the surviving Avestan texts, with ritual instructions, and many valuable personal observations on the customs and usages of the Parsis, as well as a translation of the Pahlavi Bundahishn.

The Avesta translation shocked Europe, for it presented an apparently polytheistic, ritualistic faith utterly at variance with Hyde's reconstruction. Anquetil sought, however, to disarm hostile criticism by maintaining that Zoroaster's own teaching had indeed been 'a pure theism', but 'even in the time of Abraham debased by heterodox opinions'. This was necessarily unsubstantiated conjecture, since at that stage the Gathas had not been isolated as the prophet's own words, and there was therefore no basis whatsoever for thus hazarding what he might himself have taught. However, the science of comparative philology was then being developed, and this enabled scholars to study the newly available Avestan language in conjunction with Sanskrit; and with this key to help them, they soon discovered that Darab's translation was inexact, and showed a lack of grasp of Avestan grammar. Most of those concerned were Protestant Christians, used to regarding the Bible, rather than a continuing tradition, as the source of their own religious beliefs; and so the discovery that the Parsis' understanding of their ancient scriptures was imperfect, together with travellers' tales about the apparent ignorance of the 'Gaurs', led them to conclude that the contemporary Zoroastrians no longer had a true knowledge of the tenets of their own faith. This misapprehension made it easier to accept Anquetil's theory that this had already been the state of affairs in the remote past. So Europe kept Hyde's interpretation of original Zoroastrianism as the Iranian form of an idealized Judaism, but added of necessity the rider that it had long been corrupted by its own adherents. So the seed was sown of much trouble for Western scholars (who were going to have to spend the next hundred years or so trying to maintain this theory in defiance of remorselessly accumulating facts), and also, more seriously, for the Zoroastrians themselves.

CHAPTER THIRTEEN

Under the Qajars and British

Christian missionaries and Parsi beliefs

The nineteenth century saw great changes for urban Parsis, the main factors being the growth of commerce and industry, and the impact of Western education and Protestant Christianity. The East India Company had banned missionaries, but pressure from revivalist societies in Britain was strong, and in 1813 its charter was renewed only on condition that this ban was lifted. The first missionaries arrived in Bombay (which by then had replaced Surat as the main centre of Parsi population) in the 1820s. In the same decade a movement began to establish there schools in which instruction would be given in English as well as Gujarati; and in 1827 Elphinstone College was founded to teach 'the languages, literatures, sciences and moral philosophy of Europe'. In 1840 this was combined with a school to form the Elphinstone Institute, and Parsis supplied most of the pupils there throughout the nineteenth century; and thus there was formed a Western-educated Parsi middle class, numbering doctors and lawyers, teachers, journalists and the like in its ranks.

In 1834 the British Government took over the East India Company's possessions, and became ruler of most of India. (Of the old Parsi centres only Navsari was not included, remaining contentedly part of the Hindu State of Baroda.) In matters of religion, official policy continued impartial, and no religious instruction was given in any government schools. Yet the teaching of English literature inevitably brought pupils into contact with Christian ideas, while Western science collided with many traditional Hindu and Zoroastrian beliefs. Parsi boys were at first insulated from shock in this respect by ignorance of their own scriptures. They knew the fundamental doctrines of the faith and were trained in its observances, but the Avesta itself, with its store of ancient learning and legend, was a matter for the dasturs, as much a mystery to the laity as the Latin Bible then to Roman Catholics. It caused therefore a great stir in the community when this element in their holy books was suddenly thrust on their attention by John Wilson, a Scottish missionary.

Wilson, arriving in Bombay in 1829, was impressed by the devout and upright character of the Parsis, whom he found to be a 'very influential portion' of the city's population, and he carefully prepared a campaign to bring them into the Christian fold. He studied Anquetil's translations of the Avesta and Bundahishn, together with other European writings, and then moved to the attack with sermons, pamphlets and articles in the new medium of daily newspapers. He assailed Zoroastrian dualism, and poured scorn on the ancient cosmogonic and mythical material in the Bundahishn, as well as the prescriptions in the Vendidad about the purity laws, contrasting these, unfairly, with the Christian Gospels rather than with Leviticus. (The Gathas themselves he could naturally make little of in Anquetil's translation.) Most Parsis had never heard of the Bundahishn, and were as startled by Wilson's summaries of its contents as a twentieth-century Christian would be if introduced for the first time to some of the more primitive parts of the Old Testament. A layman hastened accordingly to repudiate the whole book as 'entirely false', and probably composed by 'some enemy of our religion' (Wilson, p. 37) – a defence which proved embarrassing when Wilson triumphantly showed that much of its material was derived from the Avesta itself, which the community regarded as being in its entirety the word of God revealed to his prophet, Zoroaster.

In their perplexity the Parsis persuaded three priests to enter the lists, but they added to confusion by producing basically different defences. Two of them betrayed orthodoxy by turning for help to the Desatir ('Ordinances'), a work now generally regarded as a literary forgery, produced probably within a Persian Sufi sect, and having only the most tenuous connections with Zoroastrianism. A manuscript of it had been brought back from Iran by Mulla Kaus, and it was published in Bombay in 1818 by his son, Mulla Firoze, arousing great interest there. It consists of a text in an artificial language (with elements taken from Indian and Iranian dialects, and a largely Persian grammar), and a Persian 'translation' of this, studiously free from Arabic words; and it purports to contain the sayings of fourteen successive prophets, from 'Mahabad' (who flourished in remote pre-history) to the 'Fifth Sasan' (living just before the Arab conquest). These prophets, it was claimed, had not died, but had withdrawn from the world as the hidden 'Masters'; and the religion taught by them had prevailed, it was asserted, in Iran down the ages, differing from that commonly ascribed to Zoroaster only because in the Avesta he had clothed his teachings in allegoric words.

This claim, when accepted by Zoroastrians, gave them licence to re-interpret the Avesta freely in the light of 'Mahabadian' doctrines, which according to the Desatir included belief in a remote, impersonal God, almighty and incomprehensible; in a series of intermediate 'Intelligences'; and in re-incarnation, with progress through the chain of being to be achieved by self-denial, fasting and solitary meditation. There were some elaborate prescriptions for prayer postures, suggestive of Hindu ascetic practices, and the spirit of the work was wholly remote from the rational, practical one of orthodox Zoroastrianism. Yet it gave 'parabolic sanctuary', as Wilson put it, to those suddenly called on, without preparation or training, to defend their ancient faith; and so two of the priests concerned took refuge with it, declaring that 'what is written in the Vendidad about Hormazd and Ahriman . . . is a parable of our prophet Zartusht. He has declared a matter in secret science' (Wilson, p. 150). So the gates were opened to occultism, which strongly influences many Parsis to the present day.

The third priest, the now venerable Dastur Edal Sanjana of the Wadia Atash Bahram, presented what was essentially traditional orthodoxy, unshaken by taunts of either dualism or polytheism. Ahriman, he insisted, was an independent malign being; and a Yazad had indeed been appointed by God to preside 'over every object in earth or in the heavenly worlds' (ibid. 198–9). He put forward, however, the long-established contamination of the Gathic doctrine of the seven creations with ancient Greek theory of the four elements; and Wilson was swift to attack this on scientific grounds, remarking mockingly (ibid. 9) that Dastur Edal had lived 'for many years almost in a state of seclusion at the principal fire temple; and he seems, to a considerable extent, to have escaped the untoward march of intellect'.

This was entirely proper conduct for a high priest; and naturally Dastur Edal, like all other Zoroastrian priests then, had received only the traditional training of his calling, so that it was unreasonable to expect him to be able to counter attacks which drew on a world of knowledge wholly unfamiliar to him.

Wilson in fact gained few converts among the Parsis, but his campaign hastened the disintegrating effects which Western influences were having on the community. The educated laity felt that their priests had failed them, and the seed was sown of that contempt which, as the nineteenth century advanced, came to replace the age-old regard for the priesthood as the learned class. In Bombay especially a sense of lay superiority was fostered both by the lack of a corporate priestly body to exercise authority there, and by the fact that individual laymen made huge fortunes while their family priests continued to enjoy only the modest incomes derived from the rituals which they performed. So working priests, simply by remaining faithful to the ways of their forefathers, came to appear backward, ignorant and poor, while the laity rushed ahead to embrace progress, science and material prosperity.

Parsi religious reforms

It was not the wealthy Parsis, however, who deliberately introduced religious reforms. They were concerned with making money and spending it, often philanthropically; and in the early nineteenth century they usually still apprenticed their sons young to their own mercantile way of life, rather than putting them to unprofitable book-learning. The changes which they brought about were there-fore mostly incidental, as when they broke one after another of the purity laws in pursuit of trade, or through sheer impatience and lack of time. Thus they undertook long ocean voyages, lived and ate among juddins, introduced the first steam-boats and encouraged the use of steam-trains, in both of which fire was put to rough work, and people of different creeds travelled in close proximity. Where the rich and enterprising led, the rest of the community generally followed, so that today it is only a small number of priests (mostly those serving in the Atash Bahrams), and a few devout and highly conservative lay people, who keep the old purity laws, and even they cannot do so with the former strictness, since they no longer live in separate, almost enclosed communities.

Deliberate reforms were initiated by those of more moderate means, sent to school by their parents in the hope that a Western education would enable them to get on in the world. Opportunities for such education increased steadily through the work of Parsi philanthropists, notably Sir Jamshetji Jijibhai (the first Parsi baronet, honoured for his vast and general charities), who endowed schools for his community in both Bombay and Gujarat. Most of the early reformers emerged, however, from the Elphinstone Institute, which had some inspiring teachers. Prominent among them was Naoroji Feerdoonji, who came to Bombay as a boy from Broach. He founded the 'Young Bombay Party' and, in 1851, the Rahnumai Mazdayasnan Sabha, known in English as the 'Zoroastrian Reform Society'. Its purpose, as formulated by Naoroji, was 'to fight orthodoxy, yet with no rancour or malice . . . to break through the thousand and one religious prejudices that tend to retard the progress and civilization of the community'. This society was largely concerned with social matters; and it has been said of its founder that 'to him is chiefly due the establishment of the first girls' school, the first native library, the first literary society, the first debating club, the first political association, the first body for improving the condition of women, . . . the first law association, and the first education periodicals. The result of these organizations became apparent as years rolled on in the religious, social and domestic relations of Parsi life.' The list suggests a modern urban existence utterly remote from that of the Parsi wards of Surat a hundred years earlier; but Naoroji's energy and care for his fellowmen were entirely in the old tradition.

The reform movement aroused strong opposition from the conservative and orthodox, and, despite Naoroji's good intentions, many harsh words came to be uttered on both sides. The reformists differed among themselves as to the degree by which they wanted to modernize the faith; but the most extreme, taking their stand on the works of Hyde and Anquetil (which had been publicized by Wilson), declared that Zoroaster had preached a simple monotheism with virtually no rituals, and that to this the Parsis should return. A spokesman for this group was Dosabhoy Framjee, a journalist and writer, who too had studied at the Elphinstone Institute, and who had a boundless admiration for Western culture. In 1858 he published a book called 'The Parsees', designed to acquaint Europe with the 'history, beliefs and manners' of his community, in which he dealt confidently on this basis with matters of faith and observance.

Writings such as his convinced Western scholars that Hyde's interpretation of Zoroaster's teachings had been a just one. The accounts
by travellers of Parsi and Irani beliefs before Western impact were
forgotten, and European philologists proceeded in harmonious
agreement with 'enlightened' Parsis, while disregarding living
orthodoxy and the entire content of the putatively erroneous
Zoroastrian scriptures. Comparatively few Parsis were, however,
'enlightened', and most of the community, putting their chief
energies into earning their livings, 'most diligently continued' (as
Wilson lamented) to believe and worship as of old, while reformists
and traditionalists met in fiery argument over their heads, and
Europeans pontificated remotely.

The need for more knowledge was keenly felt by orthodox and
reformist alike; and in 1854 the Bombay Kadmis founded the Mulla
Firoze Madressa for the instruction of young priests. The teaching
given there was, however, at first only traditional, with knowledge of
such works as the Persian Rivayats being added to the basic learning
of Avestan by rote. The union of such traditional learning with
Western scholarship was brought about by a Kadmi layman,
Kharshedji Cama. No practising priest could yet consider losing his
ritual purity by making an ocean voyage; but Kharshedji, having
distinguished himself in his turn at the Elphinstone Institute, joined
his family's firm, and travelled to China and then Europe. There he
abandoned commerce, and spent the year of 1859 visiting leading
scholars in the Iranian field. With his penetrating intellect and
retentive memory he garnered enough in that short time to be able
on returning to Bombay to pursue Avestan and Pahlavi studies by
himself on Western lines; and he gathered round him a small class of
remarkably gifted young priests, which met regularly over the next
twelve years. One of them, Sheriarji Bharucha, wrote later that they
'felt as if the scales of ignorance were every day falling away from their
mental eyes. . . . Not content with teaching Avestan and Pahlavi
books only, Mr. Cama also introduced the study of comparative
grammar. . . . Of course it was not an easy task . . . to examine . . .
the old Parsi notions, opinions, doctrines and views of history. . . .
Both the teacher and the pupils had to unlearn every day many things
previously learnt.' Here again the influence of Europe streamed in,
with Western linguistic discoveries giving spurious authority to
Western pronouncements about Zoroastrian theology.

The fame of Kharshedji's classes spread and led to the foundation by the Shenshais of the Sir Jamshetji Jijibhai Zartushti Madressa 'for the purpose of teaching Avestan, Pahlavi, Sanskrit, English and other languages to the sons of Parsi priests . . . with a view to enable them to understand thoroughly the Zoroastrian religion'. Most of Cama's pupils managed to live from grants and teaching posts at this and the Mulla Firoze Madressa, for none of them, having had an education in critical scholarship, wished to continue as a practising priest. This was a problem which was to loom ever larger as the century progressed. The community clamoured for an educated priesthood; but the fact that all Zoroastrian acts of worship are performed without book means that every working priest must spend hours of boyhood learning long liturgies by heart, and must constantly refresh his memory of these throughout adult life. A compromise was gradually reached by which priests' sons attended a traditional priestly school in the early morning (rising with the sun), and then went on to share a secular education with their lay fellows for the rest of the day; but fewer and fewer of them wanted subsequently to take up the priest's calling, with its repetitive work, its relatively meagre material rewards, and its steadily diminishing standing in the community. So instead of the most intelligent of a priest's sons following his profession, it began to be the dullards, and so the prestige of the priesthood sank still further.

Haug and West on Zoroastrian beliefs

Meantime a brilliant young German philologist, Martin Haug, had made the crucial discovery that the Gathas were in a more ancient dialect than the rest of the Avesta, and alone could be regarded as the authentic utterance of Zoroaster. In the light of this, he translated these supremely difficult texts afresh, seeking in them support for the established academic dogma of the prophet's rigid monotheism; and this he found in the repeated Gathic denunciations of the 'daevas', which he interpreted as a rejection of all divine beings other than Ahura Mazda. (This was a natural mistake for a scholar familiar with the Vedas, in which the cognate term 'deva' is a general one for 'divinity'.) As for the dualism so evident in the Gathas, Haug dealt with that by drawing a fine distinction between Zoroaster's theology 'according to which he acknowledged only one God', and his 'merely philosophical doctrine' of the existence of two primeval causes; while the Amesha Spentas, he declared, were 'nothing but abstract nouns and ideas'. (These interpretations he set out again in English in his 'Essays', pp. 300 ff.) As for rituals, the silence (as he thought) of the Gathas in this respect meant that Zoroaster 'neither believed in them, nor thought them to be an essential part of religion'.

The 1860s found Haug in India, teaching Sanskrit at Poona University, and while there he lectured energetically to the Parsis about his discovery, startling them profoundly. That of all their scriptures only the Gathas represented the actual words of Zoroaster came as a great shock, and to this day some of the orthodox find it impossible to accept; but the reformists, once they had taken it in, rejoiced mightily, for Haug had provided them with exactly what they had been seeking, namely scholarly justification for rejecting everything in the faith which did not accord with nineteenth-century enlightenment. Now only the Gathas needed to be defended out of all the texts attacked by Wilson; and Haug had shown that these venerable works could themselves be interpreted as teaching just that type of simple theism which they, led by Europe, had already attributed to their prophet. As Kharshedji Cama observed: 'Since that day, there has been no more Christian polemic against the Parsis, and the Parsis say "Haug has done us a service", and they esteem him a great Zoroastrian scholar.'

While in India Haug collaborated with a remarkable Englishman, E. W. West, who was chief engineer on one of the Indian railways. There were plenty of Parsis by then working on the railways, and West took up the study of their Pahlavi literature, and by his careful editions and translations made this branch of Zoroastrian writings known to Europe. Every Pahlavi work contradicted the theories of Zoroastrian monotheism and lack of ritual; but this was all dismissed, together with the testimony of the Younger Avesta, as a corruption of the primitive faith. West himself, however, becoming steeped in the Pahlavi books, argued wisely and calmly for their importance for an understanding of Zoroastrianism. In annotating and expounding them, he was inevitably led to reflect on what were then the current controversies, and of one of these he wrote as follows: 'The Parsi religion has long been represented by its opponents as a dualism; and this accusation . . . has been advanced so strenuously that it has often been admitted by the Parsis themselves, as regards the medieval form of their faith. But neither party seems to have fairly considered how any religion which admits the personality of an evil spirit . . . can fail to become a dualism to a certain extent. If, therefore, the term is to be used in controversy, it behoves those who use it to define the limits of objectionable dualism with great precision, so as not to include most of the religions of the world, their own among the number. If it be necessary for a dualism that the evil spirit be omnipresent, omniscient, almighty, or eternal, then is the Parsi religion no dualism' (SBE, V, lxix).

Theosophy and the Parsis

In 1885 there arrived in Bombay Henry S. Olcott, who ten years earlier had helped found the Theosophical Society in New York. He had a high regard for Zoroastrianism, which he, like Haug (whose writings he knew) held to be 'one of the noblest, simplest, most sublime religions of the world'. He, however, held the Desatir to be of equal authority with the Gathas, and when it was his turn to lecture to the Parsis, he told them that their faith rested upon 'the living rock of Occult Science', because their prophet had 'by a certain course of mystical study penetrated all the hidden mysteries of man's nature and the world around him' (pp. 303, 305). These mysteries he and his followers, the magi of old, had transmitted 'under the safe cover of an external ritual'. Therefore the Parsis, far from abandoning their rituals, must preserve them with meticulous exactitude, while seeking the lost key to their true meaning. As Olcott eloquently put it (p. 311), 'the cloud gathers over the fire altar, the once fragrant wood of Truth is wet with the deadly dews of doubt'; and he urged the community to ignore the barren findings of European philologists, who sought verity 'among the dry bones of words', and who denied that dualism which was at the heart of the faith. 'The law of the Universe is a distinct Dualism . . . and the personification of (its) opposing powers by Zaratusht was but the perfectly scientific and philosophical statement of a profound truth' (ibid. 314–15). Hence his teachings (said Olcott) were 'in agreement with the most recent discoveries of modern science . . . and the freshest graduate from Elphinstone College (had) no cause to blush for the "ignorance" of Zaratusht' (ibid. 303).

Olcott's words gave the same sort of support and satisfaction to occultists as Haug's interpretations had to reforming theists; and a number of the orthodox too were pleased to hear a Westerner speak in praise of rituals. Theosophy held even more attraction for Hindus, since its attempted reconciliation of all creeds was based on Vedantic

Hinduism; and soon there was a thriving branch of the Theosophical Society in Bombay, with Hindu and Parsi members. The latter poured out a flood of books and pamphlets to spread their ideas, arguing that theosophy had been taught, esoterically, by Zoroaster himself, whom they claimed was a divine being, an Amashaspand incarnate, and so even greater than the other hidden 'Masters'. The rituals of the faith they followed Olcott in interpreting in pseudo-scientific terms, explaining those of the fire-cult, for instance, as designed to create 'pyro-electricity'. Despite their regard for the significance of their own ancient rituals, Parsi theosophists tended to adulterate Zoroastrian observances by creating new rites, heavy with symbolism, in their own homes.

Ilm-i Khshnum: Zoroastrian occultism

For this they were censured by adherents of the Ilm-i Khshnum, an exclusively Zoroastrian occult movement. This took its name, intended to mean 'Science of (Spiritual) Satisfaction', from a word 'khshnum' that occurs twice in the Gathas; and it was founded by Behramshah Shroff, who was born in Bombay of priestly stock in 1858. His parents were very poor, and he was not made priest himself, or indeed given much education of any sort. When he was seventeen he wandered off to join an uncle in Peshawar; and there, the story goes, he was taken up by a caravan of outward-seeming Muslims, who secretly wore the kusti. He travelled with them to Iran, and was led to a miraculous place on Mount Demavand where he was enlightened by the 'Masters', who explained to him the esoteric meaning of the Avesta. He returned to live in Surat, where he kept silence for thirty years. Then in 1902 he began to preach, interpreting the Avesta on an 'elevated' plane. His doctrines have been characterized as a thorough-going adaptation of theosophy, with belief in one impersonal God, planes of being, and reincarnation, much planetary lore, and a complete disregard for textual or historical accuracy. With cloudy occultism went strict orthopraxy and observance of the purity laws. Behramshah gradually gained a small following in Surat and Bombay, and, more surprisingly, won over a number of Sanjana priests at Udwada. Two Ilm-i Khshnum agiarys exist in Bombay and one in Udwada, and there is a mass of Ilm-i Khshnum literature, much of it advocating vegetarianism and an ascetic way of life.

One observance maintained by Ilm-i Khshnum is that laymen as well as priests may undergo the barashnom. This was the case for the whole Parsi community down to the eighteenth century, when (for some reason) priests in Bombay began withholding the purification from the laity. By the end of the nineteenth century it was general practice for the Parsi laity to undergo it only vicariously, paying priests to be their proxies, whereas among the Iranis it was still being administered locally to lay men and women in the 1970s.

With their regard for orthopraxy, Ilm-i Khshnum have a clear position in controversies over forms of prayer, which first arose in the nineteenth century. The reformists, influenced by Protestant Christian usage, urged that Avestan prayers should be translated into the vernacular, so that worshippers could understand what they were saying. The orthodox position was that Avestan was the sacred language, and that to pray in it was part of the age-old devotional tradition of the community, and not to be given up; and the occultists supported them, on the grounds that the ancient words produced beneficial vibrations on the ethereal plane. The reformists produced a Gujarati prayer-book, but failed to bring it into general use. The community has remained therefore united in its forms of worship.

Parsis and the printed word

Until the nineteenth century the learning of Avestan prayers was a matter of patient repetition by teacher and taught; but in the 1820s Mobad Furdoonji Marzbanji, the 'Caxton of Bombay', began printing the Khorda Avesta in Gujarati script, and soon copies of this were generally and cheaply available. This step, taken by a mobad was another blow to the status of priests. Till then they had been the guardians of the holy words, both through knowing them by heart and through being able to read them in the mysterious Avestan and Pahlavi characters; but now, transcribed into the adequate and familiar Gujarati script, they could be read by any school-child, and what had been a professional mystery was open to the many. Later one of the most gifted of Kharshedji Cama's pupils, Tehmuras Anklesaria, a Godavra priest, set up another press to print Avestan and Pahlavi works in the original scripts. In 1888 he printed the complete Yasna and Visperad with ritual instructions, and also a huge Vendidad with especially large characters, so that priests could read it easily by lamplight during the night office. The actual understanding of Avestan texts was meantime furthered by one of his fellow-students, Kavasji Kanga, who published over the years a revised Gujarati translation of the whole Avesta, as well as an Avestan grammar (in 1891) and a detailed Avestan dictionary (in 1900). In the preparation of these he made full use of the work of European philologists.

The Parsi practice of the faith

In 1898 there appeared a study of the Parsis of Gujarat, commissioned by the British Government from two orthodox Parsis, Kharshedji Seervai and Bamanji Patel (the editor of 'Parsi Prakash'). This admirably succinct work describes the beliefs, customs and daily life of 'provincial' Parsis at the end of the nineteenth century, and shows how little these had changed from earlier days. In Bombay too the Parsi community continued to hold together, not only as an ethnic body but as one united by the practice of the faith. The controversies which troubled it were largely doctrinal, and even reformists usually turned to the priests to perform the customary rites at marriage, to initiate their children, and to solemnize the soul-ceremonies of their parents; and however strongly they rejected dualism intellectually, their moral attitudes continued to be those which a long tradition of dualism had engendered, so that evil was felt to be something aggressive, to be fought and subdued. So too with the occultists: despite their intellectual acceptance of a remote, impersonal God, reality remained for them the worship of Ohrmazd and defiance of his Adversary. Effective religious beliefs (those, that is, which influence behaviour) thus remained broadly the same for Parsis of every persuasion, and it is striking how often the biographies of distinguished Parsis of the late nineteenth century present a man of the same stamp: kindly, generous and in the main forbearing; simple in his own life, disciplined, and strict in the upbringing of his much-loved children; tirelessly active, optimistic, and filled with a great desire to serve his fellow-men, to advance the cause of goodness, and to diminish evils, whether of ignorance, poverty, sickness or social injustice.

Women in the early nineteenth century still kept their traditional place in the home, where they had a major part in maintaining the domestic rites of the faith: tending the hearth fire, censing the house with brazier and incense each evening at sunset, doing the ritual cooking, in strict purity, for family observances, and training the children in their religious duties. In the latter half of the century, after the reformists had started girls' schools, women gradually began to take part also in the public life of the community, and to attend what had previously been wholly male functions, such as the gahambar feasts. By then, however, these feasts, which for so many centuries had been a means of bringing rich and poor together, were no longer, in Bombay, an occasion for all Parsis of one locality to forgather. Their houses there were too scattered, and the rich had adopted foreign ways, and were no longer ready to sit at one cloth with the poor. So the ancient custom, though still observed, had degenerated there more or less into club or social dinners, though still with a religious element.

Earlier, maintaining the gahambars had been one of the tasks of the Parsi Panchayat; but by the end of the nineteenth century this body had given up many of its former functions, relinquishing them variously to British courts of justice or to individual philanthropists. In other ways, however, its power and prestige had grown. In 1834 the Panchayat possessed relatively modest assets and no quarters of its own. In 1875 it entered into imposing premises, with its trustees administering funds amounting to 44,000,000 rupees, and acting as bankers for many smaller Parsi bodies. As the community had spread out and founded new colonies, first along the shipping routes of the British Empire, and then across India, following the railways, there came into being many new Panchayats or Anjomans (the Hindu or Persian terms were by now used interchangeably). Of them a Parsi has written: 'Wherever in India or abroad there lived five to ten Parsis or more, a Panchayat or Anjoman soon grew up and collected funds for common religious and charitable purposes. Their activities soon expanded to meeting other needs as of relief of poverty, assistance for education, providing medical care, housing and other social needs. The apex of these local Anjomans has been the Parsi Panchayat of Bombay, the custodian of the funds of most of the Panchayats in India and a few from abroad. This great co-operative pyramid of the Parsis has been the bulwark of strength, representing a modest structure of a unique Social Security system. . . . Although all the wants of the needy members may not be met adequately, one can say that no deserving Parsi need starve or grow hungry, no Parsi child need grow up without minimum education, and no sick Parsi need suffer for want of medical care' (Bulsara, p. 9).

In the late nineteenth century, it is estimated, there were about 120 such local Anjomans, about the same number of dakhmas or 'towers of silence' (this expressive term had been coined by a British journalist), and 134 lesser fire temples. (Older centres often had more than one agiary and dakhma, and some new ones lacked either, and had of necessity to bury their dead.) In Bombay two more Atash Bahrams had been consecrated, a Kadmi one, enthroned by the Cowasji brothers in 1844, and a Shenshai one installed by the Bhagaria Anjoman in 1898 – this being the eighth and last Parsi Atash Bahram. Its high priest was Jamasp M. Jamasp-Asana, a descendant of the Jamasp Asa who, with Darab Kumana, had studied under Dastur Jamasp Vilayati. Another branch of this family provided the priest-in-charge of one of the fire temples in Poona, on whom eventually was conferred the impressive title of 'Dastur of the Shenshai Parsis of the Deccan, Calcutta and Madras', while in 1909 the Parsis of Karachi named their chief priest 'Dastur of the Parsis of North-West India'. These titles (probably inspired by those of Christian bishoprics) had little reality, for outside the old 'panths' a dastur's authority was limited to his own temple (to which he was elected by the trustees), and any wider influence which he might exert depended on his personal qualities.

Irani Zoroastrians in the nineteenth century

While the Parsis thus prospered and spread out, their Irani brethren, pitifully reduced in numbers, were suffering greatly. Life for them was continually hard, but the most dangerous time was always that between the death of one king and the crowning of the next, when there was no recognized local authority. Then in Yazd and Kerman fanatics and ruffians alike 'fell upon the poor Zoroastrians, mishandled them, even killed some of them, robbed them, and especially took from them . . . their books, to burn them' (Petermann, 204). Travel was now officially forbidden them; but in 1796 a Kermani managed to flee secretly to Bombay with his beautiful daughter Golestan, who was threatened with abduction. There she became the wife of Framji Panday, a merchant, who for her sake aided 'with body, mind and money' other Irani fugitives. In 1834 their eldest son started a fund to help Irani refugees in India; and twenty years later another son helped found the 'Society for the Amelioration of the Conditions of the Zoroastrians in Persia'. One of the first actions of this Society was to send an agent to Iran, and fortunately its choice fell on the valiant Manekji Limji Hataria.

Manekji, a small trader who had travelled widely in India, was devoted to his faith and community; he was also self-reliant, resourceful, and had the tact and patience needed to negotiate on behalf of his oppressed co-religionists. He was dismayed at first to find them so reduced in numbers, the precise figures, as he reported them to the Society in 1854, being 6658 in Yazd and its villages, only 450 in and around Kerman, 50 in the capital, Tehran, and a few in Shiraz. In that same decade the number of Parsis in Bombay was estimated at 110,544 (or 20 per cent of the population), with some 20,000 in Surat, and perhaps 15,000 in the rest of Gujarat and scattered about India. Yet the Iranis, despite everything, had kept the same spirit and enterprise as the Parsis; and as soon as Manekji managed to have the pressures on them a little reduced, their 'akabir' or elders set to work with him to rebuild dilapidated fire temples and dakhmas (they had been prevented from keeping these in repair), and to do what could be done for the most destitute among them. A bold innovation (much disapproved of by the local Muslims) was the founding of schools to give Zoroastrians a basic, Western-type, education. Manekji began this activity within a year of his arrival, and soon, with the help of Parsi funds, primary schools had been established in Yazd, Kerman and many of the Zoroastrian villages; and in 1865 a small boarding school was opened in Tehran. Manekji encouraged the growth of the little colony in the capital, since Zoroastrians suffered less there than in the old centres, where prejudice against them ran deep.

Manekji struggled against oppression of every sort, striving, for instance, to bring murderers of Zoroastrians to justice. (The punishment, when he was successful, was usually a small fine, for the death of an unbeliever was of little consequence.) But his main aim, pursued over years, was the abolition of the jizya, and in 1882 his efforts were at last crowned with success, to the boundless joy and gratitude of the Iranis. Many inequalities remained, and plenty of local harassment; but from this point on they began the same ascent to wealth, through commerce, as the Parsis before them, helped like them by their talents and industry, and by their reputation for scrupulous honesty.

Irani priests had for many decades before this been making their way unobtrusively to Bombay to serve for a while at the Dadyseth

Agiary; and in the 1860s Tehmuras Anklesaria began to frequent their company there in order to learn Persian and 'Dari' from them. Later, when editing a Pahlavi text, the Dadestan i dinig, he asked an Irani friend, Mobad Khodabakhsh Farud, to make inquiries, on his return to Persia, for manuscripts of this work. To his astonishment Khodabakhsh returned a few years later bearing manuscripts not only of it, but of the Epistles of Manushchihr, the Wizidagiha of Zadspram, a Pahlavi Rivayat, a part of the Madigan i Hazar Dadestan, a longer recension of the Bundahishn, and the Nirangestan. Some of these manuscripts were unique, and the works they contained might otherwise well have perished, even at that late date, for Khodabakhsh explained that their owners had parted with them only because they knew that they would be safer with the Parsis. Tehmuras edited and printed some of the texts himself, while others were edited in the twentieth century by his son Behramgore, and by another priest, one of the finest Parsi scholars, Bomanji N. Dhabhar. Tehmuras, in part return, worked with an Irani priest to make a Persian translation of the Khorda Avesta for his community. This, and service books in Persian and Avestan script, were printed in Bombay and taken in small consignments to Iran.

The Iranis, enclosed within a society which was itself still quite untouched by progress, were naturally far more conservative than the Bombay Parsis; but not so much divided them in outlook and way of life from co-religionists in Gujarat, and Manekji, who himself came from a village near Surat, seems to have found only one practice to trouble him, that of sacrificing cows, the ancient ritual offering to Anahid, at the shrine of Banu-Pars; and such was the gratitude that the Iranis felt to him that they abandoned this at his persuasion. He made no objection to their substituting sheep and goats, which were still sacrificed by the Parsis, even in Bombay, down to the mid nineteenth century. Then gradually, under the pressure of reformists, the rite was abandoned there, and Gujarat slowly followed suit; and there are many Parsis today who sincerely deny that it ever formed part of their religious practices.

Influences from Bombay filtered back to Iran too from the late nineteenth century, but had little general effect there in the Qajar period. The half century after the abolition of the jizya was in many ways a golden age for the Irani Zoroastrians. Education and new ideas had not begun seriously to challenge old orthodoxy, and increasing wealth was largely put at the service of the faith. Yet during this time the seeds of change were sown there also. As had happened in India, the sons of priests followed the laymen's sons into the new schools, did well there, and in ever-increasing numbers abandoned their fathers' calling for secular careers. The Tehrani community grew apace, as the Bombay one had done, and since individuals were making great fortunes the communal solidarity of the years of oppression was weakened, while modern ways began to undermine age-old orthopraxy.

One more great sorrow came, moreover, to the Iranis at this time, which was that, just as life was becoming safer and more prosperous for them, a relatively large number of their community were attracted by the preaching of the Baha'is. For centuries the Zoroastrians had had to grieve for those of their fellows who were lost to Islam, but at least these had achieved by their apostasy a better worldly lot; now they had to mourn for relatives and friends who on embracing this new religion met persecutions as harsh as any that the Zoroastrians themselves had known during the worst years of oppression. Why there should have been so many converts is not simply explained, but a number of reasons suggest themselves. The founder of Babism (the fore-runner of Baha'ism) was regarded by some as the Saoshyant, his being a purely Iranian movement, and necessarily opposed to Islam. Thereafter Baha'ism developed a claim to be a world-faith, and offered the Irani Zoroastrians, as theosophy did the Parsis, membership of a wider community, in which they would have an honoured place. But since Muslims regarded Baha'ism as a pernicious heresy, adopting it sometimes led to horrible deaths.

Parsi calendar and religious reforms in the early twentieth century

In Bombay meanwhile a development took place which was designed to end the rift between Shenshais and Kadmis. Kharshedji Cama was troubled by the calendar problems which divided his community; and became convinced that, since the original Zoroastrian calendar must have remained in harmony with the seasons, this could only have been, in essence, the Gregorian one. The intercalation of an extra day every four years had simply been neglected, he supposed, in the confusions of past history. Accordingly there was founded, in 1906, the Zartoshti Fasli Sal Mandal, or 'Zoroastrian Seasonal-Year Society', whose aim was to persuade the whole community to adopt such a calendar, with a fixed spring No Ruz and a leap-day every fourth year; but its members, who called themselves Faslis, increased their numbers only slowly.

The Parsis had by that time made fine scholarly contributions to knowledge of their religion, notably through editing and publishing Pahlavi texts; but they felt the lack of progress in theological studies. So a group of reformists, again led by Cama, sent a young Bhagaria priest, Maneckji Dhalla, to New York to study under the American Iranist, Williams Jackson. Dhalla left India profoundly orthodox, as he explains in his autobiography, but during three and a half years abroad learnt to blend his traditional beliefs with Western academic dogma, and to contemn ritual. On his return he was elected their high priest by the Parsis of Karachi, a progressive, mercantile community, and thereafter he wrote several books on Zoroastrian theology and history. These contain much valuable material, but never deal rigorously with the contradictions which arose from the mixture of traditional orthodoxy with alien ideas. Thus he once wrote: 'It seems to me that we tread a very delicate path when we set aside as non-Zoroastrian all that does not appear in the Gathas' (*Zoroastrian Theology*, 77–8), and he in fact continued to venerate the yazatas as his forefathers had done, seeking their help in this life and looking to be judged at death by Mihr, Rashn and Srosh. Nevertheless on paper he was ready to describe these beings as 'pre-Zoroastrian divinities', belief in whom had been 'engrafted' on the pure monotheism which Zoroaster had taught. Dhalla was able to live with such contradictions, it seems, partly because of a lack of strong concern for logical consistency, partly because the life of the spirit was for him more important than that of the intellect, the practice of the faith than its theology. It was natural, therefore, that among his writings there should be a purely devotional work, called 'Homage unto Ahura Mazda', which has been widely read and used by Parsis. In it Dhalla explicitly accepted a modern Western version of the old Zurvanite heresy, according to which Ahura Mazda himself was the hypothetical 'father' of the twin Spirits of Y 30.3, who were now identified as Spenta Mainyu (regarded as wholly distinct from Ahura Mazda) and Angra Mainyu. Yet though Dhalla thus, under foreign influences, abandoned the fundamental doctrine of the absolute separation of good and evil, his book still breathes the sturdy, unflinching spirit of orthodox Zoroastrian dualism. 'As a soldier takes the oath of fealty to the king, so is every Zoroastrian arrayed on the side of the King of kings to fight a stubborn fight, a courageous

fight . . . against . . . falsehood, inequity, vice and wickedness . . .
I will fight Angra Mainyu, hand to hand and foot to foot and hurl him
headlong' (op. cit. 135). 'Let me not' (he prayed) 'be a visionary, or a
dreamer' (ibid. 246); rather he sought to be one who was tirelessly
active in the cause of righteousnes, of Asha. Zoroastrianism, he
declared, is 'the most . . . buoyant, optimistic, hopeful, youthful
religion' (ibid. 241), 'for thou, Ahura Mazda, art hope itself . . .
Zarathushtra gives us thy message of Hope – hope in the ultimate
triumph of good over evil, and hope in the destruction of' the
Kingdom of wickedness and the coming of thy Kingdom of
Righteousness!' (ibid. 117).

Despite doctrinal innovations and uncertainties, Dhalla's work
remained thus orthodox in spirit. Nevertheless he clashed with traditionalists by attacking what he regarded as outworn rituals, the saying
of prayers by rote, and the exclusion of non-Zoroastrians from
religious observances; and he expressed himself in such matters with
characteristic Parsi vigour. 'May the breath of Vohu Manah' (he
prayed) 'blow the mists of superstition and credulity, that generate
orthodoxy, from my mind and illumine it with the gleams of the
sunshine of needful reform. . . . Let me discern the signs of the age I
live in. Let me be in harmony with it' (ibid. 276, 277).

In accordance with such aspirations, Dhalla was a prime mover in
establishing an annual Zoroastrian Conference to continue the work
of the nineteenth-century reformists. Its first meeting, in 1910, was
stormy; but thereafter the organizers concentrated their main efforts
on practical, uncontroversial matters, such as technical and educa-
tional projects for the welfare of the community. (Industrialism had
by then reached Bombay, and the Parsis were adapting themselves to
owning and to working in factories, both of which activities disrupted
old patterns of life.) Relative peace, therefore, reigned at its
proceedings; and in 1913 its President felt able to address the opening
meeting with satisfaction in the following words: 'Our
religion . . . is singularly free from dogmas, and is so simple in its
tenets that it differs but little from Unitarianism or Rationalism', thus
contrasting, he claimed, most favourably with other creeds. As an
observer commented (Moulton, 175), the danger of such an attitude
was its negative emphasis. 'Reforming Parsis are so busy denying and
denouncing that they have difficulty in assertion.' Yet at this very
time visitors to Bombay were recording the impression made upon
them by the evening gathering of Parsis at the sea's edge to say their

kusti-prayers, 'Going and coming all silent and quite informal, worshipping together and yet each alone. On feast days there are thousands lining the shore, and every day the number mounts up into the hundreds. Some stay but five or ten minutes, some half an hour or more . . . either reading additional prayers from a prayer-book . . . or making spontaneous prayers of their own. . . . The dome of the eternal heavens is the cathedral, the setting sun acts as altar, and the . . . evening sky, bending over the endless reaches of the Indian ocean, lends a framework' (Pratt, 335–6). Despite all the forces of change, the devotional life of the community thus continued, even in industrialized Bombay, to flow placidly along old channels, with prayer being offered at the appointed times to the Creator in the setting of his own creations; and this was something of which reformist and traditionalist could alike approve.

CHAPTER FOURTEEN

In the twentieth century

Urban Parsis

For both communities the chief strongholds of simple, untroubled orthodoxy had been the villages and country towns; but the twentieth century has seen the erosion of this rural life, and by its latter half most Zoroastrians have become city dwellers. For the Parsis this process, already well advanced by 1900, was hastened by the movement for India's independence. This was patriotically supported by individual Parsis, among whom had been founder-members of the Congress Party; but in time it unleashed some Hindu hostility against the community, which was thought to have prospered unduly under British rule. In the 1930s there was a boycott of Parsi farms in Gujarat, which forced their owners to sell. Others suffered through prohibition (introduced in Gujarat in 1937), for some Parsi villages were given over to growing the toddy-palm. There was an exodus therefore of country people to Bombay. There too the golden age of prosperity for the Parsis was over, with Hindus and Muslims now competing strongly where they had once led; but the Parsi Panchayat still disposed of large funds, and the trustees strove to keep the 'devil of unemployment' away from their co-religionists by creating training schemes, and they provided also subsidized communal housing. Some of the more conservative among them were uneasy at engaging in such new activities, but they were only an extension of those by which down the centuries the 'akabir' had sought to care for the poorer members of the community.

Parsi philanthropists in general shared the trustees' instinct for keeping to familiar ways; but one who had broken earlier away from tradition was the pioneer industrialist, Jamshedji Tata (himself a Bhagaria priest in minor orders), who established scholarships for able boys of any creed to study science and technology. No one arose to make similar endowments for the humanities, and outside the two Madressas little provision was made for the scholarly study of Zoroastrian history and religion, and those who were drawn to these subjects had to pursue them in their spare time. With Parsi energy and devotion several did so, among them two fine historians, Shapurshah H. Hodivala and Dara Meherji-Rana. The best known to the world at large was Jivanji J. Modi, who was hereditary priest-in-charge of a Bombay fire temple, a graduate of both Elphinstone Institute and the Sir J. J. Madressa, and for fifty years full-time secretary of the Parsi Panchayat. He wrote many books and articles on Parsi rituals and customs, history, beliefs and folk-lore, and received much recognition from foreign learned societies. His major work in English, published in 1922, was 'The Religious Ceremonies and Customs of the Parsees', written partly to record observances which were then being abandoned in the rush of industrialized life.

The founding of new fire temples continued, however. These included a Fasli one, called the 'Atesh-kade', established in 1937, whose first priest-in-charge, markedly a reformist, became drawn into association with the 'Mazdaznans'. They were yet another eclectic, occultist American group, whose founder, one Otoman Hanish, claimed visionary enlightenment. He had come across the English translation of the Avesta (in the Sacred Books of the East), and blended elements from what he apprehended of Zoroastrianism from it with others from Hinduism and Christianity, used fire as a cult-symbol and added breathing exercises, song and dance. In the 1930s a wealthy follower of his, calling herself 'Mother Gloria', arrived with a few others in Bombay, intending to restore to the Parsis the true message of Zoroaster, lost to them through the error of ages. The wrath of the orthodox was deep, and probably startled the well-meaning lady by the vigour of its expression. She nevertheless remained in Bombay for a number of years before returning to the USA, where the movement still has a small following.

In the twentieth century

Zoroastrians in modern Iran

Meantime the Irani Zoroastrians were pursuing a course which was to turn them also, in a mere half-century, into a mainly urban community, with Tehran having the same dominant role in their society as Bombay in that of the Parsis. In 1900 it was still Yazd and its villages which had the largest Zoroastrian population, of some 10,000 souls; and there was much traditionally pious activity there, with the repairing of old fire temples and shrines, and the building of new ones, and the making too of water-tanks, and other useful public works. Money was also spent by individuals in endowing gahambar observances, and the Gahambar Khane, where communal religious services and feasts were held, was rebuilt on an impressive scale. The new schools were a progressive element, and they included the first Iranian school for girls, founded early in the century by Sohrab Kayanian, head of the Zoroastrian Anjoman of Yazd. In the 1850s both Yazd and Kerman, under guidance from the Parsi agent, Manekji, had turned their traditional councils of elders into elected Anjomans, each with a secretary and written minutes; but with these, as with the Parsi Panchayat, the hereditary principle persisted. In Yazd the priests had their own separate assembly, under the Dasturan dastur, which exerted considerable authority in religious matters.

Although individual merchants had attained wealth, and through it influence, the Zoroastrians of Yazd and Kerman were still despised, bullied, and sometimes brutally mistreated. Matters were easier in Tehran; but in 1900 the ways there were rough and dangerous, and the Zoroastrians of southern Persia found it easier and more profitable to maintain their links with Bombay. The Tehrani community numbered then only about 325 souls, and had only one communal place of worship, a little shrine to Bahram Ized, divinity of the way. (This had been built about 1830, when Zoroastrian villagers used to travel up on foot from the south, in groups of 200 or so, to seek summer work in the gardens of the capital.) They founded their Anjoman in 1898, and ten years later established an Adaran fire, tended by priests from Yazd. The temple in which it was installed was built on the Parsi plan, with the sacred fire set in a metal container in a central sanctuary, visible to all who entered; and this testifies both to the safety of life in Tehran, and to the changed relations between the two Zoroastrian communities, with the Iranis, grateful for help and impressed by the Parsis' achievements, conceding to them the sort of authority which the Parsis had earlier looked for from those in the mother-country.

Before the Anjomani fire was installed, a Dadgah fire had been maintained at his own house by the great merchant-banker, Jamshid Bahman Jamshidian, who by his own exertions had made himself one of the wealthiest and most influential men in Iran. He had a Zoroastrian love of justice, and sought it not only for his own community, but for all the oppressed of the land; and this led him to support the movement for constitutional reform. After many difficulties a parliament, the Majles, was established in 1906, and he was among the first members to be elected. So after over 1000 years a Zoroastrian voice was heard again in the councils of Iran. In 1909 it was agreed that each of Iran's minorities should return one representative to the Majles, and the first official Zoroastrian deputy was Kay Khosrow Shahrokh. This remarkable man, of a traditionally learned Kermani family, had been sent by Manekji as a boy to study in Bombay, where he was profoundly impressed both by the Parsis' own progress, and by what he learned among them of the glories of ancient Iran. (This was something which teachers at the Elphinstone Institute, reared in classical studies, could tell their pupils about; and it was in the nineteenth century that the name 'Cyrus' became current among the Parsis, and the symbol of the winged disc from Persepolis was adopted by them as the Zoroastrian symbol, to appear proudly over the gates of fire temples and schools.) So Kay Khosrow returned with two ambitions; to help his own community to advance, and Iran to regain her dignity among the nations. He did much to further both aims, for he was Zoroastrian deputy for thirteen sessions of the Majles, and was one of Iran's most tireless and devoted public servants for over thirty years.

In 1925 the Majles deposed the last Qajar, and enthroned Reza Khan, his prime minister, in his stead. He, as Reza Shah Pahlavi, sought to increase Iran's wealth by modernization, and at the same time to deepen the nation's sense of pride and identity by evoking the unique splendours of its imperial past. These aims led to accord between the king and the Zoroastrian deputy; and it is held to be a result of this that when Reza Shah introduced a Gregorian-type solar calendar, he chose Zoroastrian names for its months.

Some feeling for the pre-Islamic era had always been kept alive in Iran by Firdausi's Shahname, but the religious element in the epic was deliberately slight. Now, linked with the new patriotism, there began an awakening of interest not only in the old days but in the old faith. One of the foremost workers in this field was Ibrahim Pur-Davud, who, like Shahrokh, was an ardent patriot and idealist. Though of Muslim parentage, he became convinced that Persia would best achieve greatness again if her inhabitants abandoned a philosophy of submission to fate, and 'like our valiant and truthful ancestors' learnt to regard life as a perennial struggle between good and evil, in accordance with the religion of Zoroaster. He set himself therefore the arduous task of making the Avesta known to his fellow-countrymen in Persian translation. He based his versions on the work of European scholars, and principally on that of the great German lexicographer, Christian Bartholomae; and in presenting Zoroastrianism to Muslim Iran he was naturally happy to stress the theory of Zoroaster's rigid monotheism, without any taint even of theological dualism. 'The contest is only between the spirits of goodness and evil within us in the world. . . . Good thoughts, good words, and good deeds, stand as the fundamental principles of the religion of Zarathustra. And this is a perennial source of glory and pride to Iran and the Iranians, that once in that land one of its sons gave this grand message to humanity, to keep themselves aloof even from bad thoughts' (pp. 48, 50–1).

The Zoroastrians warmly welcomed Pur-Davud's efforts to win recognition for the nobility of their faith among those who had so long despised it as polytheism and fire-worship. His translation of the Gathas was printed in Bombay under Parsi auspices, and his work in general was hailed by them as a harbinger of coming goodwill and understanding among all the inhabitants of Iran. Unquestionably it contributed greatly to the increased respect felt for the old religion by educated, liberal Iranians, some of whom were led to read other works written by Irani Zoroastrians for the enlightenment of their own community. Among these were two by Kay Khosrow Shahrokh, the 'Ayin-i Mazdesnan' and 'Furugh-i Mazdesnan', through which he sought to present to the Iranis the Parsi reformists' ideas about their ancient faith (as possessing originally a simple theology, a high ethical code and virtually no observances).

Since the reformists' ideas derived originally from Europe, there was harmony between Shahrokh's expositions and those of Pur-Davud; but these ideas had less immediate impact on the orthodox in Iran than had been the case earlier in India, because most of them still lived in the provinces, where they quietly pursued old ways, and felt little need to read or to trouble themselves with novel expositions of the faith. In the 1930s, however, one proposed innovation was forced on the attention of the whole community. While in India Kay Khosrow had been impressed by arguments in favour of the 'fasli' calendar, and he saw its adoption as both desirable in itself, and a means of bringing the Zoroastrian reckoning into close accord with the new national one. He convinced Sohrab Kayanian in Yazd, and Sorush Sorushian, head of the Zoroastrian Anjoman in Kerman; and in 1939, after years of reasoning and exhorting, the reformers persuaded the whole Irani community to adopt the fasli calendar, named by them the 'bastani' or 'ancient' one (since this they truly believed it to be). The greatest difficulty had been in winning over Yazd; and many people there continued to be troubled by the thought that they were doing wrong in using an alien, secular form of reckoning for calculating their holy days. So after a short time, led by their priests, they reverted to the 'qadimi' or 'old' calendar. Since 1940, therefore, the small Irani community has observed two calendars, so that in the 1970s Tehranis and Kermanis celebrated the religious No Ruz (on 1 Farvardin) in March, and most Yazdis in late July. The Parsis continued to have three calendars, that is the two observed in Iran and their own Shenshai reckoning (with No Ruz then in August).

An ancient usage which the Tehrani reformists were prepared to abandon under pressure from the Shah, as not in harmony with modernization, was the rite of exposure of the dead. So in 1937 they established an 'aramgah' or cemetery (literally 'place of rest'), and abandoned the hillside dakhma built by Manekji. Against scriptural precept (that the dead should be laid in barren places) the 'aramgah' had running water, trees and greenness; but care was taken to isolate the corpses from the good earth by the use of coffins placed in cement-lined graves (a more expensive process, inevitably, than exposure in a communal tower). Two years later Sorush Sorushian established an 'aramgah' in Kerman also, but the dakhma there continued in use, as a matter of personal choice, until the 1960s, and it was not until 1965 that the Yazdis began using a cemetery. A decade later it was only Sharifabad, with its long priestly tradition of orthodoxy, which still maintained and used its dakhma. Since the beginning of the century there had been Parsis too who gave preference to burial over exposure, and in crowded Bombay a movement had grown up for using crematoria. This had greatly distressed traditionalists, and most priests refused to perform rites for the dead in such circumstances. The towers of silence remain in use there in beautiful gardens on Malabar Hill; but this once lonely place is now ringed by tall apartment buildings, and many criticisms of the custom are voiced from within and without the community.

Southern Persia changed comparatively little during Reza Shah's reign, but with new security the Zoroastrians of Yazd increased their numbers to about 12,000. The 1940s brought occupation of Iran by British and Russian troops, with some intensive road-making, and the introduction of motor transport on a large scale. When the foreigners withdrew, they sold a number of their vehicles locally, and soon buses and cars were hastening to and fro between the provinces and Tehran, for the capital had begun to exert a strong pull in many ways. It had the only university in the country, industry was thriving, and rapid Westernization was making life there more varied and attractive. For Zoroastrians it had the added advantage that there was virtually no discrimination against them there. There was a falling off moreover of trade with independent India, and years of drought were reducing the yields of farms. There was therefore a steady movement northward, and between 1945 and 1965 the Zoroastrian population of Yazd is reckoned to have halved, while that of Tehran swelled correspondingly. The number of working priests shrank even more drastically, so that from over 200 in the 1930s they were reduced to no more than ten, and there was no longer an acknowledged high priest among them, a Dasturan dastur. They thus lost most of their old authority in Yazd, and gained no new voice to compensate in Tehran, for most of the priests and priests' sons who left for the capital took up secular callings there. Kerman too lost a high proportion of its Zoroastrian population to the northern city. The last village family of Zoroastrians left the district in 1962, and there were by then only three or four working priests in the town of Kerman itself.

The laity thus gained authority in the Irani community even more rapidly and thoroughly than among the Parsis; and with wealth and enterprise becoming concentrated in Tehran, the Anjoman there acquired the same role of leadership as the Bombay Panchayat. It too was a lay body, largely concerned with furthering social and philanthropic work, and its elected members included both orthodox and reformist – for the flight from the south had brought numbers of traditionally orthodox Zoroastrians to the capital, many of whom tried to maintain their old observances as best they could in the new conditions of city life. The reformists were anxious, however, to persuade the whole community to achieve a 'rational devoutness', and to abandon many rituals and practices. They founded societies for discussion and inquiry, published books and journals, sent down lecturers to Yazd and Kerman to urge the need for progress, and in the 1970s began to bring children up from there to summer camps, to introduce them to modern ways.

Parsis in independent India and Pakistan

Meantime the end of British rule in India in 1947 had brought great changes for the Parsis, threatening the ties which bound their community together. The 5000 or so Parsis of Karachi, Lahore and Quetta found themselves living in the Muslim state of Pakistan, and obliged to learn Urdu in preference to Gujarati. A number emigrated from there and from India, mostly to England, Canada and the USA; but the majority remained, whether as Indians or Pakistanis, and played a valuable part in the life of the two states, contributing (in proportion to the size of the community) a striking number of public figures – soldiers, airmen, scientists, industrialists, newspaper editors. (Public service had long been regarded by Parsis as a religious obligation, a part of their duty, each according to his ability, to care for their fellow-men.) India being a secular state, there was no planned discrimination there against Parsis, and that they suffered at all as a religious community was incidental. Thus measures begun for economy during the 1939–45 war, and continued after independence, included a ban on all public banquets, and so virtually put an end to the age-old observance of communal gahambars. It also became difficult to import wool for weaving kustis (by now the task of priests' wives in India, and laywomen in Iran), and the Parsi Panchayat had to make urgent representations to obtain a special quota. Religious schools were obliged to open their doors to all comers, and so it was no longer possible to maintain a truly Zoroastrian atmosphere in the Parsi ones. Apart from such government actions, material progress continued its remorseless erosion, and as the hearth fires went out in Zoroastrian homes in Bombay as in Tehran (replaced by electricity, oil or gas) a centre for family devotions vanished with them, while the enticements of new interests and diversions encouraged increasing neglect of religion, an indifference more deadly than all the clash of controversy.

Recent interpretations of Zoroastrian belief

For those Parsis in India who remained actively devout, and still sought ways of interpreting their ancient faith, there was naturally an inclination now to turn away from a Christian approach, and seek affinities in Indian religion. Some, accustomed by theosophy to linking different creeds, grafted on to their Zoroastrianism veneration for modern 'gurus' such as Meher Baba, who offered a variety of paths to spiritual salvation; and pictures of such sages came to adorn many Parsi homes, beside idealized portraits of their own prophet. Others sought to interpret the Avesta in the light of the Vedas, and the Parsi Association of Calcutta went so far as to publish, in 1967, a translation of the Gathas by a Hindu scholar who identified the Avesta as the missing 'fifth Veda', and saw Zoroaster's own Gathas as forming the earliest scripture of the Chishti cult. A more solid work was that of Irach Taraporewala, 'The Divine Songs of Zarathushtra' published in 1951. In this the author (a lawyer) first gave a literal translation of each Gatha, which essentially, like that of Pur-Davud, followed Bartholomae's rendering, and then, after an interpretive commentary, provided a second, free translation, designed to render the 'thought' behind the actual words, and to show (as he said, p. xi) 'how all the great ideas I had so highly admired in Sanskrit Scriptures were also discoverable in the Avesta'. Although in general Taraporewala rejected European translations as too literal, he adopted unquestioningly the European assumption that 'it would, of course, be utterly wrong to read the ideas of Later Zoroastrian Theology into the Gathas' (p. xii); and this assumption allowed his second rendering to be almost as free and subjective as those of the occultists. Since then, other translations of the Gathas have been made by Parsi and Irani laymen, who have all proceeded in this same way, of taking an existing translation and re-interpreting it in the light of their own inspired thoughts. The high priests of the Anjoman and Wadia Atash Bahrams of Bombay (Dastur Kaikhosroo Jamasp Asa and Dastur Firoze Kotwal) have continued the exacting task of editing and publishing Pahlavi texts – an activity which has been welcomed by the international academic community; but Avestan studies have been neglected of late by trained Parsi scholars, probably because of the daunting philological requirements for their pursuit.

The problem of interpreting the Gathas lies at the heart of the theological difficulties which confront modern Zoroastrians. Clearly whatever the doctrines were which their prophet taught over 3000 years ago, these need to be re-interpreted for his contemporary followers, as do the teachings of all other prophets for their own communities. What is unusual in the case of Zoroastrianism is the wide diversity of opinion as to what their prophet originally taught, let alone how this should be understood today; and the blame for this confusion lies largely with the West, and the ruthless self-confidence of nineteenth-century scholars and missionaries. The doctrines of the faith, adumbrated only in the Gathas, are made clear in the tradition, preserved in the surviving Avestan and Pahlavi books; but down to the nineteenth century their testimony, inaccessible to most of the community, was supplemented by the magisterium of the living Zoroastrian church. It was the abrupt impact of Western culture which shattered the confidence of many Parsis in this, making them, like juddins, concentrate on the Gathas, seeking Zoroaster's own message there; but without the key provided by the tradition these ancient devotional texts remained bafflingly enigmatic, and so the versions of them, whether produced by Parsis, Iranis, or Western scholars, varied so much from one another that they caused bewilderment. Matters have now been further complicated with the reversal by Western scholars of nineteenth-century assumptions, because of slow recognition of the subtle allusions in the Gathas to the links between the Amahraspands and their creations, to the lesser yazatas and to the essential rituals of the faith. So the West has now destroyed the basis which it originally provided for Parsi reformists, although this has yet to be realized within the community itself. A few of the orthodox continue serenely untroubled by all this; but many Zoroastrians, in a literate age, long for a simple, noble, lucid scripture on which to base a unified faith, and this is a longing which seems doomed to remain unfulfilled, because of the immense antiquity of their tradition.

Western attacks on this tradition were damaging not only to doctrinal unity but also to communal pride; for once the reformists had accepted the theory that their prophet's teachings were early corrupted, then they had to think that their ancestors had lived by, and in many cases suffered and died for, beliefs which were false. Far from honouring them for faithfulness, they found themselves reproaching them for error. Moreover, by this theory, Zoroaster's own doctrines could have had no influence on religious history, having been almost at once lost to sight. The reformists have thus had to abandon a great heritage. The orthodox were not deprived in this way; but under attack they tended to entrench themselves behind orthopraxy, and to conduct the battle over observances rather than doctrine. So they too gave no thought to the influence which their religion has had upon other faiths – indeed such considerations are basically irrelevant for those who believe that they are themselves engaged in preserving God's true revelation to mankind. Yet awareness of the historical facts might well be a source of strength and proper pride to others in a small community, struggling not to be engulfed in the general sea of humanity.

International dispersion

The reasons why Zoroastrians should feel their identity especially menaced in the twentieth century are various. There is the dispersal of the Parsis, with less close ties than formerly between those overseas and Bombay and Gujarat; and partly in consequence there is more marrying out of the community, and this, with a sharply falling birthrate, is whittling away its numbers. These latter problems are shared by the Iranis, and both groups face the increase of secularism among their members. Population statistics do not show, therefore, how many believing Zoroastrians there are in the world; but the round figures for the community in 1976 were a total of 129,000 souls, with 82,000 in India, 5000 in Pakistan, and 500 in Ceylon; 25,000 in Iran (of whom about 19,000 then lived in Tehran); 3000 apiece in Britain, Canada and the USA, and 200 in Australia. There were also small groups still in Hongkong and Singapore, but old colonies in Aden, Shanghai, Canton and elsewhere had had to be abandoned, sometimes with an almost total loss of individual and communal assets. Iran had, however, encouraged Parsis to settle there and become citizens, and a number of them have done so.

Scattered across the world in this way, the Zoroastrians have kept their energy and resourcefulness, and every local community has produced its 'akabir', who organized the means of achieving social, charitable and religious goals. The older colonies in places like London and Hongkong have had Zoroastrian Associations for many decades, and the new ones have swiftly created them. In the 1970s the Parsis created a Federation of Zoroastrian Anjomans of India; and in 1975 the first North American Zoroastrian Symposium was held in Toronto. Air-travel made it possible to hold a first World Zoroastrian

Congress in Tehran in 1960, with subsequent ones in Bombay in 1964 and 1978. These had the broad aims of establishing contact between the various Zoroastrian groups, and creating a forum where matters of common concern could be discussed. The second North American Zoroastrian Symposium took place in Chicago in 1977. The main questions considered at such gatherings are these: how to arrest the decline in numbers of the priesthood (now reaching a desperately low level even in Bombay); what part ritual and ceremony should have in religious life; how to study and learn about the faith; how to bring up children in the religion; whether the spouses and offspring of mixed marriages (with a juddin partner) may be received into the faith; whether conversion of juddins is permissible; and how to conduct funerary rites. There is ample matter here for debate, and nearly always a wide variety of opinions, from extreme reformist to strict orthodox, even in the newest colonies. One thing which helps sustain Zoroastrians is the knowledge that their community is no longer alone in its troubles (as seemed the case in the nineteenth century), but that the rising tide of secularism threatens to overwhelm other faiths also, however numerically strong, who likewise must battle against it, and strive to reinterpret doctrine and re-examine ritual. They also have justifiable confidence in themselves, and can still draw on those qualities of courage, hope and readiness to defy adversity which Zoroaster's teachings have so remarkably instilled in his followers down the centuries.

Bibliography

This brief bibliography has two aims: to expand the short references given in the text, and to provide a guide to the chief primary sources and some of the abundant secondary literature. With rare exceptions, articles in journals are not cited; and the references to books are confined in the main to a selection of works in the English language. The primary sources are also cited wherever possible in English translations. (The distinction made for Chapters 5–10 between primary sources and secondary literature is dropped for the later chapters.)

Many useful articles on aspects of Zoroastrianism can be found in Hasting's *Encyclopaedia of Religion and Ethics*.

Chapters 1–4

THE YASHTS

The only complete English translation remains that of J. Darmesteter, *The Zend-Avesta*, part II, *The Sirozahs, Yashts and Nyayesh*, SBE, vol. XXIII, Oxford 1883, repr. Delhi 1965. This gives a general idea of their content, but is out-of-date in many respects. A complete English translation of the *Mihr Yasht* (Yt 10) is provided by I. Gershevitch, *The Avestan Hymn to Mithra*, Cambridge 1959, repr. 1967.

THE YASNA

The only complete English translation remains that of L. H. Mills, *The Zend-Avesta*, part III, *The Yasna, Visparad, Āfrīnagān, Gāhs and Miscellaneous Fragments*, SBE, vol. XXXI, Oxford 1887, repr. Delhi 1965.

Bibliography

THE GATHAS

There is no standard translation in any language. The German one by C. Bartholomae, published in 1905, was rendered into English, with small modifications, by J. H. Moulton, *Early Zoroastrianism*, London 1913, repr. 1972, pp. 343–90. This may be compared with that of Mills in his *Yasna* translation (see above). Maria W. Smith published a translation, also based on Bartholomae's but modified by her own syntactical ideas, in *Studies in the Syntax of the Gathas of Zarathushtra*, Linguistic Society of America, Philadelphia 1929, repr. 1966. A French translation by J. Duchesne-Guillemin was put into English by Maria Henning, *The Hymns of Zarathushtra*, Wisdom of the East Series, London 1952. In the same year there appeared, also in London, *The Songs of Zarathushtra, The Gathas*, by F. A. Bode and Piloo Nanavutty, Ethical and Religious Classics of East and West. This has no claims to scholarly originality. In 1951 Irach J. S. Taraporewala published in Bombay *The Divine Songs of Zarathushtra*, in which he gave a close English translation of Bartholomae's German rendering, and then his own free interpretation. The most recent version is by S. Insler, *The Gathas of Zarathushtra*, Acta Iranica, third series, vol. I, Leiden 1975.

VENDIDAD

The only complete English translation remains that of J. Darmesteter, *The Zend-Avesta*, part I, *The Vendīdād*, 2nd ed., SBE IV, Oxford 1895, repr. Delhi 1965.

BUNDAHISHN

Two recensions exist. The shorter one, known as the *Indian Bundahishn*, is readily accessible in the out-of-date translation (with valuable notes) by E. W. West, SBE V, Oxford 1901, repr. 1965. The longer *Iranian* or *Greater Bundahishn* was translated into English by B. T. Anklesaria, *Zand-Ākasih*, Bombay 1956.

RITUALS

A summary of the main rituals of Zoroastrianism was given by M. Haug at the end of his *Essays on the Sacred Language, Writings and Religion of the Parsis*, 3rd ed., London 1884. A discursive but very thorough description of almost all existing observances was provided by J. J. Modi, *The Religious Ceremonies and Customs of the Parsees*, 2nd ed., Bombay 1937; and his material on the main ceremonies was condensed by J. Duchesne-Guillemin in *La Religion de l'Iran ancien*, Paris 1962, ch. 2, translated into English by K. M. Jamaspa Asa as *Religion of Ancient Iran*, Bombay 1973.

Bibliography

THE TRADITION OF ZOROASTER'S LIFE

Most of the Pahlavi material was translated by E. W. West, 'Marvels of Zoroastrianism', SBE XLVII, Oxford 1897, repr. Delhi 1965. This and almost all the later material was drawn on, uncritically, by A. V. W. Jackson for his *Zoroaster, the Prophet of Ancient Iran*, New York 1899, repr. 1965.

Chapter 5

PRIMARY SOURCES

Arrian, *Anabasis of Alexander*, vol. II, Loeb Classical Library.
Herodotus, *History*, Books I and III, Loeb Classical Library.
Kent, R. G. *Old Persian, Grammar, Texts, Lexicon*, New Haven, Connecticut, 2nd ed., 1953. (This contains English translations of almost all the Achaemenian inscriptions.)
Strabo, *Geography*, vol. VII, Loeb Classical Libary.

SECONDARY LITERATURE

Frye, R. N., *The Heritage of Persia*, London 1962, new ed. 1976. (A concise general history of pre-Islamic Iran, with valuable bibliographies.)
Ghirshman, R., *Iran, from the Earliest Times to the Islamic Conquest*, Pelican Archaeology Series, London 1954. (Full of archaeological data, but boldly speculative in much of the interpretation.)
Olmstead, A. T., *History of the Persian Empire*, Chicago 1948, repr. 1959. (Vigorously written, learned, but with many inaccuracies and misleading reconstructions.)
Schmidt, E. F., *Persepolis I, Structures, Reliefs. Inscriptions*, University of Chicago Oriental Institute Publications, LXVIII, 1953. *Persepolis II, Contents of the Treasury and Other Discoveries*, ibid., LXIX, 1957; *Persepolis III, The Royal Tombs and other monuments*, ibid., LXX, 1970. (These massive works are superbly illustrated.)
Stronach, D., *Pasargadae*, Clarendon Press, Oxford 1978. (Another massive work, again splendidly illustrated.)
Zaehner, R. C., *Zurvan, A Zoroastrian Dilemma*, Oxford 1955. (This contains almost all the texts relating to Zurvanism, mostly with English translations. Much of its theory was subsequently revised or abandoned by the author.)
The Dawn and Twilight of Zoroastrianism, London 1961, repr. 1976. (A strongly Christian interpretation, which leaps from the Achaemenians to the Sasanians. Basically unsound, but with valuable insights, and many quotations of texts.)

Bibliography

Chapter 6

PRIMARY SOURCES

Josephus, *Jewish Antiquities*, Loeb Classical Library.
Pausanias, *Description of Greece*, V, transl. J. G. Fraser, London 1898.
Strabo, see previous chapter.

SECONDARY LITERATURE

Colledge, M. A. R., *The Parthians*, Ancient Peoples and Places, London 1967. (Superficial on the religion.)
Debevoise, N. C., *A Political History of Parthia*, Chicago 1938.
Newell, E. T., 'The Coinage of the Parthians', in *A Survey of Persian Art*, ed. A. U. Pope, London 1938, vol. I, pp. 475–92. (This massive volume, with its accompanying plates, contains much valuable material for pre-Islamic Iran.)
Rawlinson, George, *The Sixth Great Oriental Monarchy, the Geography, History and Antiquities of Parthia*, London 1873. (Still reliable in many respects, being based largely on classical sources.)
Rosenfield, J., *The Dynastic Arts of the Kushans*, Berkeley, California, 1967. (Contains a useful survey, with illustrations, of Kushan history and the coinage.)

Chapters 7–9

PRIMARY SOURCES

Arda Viraz Namag, ed. and transl. by H. Jamasp Asa and M. Haug, Bombay and London 1872.
Basil, St, *Collected Letters*, Loeb Classical Library, vol. IV.
Biruni, *The Chronology of Ancient Nations*, transl. by C. E. Sachau, London 1879, repr. 1969.
Braun, O. (transl.), *Ausgewählte Akten persischer Märtyrer*, Bibliothek der Kirchenväter, vol. 22, 1915.
Dadestan i Menog i Khrad, ed. and transl. by E. W. West, *The Book of the Mainyo-i-Khard*, Stuttgart and London 1871.
Dhabhar, B. N. (transl.), *The Persian Rivayats of Hormazyar Framarz and Others*, Bombay 1932.
Ehrlich, R. (transl.), 'The Celebration and Gifts of the Persian New Year (Nawrūz) according to an Arabic source', *Dr. J. J. Modi Memorial Volume*, Bombay 1930, 95–101.
Firdausi, *Shahname*, transl. by A. G. and E. Warner, vols VI–IX, London 1912–25.

Bibliography

Grignaschi, M. (transl.), 'Quelques spécimens de la littérature sassanide. . .',
Journal asiatique, 1966, 16–45.

Hoffman, G. (transl.), *Auszüge aus syrischen Akten persischer Märtyrer*,
Leipzig 1880, repr. 1966.

Kirder's inscription at Sar-Mashhad has been transliterated and translated into
French by P. Gignoux, *Journal Asiatique*, 1969, pp. 387–418.

Madigan i Hazar Dadestan. An idea of the contents of this difficult work may
be had from the pioneer transl. by S. J. Bulsara, *The Laws of the Ancient
Persians*, Bombay 1937.

Mas'udi, *Les Prairies d'Or*, text and French transl., ed. Ch. Pellat, vol. II,
Paris 1965.

Saddar Bundahesh, almost completely transl. into English by B. N.
Dhabhar, *Rivayats* (see above).

Nöldeke, Th. (transl.), *Geschichte der Perser und Araber zur Zeit der
Sasaniden aus der arabischen Chronik des Tabari*, Leiden 1879.

Tansar Name, transl. M. Boyce, *The Letter of Tansar*, Rome 1968.

Vis u Ramin, transl. G. Morrison, *Vis and Ramin*, New York and London
1972.

SECONDARY LITERATURE

Bailey, H. W., *Zoroastrian problems in the ninth-century books*, Oxford
1943, repr. 1971.

Christensen, A., *L'Iran sous les Sassanides*, 2nd ed., Copenhagen 1944. (The
only solid, fairly up-to-date history of the period. For chapter 7,
Christensen's 'Sassanid Persia', *Cambridge Ancient History*, vol. XII, ch.
4, is relevant.)

Pavry, J. C., *The Zoroastrian Doctrine of a Future Life from Death to the
Individual Judgment*, New York 1929. (Deals with the subject in the
Avesta and Pahlavi books.)

Rawlinson, G., *The Seventh Great Oriental Monarchy, the Geography,
History and Antiquities of the Sasanian . . . Empire*. (Out of date, but still
useful.)

Zaehner, R. C., *The Teachings of the Magi, A Compendium of Zoroastrian
beliefs*, Ethical and Religious Classics of East and West, London 1956,
repr. 1976. (A useful collection of Pahlavi texts in translation, from
Sasanian and post-Sasanian times, with linking commentary.)

Chapter 10

PRIMARY SOURCES

Baladhuri, *Futuh al-Buldan*, transl. P. K. Hitti and F. C. Murgotten, *The
Origins of the Islamic State*, vol. I, New York 1916.

Dadestan i dinig, part I, transl. E. G. West, SBE XVIII.

Bibliography

Dhabhar, see chapters 7–9.

Dinkard, ed. with Eng. transl. by P. B. and D. P. Sanjana, 19 vols, Bombay, completed in 1928.

Epistles of Manushchihr, transl. E. G. West, SBE XVIII.

Ibn Isfandiyar, *History of Tabaristan*, transl. E. G. Browne, Gibb Memorial Series II, London 1905.

Narshakhi, *History of Bukhara*, transl. R. N. Frye, Cambridge, Mass. 1954.

Rivayat of Adurfarnbag, ed. and transl. in 2 vols by B. T. Anklesaria, Bombay 1969.

Shkand-gumanig Vizar, French transl. by P. J. de Menasce, Freiburg-in-Switzerland 1945.

Siyasat Name, transl. by H. Darke as *The Book of Government of Nizam al-Mulk*, London 1960.

Wizidagiha i Zadspram, ed. with English summary by B. T. Anklesaria, Bombay 1964.

SECONDARY LITERATURE

Browne, E. G., *A Literary History of Persia*, vol. II, Cambridge 1906, repr. 1928.

Dennett, D. C., *Conversion and the Poll-tax in Early Islam*, Harvard Historical Monographs, XXII, 1950.

Monnot, G., *Penseurs musulmans et religions iraniennes, ʿAbd al-Jabbar et ses devanciers*, Librarie philosophique J. Vrin, Paris 1974.

Nyberg, H. S., 'Sassanid Mazdaism according to Moslem sources', *Journal of the K. R. Cama Oriental Institute*, 39, 1958, 3–63.

Tritton, A. S., *The Caliphs and their Non-Muslim Subjects*, London 1930, repr. 1970.

Chapter 11

Browne, E. G., *A Literary History of Persia*, vol. III, Cambridge 1920.

Chardin, J., *Voyages en Perse et autres lieux de l'Orient*, Amsterdam 1735, vol. II.

Commissariat, M. S., *A History of Gujarat*, vol. I, Bombay 1938.

Drouville, G., *Voyage en Perse fait en 1812 et 1813*, 3rd ed., vol. II, Paris 1828.

Geldner, K. F., intro. to the *Avesta*, vol. I, Stuttgart 1896.

Hodivala, S. H., *Studies in Parsi History*, Bombay 1920.

Jordanus, *The Wonders of the East*, transl. and ed. by H. Yule, Hakluyt Society, London 1863.

Bibliography

Chapter 12

Anquetil du Perron, H., *Zend-Avesta, Ouvrage de Zoroastre*, 2 vols, Paris 1771.

Chardin, see previous chapter.

Commissariat, see previous chapter.

Daulier-Deslandes, A., *Les Beautez de la Perse*, Paris 1672, transl. A. T. Wilson, London 1926.

Figueroa, see *L'ambassade de D. Garcias de Silva Figueroa*, transl. into French by A. de Wicquefort, Paris 1669.

Fryer, J., *A New Account of East India and Persia, 1672–1681*, ed. W. Crooke, Hakluyt Society, London 1915, vol. II.

Lord, Henry, *A Display of Two Forraigne Sects in the East Indies*, London 1630.

Mandelslo, A. von, *Supplement to the Voyages and Travells of the Ambassadors sent by Frederick Duke of Holstein to the Great Duke of Muscovy*, transl. J. Davis, London 1669.

Master, Streynsham, quoted by H. Yule (ed.), *The Diary of William Hedges Esq.*, Hakluyt Society, London 1888, vol. II.

Niebuhr, K., *Travels through Arabia and Other Countries*, Eng. transl. by R. Heron, Edinburgh 1792.

Ogilby, J., *Asia*, London 1673.

Ovington, J., *A Voyage to Surat in the Year 1689*, ed. H. G. Rawlinson, Oxford 1929.

Pietro della Valle, see *Fameux voyages de Pietro della Valle, gentilhomme romain*, transl. into French by E. Carneau and F. le Comte, Paris 1661–3.

Stavorinus, J. S., *Voyages to the East Indies*, transl. from the Dutch by S. H. Wilcocke, London 1798, vol. II, repr. 1969.

Tavernier, J. B., *Six Voyages en Turquie, en Perse et aux Indes*, Paris 1676, anon. Eng. transl., London 1684.

Chapters 13 and 14

Boyce, Mary, *A Persian Stronghold of Zoroastrianism*, Oxford 1977. (An account of life in the highly traditional village of Sharifabad.)

Browne, E. G., *A Year amongst the Persians*, Cambridge, 2nd ed., 1926, repr. 1927, chs 13–15. (Interesting passages on the Zoroastrians of Yazd and Kerman.)

Bulsara, J. F., *Bird's Eye Picture of the Parsis*, Bombay 1969.

Dhalla, M. N., *Zoroastrian Theology*, New York 1914. *History of Zoroastrianism*, New York 1938. *Homage unto Ahura Mazda*, Karachi 1943. *Autobiography of Dastur Dhalla*, transl. into Eng. by G. and B. S. Rustomji, Karachi 1975.

Bibliography

Dosabhoy Framjee, *The Parsees: their History, Manners, Customs and Religion*, London 1858. Expanded, after the author had taken the surname Karaka, into *History of the Parsis*, 2 vols, London 1884.

Duchesne-Guillemin, J., *The Western Response to Zoroaster*, Oxford 1958. (The early chapters contain a summary of Western studies on Zoroastrianism, the final ones are concerned with Zoroastrianism, ancient Greece, and Israel.)

Jackson, A. V. W., *Persia Past and Present, a Book of Travel and Research*, New York 1910, chs 23, 24. (Detailed material on the Zoroastrians of Yazd.)

Kulke, E., *The Parsees in India, A Minority as Agent of Social Change*, Weltforum Verlag, Munich 1974. (Marred by inaccuracies, but interesting materials, with bibliography, on the Parsi community in modern times.)

Moulton, J. H., *The Treasure of the Magi, A Study of Modern Zoroastrianism*, Oxford 1917, repr. 1971.

Murzban, M. M., *The Parsis in India*, an enlarged, annotated and illustrated English transl. of Delphine Menant, *Les Parsis*, 2 vols, Bombay 1917.

Olcott, H. S., *Theosophy, Religion and Occult Science*, London 1885.

Petermann, H., *Reisen im Orient*, vol. II, Leipzig 1865.

Pratt, J. B., *India and its Faiths*, London 1916.

Pur-Davud (Poure Davoud), I., *Introduction to the Holy Gathas*, transl. into English by D. J. Irani, Bombay 1927.

Seervai, K. N. and Patel, B. B., 'Gujarat Parsis', *Gazetteer of the Bombay Presidency*, vol. IX, part 2, Bombay 1899.

Taraporewala, I. J. S., see bibliography to Chapters 1–4.

Wilson, J., *The Parsi Religion . . . unfolded, refuted, and contrasted with Christianity*, Bombay 1843.

General

A number of books concerned with the art and archaeology of ancient Iran show Zoroastrian material. The following (all of which have further bibliographies) are among those available in English:

Ghirshman, R., *Persian Art: the Parthian and Sasanian Dynasties*, London and New York 1962.

Godard, A., *The Art of Iran*, London 1965.

Lukonin, V. G., *Persia* II, transl. by J. Hogarth, Archaeologia Mundi, Geneva 1967.

Porada, Edith, *Ancient Iran, the Art of Pre-Islamic Times*, Art of the World Series, London, 1965.

The following works are rich in specifically Zoroastrian illustrations:

Hinnells, J. R., *Persian Mythology*, London 1973.

Molé, M., *L'Iran ancien*, Religions du Monde, Paris 1965.

Index

Note: because of the length of Zoroastrian history, religious terms regularly have more than one form. Where the oldest form is in frequent use it is given first, and the later form is put after it in brackets, e.g. yazata (yazad). If the later form is the familiar one, the position is reversed, but then the chronological relationship is indicated, e.g. Ātash Bahrām (older Ātakhsh ī Varahrān). Cross-references are given where the forms are not closely alike, e.g. Ahura Mazdā *see* Ohrmazd.

Long vowels are marked for religious terms and historical names, but not for personal names of modern times, or for well-known place-names.

Index

jurers in his jurisdiction, 181; his
independent existence asserted by
Parsi orthodox, 198; accepted
instinctively by reformists, 207, 214;
regarded by some Western scholars as
the son of Ahura Mazdā, 213

Ahuna Vairya (Ahunvar), 34–5, 37,
135, 161

Ahura Mazdā, Ahuramazda, see
Ohrmazd

ahuras, 9, 10, 11, 16, 19, 26

Airyaman, 10, 28, 35

Airyanem Vaējah, 40, 93

Airyēmā ishyō, 35, 38

Aiwisrūthra, the first night-watch, 32

akābir, 'great ones', leaders of the community, 186, 192, 193, 210, 217, 226

Akbar, 176, 182, 183, 185, 186

Alexander, 78–9, 175

al-Muqaffaᶜ, 150

Amahraspand, see Amesha Spenta

Ameretāt (Amurdād), the Amesha
Spenta 'Long Life' or 'Immortality',
22; lord of the fourth creation, plants,
23; scatters essence of original Plant,
25; aided by Zam, 41; a day and
month dedicated to her, 71, 73; her
name-day feast, 73; her worship
attested in Armenia, 84

Amesha, 'Immortal', 11

Amesha Spenta (Amahraspand), 'Holy
Immortal', general term for
beneficent divinities evoked by
Ahura Mazdā, 21; name first attested
in Yasna Haptanhāiti, 37; used
particularly of the six great Beings of
Zoroaster's revelation (seven when
Spenta Mainyu, i.e. Ahura Mazdā
himself, is included), 22; these six
close to Ahura Mazdā and one
another, 23, 58; with Ahura Mazdā
are lords of the seven creations, 21,
23, 24, 181, 225; hence physically
represented in the yasna, 23; inspire a
comprehensive morality, 24; turn
Ahriman's evil to good, 25; pantheon
organized round them, 41–2; receive
calendar dedications, 71–3;

'subalternate spirits', and the servants
of Ahura Mazdā, 179, 185;
interpreted by some Western scholars
as abstract ideas, 202–3

Anagra Raocha, 71

Anāhīd-Ardashīr, sacred fire, 114

Anāhita (Anāhīt, Anāhīd), a yazata,
representing the assimilation to
Aredvī Sūrā (q.v.) of 'Anaitis'
61–2; identified by Greeks with
Aphrodite and Artemis, 61, 89;
worshipped with images in temples,
62–3, 79, 85; beloved in Armenia, 84;
tutelary divinity of the Sasanians,
101, 115, 116, 135, 142; sacred fire in
her Istakhr temple, 106, 114;
represented in investiture scenes,
107, 116; venerated in Muslim times
as Shahrbānū, 151; and as Bānū-
Pārs, 163, 164, 211

Anaitis, see Anāhita

anarya (anēr), 'non-Iranian', 47, 51, 56,
151, 154

andarz, 136

Angra Mainyu, Anra Mainyu, see
Ahriman

animals, the fifth creation, 12;
represented in the yasna, 12; under
guardianship of Vohu Manah, 23;
honoured at fifth gāhāmbār, 33

anjoman, local Zoroastrian assembly,
172; separate priestly anjomans, 186,
218; widely established by Parsis,
208, 209; by Iranis in Yazd and
Kerman, 218; in Tehran, 222–3;
federation of Anjomans of India, 226;
synonym of panchāyat, q.v.

Anjoman Ātash Bahrām in Bombay,
209, 225

Anklesar, 167, 170

Anklesaria, Behramgore, 211

Anklesaria, Tehmuras, 206, 211

Anquetil du Perron, 194–5

Anshan, Elamite kingdom, 49

Apam Napāt, see *Varuna

Apama, 80

Apaosha, 7

Āpas (Ābān), yazatas, the 'Waters',

238

Index

Ātash Niyāyesh, 63
ātash-zōhr, 185; cf. zaothra
athaurvan, 18, 66
Atossa, 51, 54
Atropatene, see Azarbaijan
*āturōshan, 85
Avesta, the Zoroastrian holy texts, 3, 18, 40; the 'Younger Avesta', 17–18; almost entirely Eastern Iranian, 50; orally transmitted, 50, 94; much of it said to be lost through Alexander's conquest, 79; tradition of its subsequent transmission, 94, 103, 113–14, 133; canon established under Ardashīr, 103; written down in sixth century A. C., 134–5; the great Sasanian Avesta, 135, 136, 156, 161; surviving texts almost entirely liturgical, 165; translated, into Pahlavi, 136, into Sanskrit, 168, into Gujarati, 169, 190, 207, into modern Persian, 211, 220; until nineteenth century its study left to priests, 197; regarded by orthodox as revealed in its entirety to Zoroaster, 197; first printed in Bombay, 206, 211
Avestan alphabet, 134–5, 169, 206
Avestan language, 3, 18; the language of prayer and worship, 46–7, 206
Avestan manuscripts, 165–6, 168, 170, 181, 189, 190, 209
Avestan people, 18, 39, 40
Avroman documents, 96–7
āyadana (Parthian āyazan), 60, 89, 90
Āyadgār ī Zarērān, 126, 170
Ayāthrima, 33
Azarbaijan (older Atropatene), 93, 165

Babylonian influences, 61, 62, 68, 72, 74; see also Mesopotamian
Bactria, 40, 80, 81, 83, 93, 98
baga, 11, 56
Baghdad, 151
bagīn, 85, 88–9, 107
bagnapat, 98, 107
Bahā'ism, 212
Bahman, see Vohu Manah

Bahman, author of the Qissa-i Sanjān, 166, 172
Bahrām, see Verethraghna
Bansda, 171, 172
Bānū-Pārs, 163, 164, 211
barashnom, 45–6, 139, 154, 173, 174, 193, 206
baresman (barsom), 5, 67, 85, 89, 107, 138
Bartholomae, Christian, 220, 224
bashn, bashnbad, 107
Basil, St, 110, 111
bāstānī calendar, 221
behdīn, 'of the good religion', a Zoroastrian, 184
Behistun, 58, 89
Behramshah Shroff, 205
Berossus, 62
Bhagaria Ātash Bahrām in Navsari, 188, 192
Bhagarias, 167, 172, 182, 188, 189, 190, 193, 209, 217
Bhagarsath Anjoman, assembly of Bhagaria priests, 192
Bharucha, Sheriarji, 201
Bharuchas, 167
Bombay, 176, 187, 189, 192, 196, 199, 201, 205, 206, 207, 209, 210, 212, 214, 217, 218, 219, 223, 227
brazmadāna, 61, 89
Bridge of the Separator, see Chinvato Peretu
Broach, 167, 171, 172, 176, 186, 189, 190, 200
Buddhism, 1, 77, 83, 84, 100, 111, 112, 120
Bukhara, 147
bull, sacred, see varasya
Bull, the Uniquely Created, 12, 25
Bundahishn, Pahlavi term for Creation, 25, 28
Bundahishn, Pahlavi book, 136, 155, 195, 197, 211
burial, 13–14, 120, 121
Byzantium, Byzantines, 110, 113, 128, 139, 142, 145

Calcutta, 209, 224

Index

calendar, Zoroastrian: created under later Achaemenians, 70–3; in the Parthian period, 92; first Sasanian reform, 104–6, 114; second Sasanian reform, 128–9; in eleventh century A.C., 159–60; solitary intercalation by Parsis, 166–7; disputes over Kadmī and Shenshāī reckonings, 189–90; faslī (bāstānī) reckoning, 212–13, 221

Cama, Kharshedji, 201, 202, 203, 206, 212

Cambay, 165, 167, 169, 170, 176, 185

Cambyses, 53–4

cattle, under the guardianship of Vohu Manah, 23; see also animals

cattle urine, see gōmēz

cemeteries, 221

Chahil, 170

Changa Asa, 172

Chardin, 164, 179

charity: by the individual, 121–2, 180, 187, 200, 218; communal, 186, 193, 208

Chinvatō Peretu (Chinvat Bridge), 'Crossing of the Separator', 13, 14, 27, 45, 115, 181

Chionites, 124

choice, a vital element in doctrine and ethics, 20, 21–2, 24, 36, 69

Christianity, Christians, 1, 77, 84, 99, 100, 110, 111, 112, 119, 120, 121, 128, 139, 140, 141, 146

confession, formal, 58, 143

conversion to Zoroastrianism, 47, 124, 134, 174, 193

cord, sacred, see kustī

corpse, unclean, 44, 52, 59

cosmogony, 11–12, 21

Cowasji Ātash Bahrām, 209

creation, 25

creations, the seven, 11, 21, 23; represented in the yasna, 11, 23; attacked by Angra Mainyu, 25, 43; protected by purity laws, 43, 52–3, 59, 60; doctrine contaminated by Greek theory of the four elements, 113, 119, 122, 123, 198

Creator, i.e. Ohrmazd, 21, 30, 69, 71, 92, 122, 155

cult, 3–6

cypress of Khorasan, 158

Cyrus the Great, 49, 50–3, 219

Dādestān ī dīnīg, 154, 211

Dādestān ī Mēnōg ī Khrad, see Mēnōg ī Khrad

Dādgāh (older Ādurōg ī pad dādgāh), 110, 141, 187, 218

Dady Seth, 190

Dadyseth Ādārān/Agiary, 190, 210–11

Dadyseth Ātash Bahrām, 190, 193

Daēnā (Dēn), yazata of Religion, 71; personified conscience, 115

daēva (Old Persian daiva, Middle Persian dēv), 'Shining One', 11; term restricted by Zoroaster to ancient gods of war and strife, whom he rejected, 11, 19, 21, 30, 36; wicked by nature and choice, the servants of Angra Mainyu, 21–2, 25; will perish at Frashō-kereti, 28; a temple of theirs destroyed by Xerxes, 56; believed by iconoclasts to inhabit images, 109; daēva-worship persisting locally, 115; daēvas identified with yazatas by Haug, 202

Dahmān Āfrīn, 72

daiva, see daēva

dakhma, 13–14, 157–8, 170, 173, 180, 185, 187, 191, 192, 193, 209, 210, 221–2

Dārāb Kumāna, 189, 194

Darī, 178, 211

Dar-i Mihr, 180, 187

Darius the Great, 54–6

Darius III, 64, 78

Dastūrān dastūr / Dastūr dastūrān, of Yazd, 164, 172, 181, 191, 218, 222; of Kerman, 165, 191

dastūrs, 157, 184, 197, 209

date of Zoroaster, 1, 3, 18, 49, 92–3

death, 12, 20–1, 25, 26, 44

Demāvand, 205

Desātir, 197–8

Dhabhar, Bomanji N., 211

Index

Index

Index

Index

Māni, 111–12, 114

Manichaeans, Manichaeism, 111–12, 130, 155

manthras, 18, 37, 139

Manthra Spenta, 71

Manushchihr ī Gōshnjam, 153–4, 160

Mardānfarrokh, 155, 160

Margiana, 40

marriage, 31, 193, 226

Mazdā, *see* Ohrmazd

Mazdak, 130–1

Mazdayasna, a worshipper of Mazdā, 35–6, 69, 115, 116

Mazdaznāns, 217

Mazyār, 153

Medes, Media, 48–9, 93, 94, 136

Median script, 80, 96

mehean, 89

Meherji Rāna, Dastur, 182, 183

Meherji-Rana, Dara, 217

mēnōg, 25, 27

Mēnōg ī Khrad, Dādestān ī Mēnōg ī Khrad, 136–7, 168, 190

menstruation, 45, 139, 180

Mesopotamian influences, 90, 95; *see also* Babylonian

Middle Persian, *see* Pahlavi

Mihr, *see* Mithra

Mihrabān Kay Khosrow, 166, 170

Mihrām-Gushnasp, 137–8, 139–40

Mihr-Narseh, 121–2

Mihr-Shābuhr, 121

Misvan Gātu, 27

mithra, covenant, verbal undertaking, 8

Mithra (Mihr), yazata of the covenant, and of loyalty, 8, 9; lord of ordeal by fire, 8, 9; and so of fire and the sun, 9, 10, 119, 137, 181; one of the three Ahuras, 9–10, 21; war-god and judge, 10, 119; presides over judgment of the soul at death, 27, 45, 181, 213; protects morning hours, 32; aids Khshathra Vairya, 41; one of chief triad of Achaemenian divinities, 62; day and month dedicated to him, 71, 72; his feast-day, 72, 73; identified by Greeks with Apollo, 82;

temples named generally for him, 89 (mehean), 180 (Dar-i Mihr); represented, on Kushan coins, 83, and on a Sasanian monument, 107; his worship in Armenia, 84; his yasht, 135; a shrine to him in later times, 164

Mithradates I of Parthia, 81, 88, 90

Mithradates II of Parthia, 81

Mithraism, 99

*Mithrakāna (Mihragān), 72, 73

mōbad (older *magupati, magbad), 65, 78, 97–8, 114, 119, 157

Mōbadān mōbad, 122, 133, 134, 160, 163, 164

Modi, Jivanji J., 217

monotheism, an original monotheism taught by Zoroaster, 19–20; and believed in by his followers, 123, 179, 185; a continuing form assumed by Western scholars, 194, 195, 202; this adopted by Parsi reformists, 203; and by Irani reformists, 220

moon, 25, 26

Moon, yazata, *see* Māh

Mulla Firoze Madressa, 201, 202

Nairyōsanha (Narseh), messenger-yazata, 116

Nanai, 90

naojōt, 174

Naoroji Feerdoonji, 200

Naqsh-i Rajab, 109

Naqsh-i Rustam, 57, 59, 107, 108, 109, 116

Nariman Hoshang, 172–3

Narseh, king, 116

nasks, 135, 136

'nature' gods, 6–7

nāvar, 174

Navsari, 167, 170, 172, 173, 182, 188, 189, 192, 196

Neryōsang Dhaval, 168–9

New Day, *see* Nō Rūz

nīrang, 166, 174

Nīrangdīn, 173

Nīrangestān, 211

Nīsā, 89–90, 91, 92, 95, 96

nobles, and the Sasanian clergy, 137, 138

Nō Rūz, 'New Day', the seventh feast of obligation, devoted to the seventh creation, fire, 34; foreshadows Frashō-kereti, 34, 73; probably celebrated at Persepolis, 57; in spring under the Achaemenians, 72; two Nō Rūz festivals after first Sasanian reform, 105; an autumn observance under Parthians and early Sasanians, 106; its link with gāhāmbārs weakened by Sasanian calendar reforms, 106, 129; its celebration in Sasanian times, 124, 129–30; moved again to spring month, Ādur, 128; brought back to 1 Fravardīn, 159–60; 'Greater Nō Rūz' celebrated as Zoroaster's birthday, 180; present dates of the feast's celebration, 221

nōzūd, 174

Nūsh-i Jān Tepe, 51

occultism, occultists, 198, 207, 224

offerings: to water, 4; to fire, 4, 63–4, 65; for the dead, 13, 14, 45, 66, 143; to temple fires, 86, 143; for the souls of the living, 108–9

Ohrmazd (older Ahura Mazdā, Ahuramazda), lord of Wisdom and greatest of the three Ahuras, 9; seen by Zoroaster in vision, 19; proclaimed by him as the one uncreated God, 19–20; and as Creator, 20, 21; the five daily prayers addressed to him, 33; the religion called for him Mazda-worship, 35–6; name and title fused in Old Persian, 55; in the inscriptions of Darius, 55–6; with Mithra and Anāhita, 61–2; in Zurvanism, 68, 69; four days and a month dedicated to him, 71, 72, 73; identified by the Greeks with Zeus, 82, 107; anthropomorphically represented under Parthians and Sasanians, 82, 107, 142; called Aramazd

in Parthian Armenia, 84; controls world through wisdom, 136–7, 149

Olcott, Henry S., 204–5

oral transmission: of the Avesta, 17, 50, 79, 136, 202, 206; of the doctrines of the faith, 17, 110–11, 220–1, 225; of the secondary literature, 126

ordeal: by water, 8–9; by fire, 9, 28, 118, 181

padan, 189

Pahlavi, or Middle Persian, language, 17, 96, 107, 108, 116–17; literature, 17, 116–17, 136–7, 153–6, 159, 165, 203, 213, 224; script, 80, 96, 136, 150, 155, 159, 169, 206; manuscripts, 165–6, 170, 171, 181, 190, 211

Paikuli, 118

Paitishahya, 33

panchāyats, 192, 208; see also Pārsī Panchāyat of Bombay

panth, 167, 171, 189, 209

panthaki, 167

Paradise, 77

parīk (older pairīkā), 85

Parni, 81

Pārs (Persis, Persia, Arabo-Persian Fārs), 49, 57, 79, 81, 87, 101, 117, 123, 135, 136; after the Arab conquest, 147, 152, 156, 159, 162

Pārsī Panchāyat of Bombay, 192–3, 208, 216–7, 218, 223

Pārsī Prakash, 183

Pārsīs: the original migration, 156–7, 166; settlement in Gujarāt and early history, 166–8; Sanskrit learning, 168–9; early contacts with the Irani community, 170, 172, 173; developments in observance, 174–5; founding of lesser temple fires, 187–8; great changes in the nineteenth century, 196 ff.; spreading through lands of British Empire, 208 et passim

Parthia, 81, 136

Parthian language, 81, 96, 107, 108, 116–17; script, 80, 96, 116; literature, 126

247

Index

Index

Index

Ahura Mazdā, 21; regarded by some Western scholars as his son, 213

Sraosha (Srōsh), yazata of Obedience and guardian of prayer, 10; invoked by Zoroaster, 21; one of the judges of the soul, 27, 181, 213; protects the second night-watch, 32; a day dedicated to him, 71; Ahura Mazdā's vice-regent on earth, 74; his yasht, 74

Srīsōk, 87

Staota Yesnya, 38, 95, 125

Strabo, 85

sudra (or sedra), 31–2, 172, 174

summer, the Ahuric season, 32, 34

sun, 7, 9, 10, 12, 23, 25, 26, 53, 119, 178, 181

Sun, yazata, see Hvar

Surat, 176, 182, 183, 185–6, 187, 188, 189, 192, 196, 205, 210

Surat Ātash Bahrāms, 190

Suratyas, 189

Surkh Kotal, 83

Susa, 57, 89

Tabaristān, 102, 153

Takht-i Suleymān, 124

Tansar, 102–3, 107, 108, 135

Tāq-i Bustān, 142

Taraporewala, Irach, 224

Tata, Jamshedji, 217

Tehran, 192, 210, 212, 218, 222, 223, 226

temples: unknown in pagan religion, 6; or in early Zoroastrianism, 46, 60; introduced with cult of Anāhita, 63, 65; consequences for religious life, 65; in Asia Minor, 85; destruction by Macedonians, 78–9; see also fire temple, āyadana, bagin

Theodoretus, 121

theosophy, 204–5, 212, 224

three, the sacred number, 4, 31, 57, 59; in funerary rites, 12–13

Three Times, 26, 67, 68–9, 70, 74

Tiri (Tīr), yazata, assimilated to Tishtrya, 62, 79; a day and month dedicated to him, 71, 72; his feast-day, 73

Tiridates I of Armenia, 84, 97

*Tirikāna (Tiragān), 62, 73

Tishtrya (Teshtar), yazata, 7; assimilated the concept of Tiri, 62, 71, 72, 73; a shrine to him, 164

tolerance, shown by Cyrus, 51–2; by Darius, 56; by Arsacids, 94, 98, 100, 108; by Sasanians, 112, 120, 133, 141; undermined by proselytizing and persecutions by other faiths, 100, 111, 119, 120, 121, 128

tombs of Achaemenians, 52–3; of Arsacids, 90; of Sasanians, 121

tower of silence, see dakhma

Tree of All Seeds, 7

Tūirya (Tūr), name of an Iranian people, 40

Turkābād, 163, 164, 165, 172, 191

twin Spirits, 20; in Zurvanism, 68; in modern Western version of the Zurvanite heresy, 213

Udwada, 188, 205

Ukhshyat-ereta, 75, 181

Ukhshyat-nemah, 75

urvan (ruvan), 12, 15

Ushah (Ushahin), the second night-watch, 32

Uzayara (Uzērin), the third day-watch, 32

Vahagn, see Verethraghna

Vahman, see Vohu Manah

Vahrām, see Verethraghna

Vahrām I, 114

Vahrām II, 114, 115

Vahrām V, 121, 123, 124, 159

Vahrām Chōbēn, 141–2, 157

Vahrāmshād, 153

vāj (bāj), 138–9, 143

Valakhsh, see Vologeses

Vankaner, 167

varasya, 174

Variav, 167, 171

*varuna, 'oath', 8

*Varuna Apąm Napāt, yazata of the oath, and truth, 8; lord of the ordeal by water, 8–9; and so of water,

Index

Index